Retirem

Retirement

A GUIDE TO GOOD LIVING

RENEE MYERS

The Crowood Press

First published in 1990 by
The Crowood Press
Gipsy Lane, Swindon
Wiltshire SN2 6DQ

© Renee Myers 1990

All rights reserved. No part of this publication may be reproduced or transmitted in any form or by any means, electronic or mechanical, including photocopy, recording, or any information storage and retrieval system without permission in writing from the publishers.

British Library Cataloguing in Publication Data
Myers, Renee
  Retirement: a guide to good living
  1. Great Britain. Retirement. Planning
  I. Title
  646. 79
ISBN 1 85223 336 2

For Cynthy and Martin who are such fun to be with

Typeset by Hope Services (Abingdon) Ltd
Printed in Great Britain by
Billing & Sons Ltd, Worcester

Contents

1	Thinking About Retirement	1
2	When to Retire	14
3	Making the Best of the Rest	25
4	Education – No One is Too Old	36
5	Hobbies and Pets	48
6	Gardening is Good for You	57
7	Leisure, Recreation and Holidays	72
8	It Pays to Keep Busy	89
9	Relationships	105
10	The Importance of Sex	116
11	It Runs in the Family	131
12	Age is Not the Problem	137
13	Staying Mentally Well	146
14	Drugs and the Relief of Pain	156
15	Exercise Means Fitness	168
16	The Best Food for You	180
17	Are You the Right Weight	189
18	Look Younger Longer	198
19	Young at Heart	211
20	The Five Senses	219
21	Dancing Feet	228
22	Keeping the Works in Order	235
23	Relaxation and Sleep	245
24	The Key to Good Health	255
25	Private Health Care	264
26	Complementary Treatment	270
27	The Carers	279
28	A Place of Your Own	289
29	Money Matters	300
30	You and The Law	310
31	Making a Will	322
32	Accentuate the Positive	327
	Useful Addresses	336
	Index	348

Acknowledgements

There are so many people who have played a tangible and deeply appreciated part in the writing of this book: those who volunteered to share their experiences and responded to questions in such a frank and open way; colleagues who offered the benefit of their wisdom and expertise and the friends who made helpful suggestions.

My love and thanks go to my relatives who have borne with my absence from precious family evenings through months of writing and rewriting and to my husband, Jack, who is so busy in retirement but found all the time for me that I needed and in the process was forced to learn to cook.

To our grandchildren Debbie, Samantha, Hannah, Toria, Lucy, Mark, Daniel, Steven, Ben and Nadia – there will be time for you again.

(The people and experiences I have written about are all real but in order to preserve privacy I have not used actual names unless I have had permission to do so.)

Foreword

You didn't expect to find me here did you? Well, you wouldn't, I mean – me! Retire? Slung out – posssibly – but retire! Not on your Nellie! But after looking through this book I realised that it is not about retirement but about changing occupations, which is vastly different. Mind you, even if I thought about changing my job – who would have me? Would you? I like what I do. I like people you see and so does Renee Myers. She likes people and she understands them and when you browse through her book you'll feel as though you are talking to her. That's something I enjoy doing and I am all for following her advice. It's all good stuff you know.

Never retire, keep going, keep smiling and the best of luck.

Frankie Howerd

Prologue

'What shall I do when I am grown up?', asked my eleven-year-old grandchild. 'And what shall I do now that I have been grown up?' I asked myself.

Is there some special attribute that distinguishes those of retirement age from other generations? We all tend to categorize by age. At this age we do this, at that age we do that. It's nonsense. Why should an entire group of people be bound by society's notion of how they should behave, dress, eat or even think?

There is no need to conform. Provided only that we are able, fit and willing, we can continue to enjoy whatever we have previously enjoyed.

This book is about living longer and staying younger. It is meant to discourage anyone from thinking that retirement means a withdrawal from life, a slide into decrepitude. Far from it. It can mark a beginning, a fresh start.

1 Thinking About Retirement

The 'Golden Years'

There has never been a time in history when people can so easily attain greater age and yet continue to enjoy youthful pleasures. The stories about how people end their working lives with misgivings that the good times are over and they can look forward only to days of failing strength and loss of independence, have gone out of the window. Those who are coming up to the age of retirement should anticipate with enjoyment a score or more of years. Years of good health, new activities, zestful and pleasurable years, perhaps the best of all.

Attitudes have changed and must change a good deal more. Raise the subject of retirement among any age group, the young, not-so-young, the immediate pre-retired as well as the elderly and the response is too often a negative one. The age of retirement should be a time that we all look forward to with positive feelings. There are many treats in store and these should indeed be the 'golden years'.

Good Prospects

The prospects for those who are facing retirement have never been so varied or so good. No longer employees, they become retirees, an increasingly important part of the community, forming one of the largest sections in today's society. A group in which everyone takes an interest because those who live long enough will one day also belong to it.

However cheerfully one may look forward to lazier days there may be a pang of regret on leaving familiar routines; rising at regular times, travelling to work and meeting with colleagues of long standing. More than likely one has to contemplate a drop in income, but on the bonus side there will be a drop in expenditure, with requirement for fewer formal clothes and reduced travelling expenses.

With the position as an income earner at an end, one can expect to feel a loss of some of the status previously enjoyed. Provided all the changes are anticipated and looked at constructively, it is easier to cope with the social and economic effects and make the most of the good things ahead.

Early retirement may bring a change in occupation, an opportunity to take on a second, perhaps quite different form of employment. As an example, the Forces offer careers which provide general education as well as training, limited service terms and pensions. There is the option of release from contract at around the age of forty, with freedom to take up second and often more lucrative careers.

A proportion of teachers and lecturers take early retirement in their fifties, intending to take on other employment, either to develop personal interests or to augment their pensions. In many other fields employees elect for premature retirement for similar reasons. They may feel that they have had enough of one particular line of work, are in need of a change and determine to do something different, perhaps more personally satisfying or enjoyable during the next part of their lives.

There may be a need to supplement pensions to maintain living standards or make home improvements, possibly to provide money for special holidays or hobbies. Some will want to provide for education for a grandchild. And some may marry late for the first time or re-marry, taking on fresh responsibilities such as a new family.

Leaving a Business

It is understandable when the self-employed feel reluctance to relinquish control of a business which they started and of which they feel an integral part. One could feel a sense of responsibility for colleagues and associates who are part of the daily routine. A business in which one is a success, still needed and appreciated, can feel too important a part of life to surrender voluntarily. People in such a position are often resistant to advice or persuasion to retire or consider handing over the reins.

Anyone who is addicted to their work, preferring to keep going indefinitely without thought of giving up, should think again. They could be missing a great deal. The familiarity of established routines may give a secure feeling but the freedom of choice following retirement opens up new vistas.

Value of Age

There is much emphasis in today's society on the value and attraction of youth and a resistance to being labelled ageing or old. It is not easy to accept that one is in the category of 'elderly' and perhaps preparing for the last part of the journey through life. We must avoid being negative; ageing is inevitable but we have a choice about how we deal with it.

The slowing-down process should not begin until the very elderly years when it is natural. Staying busy for as long as possible is the way to stay youthful and healthy in mind and body.

When it is Wise to Retire

We want to retire with many years of good physical and mental health ahead to enjoy. In our late seventies there are changes in physique, our bones are less strong, losing mass and becoming fragile. Our resistance to ordinary ills may reduce and we may ourselves recognize that physical and mental powers are not what they once were. Should we not seek some respite to enjoy leisure rather than continue actively engaged by work until life's end?

One man regrets that he delayed retirement so long. Henry was seventy-two and finally faced selling his grocery shop, for he could no longer manage to lift goods or roll up the heavy front shutters. Reluctantly, he sold out and having handed over the business set about completing some woodwork in the house for his wife. A friend offered to pay him for similar work and he found his skills as a carpenter in demand.

He now feels fitter, more relaxed and takes days off to go fishing when he wants to. His wife hopes that he will join her in her activities as a friend of the local hospital but, as he says, 'Later perhaps, but I love this freedom and I've got plenty of time.'

There is good reason for retirees to feel optimistic about their chances of enjoying the later years. They can expect to live longer and be in better health than were their parents. Today's late middle-aged can anticipate a life-span equal to the average age of both their parents, plus two years. And there are confident predictions that a few decades hence, life expectancy will be even greater.

Married couples may disagree about when retirement should take place and feel concerned about how they will fill the days. But these fears generally prove groundless and the years of shared and relaxed time, often more carefree than they have previously experienced, may prove to be the sweetest they have known.

Maintaining Standards

We should all like to think that we can commence the years of retirement without too much of a drop in our income or standard of living. It is natural to want to maintain an economic status equal to that of our friends and associates, to continue to have the kind of comforts and luxuries we have become used to. It may not be feasible to achieve this but sensible preparation and planning will at least ensure that the appropriate steps have been taken.

As early in life as possible, financial advice should be sought and no time lost in taking up an insurance or pension scheme. Provision made in youth or middle age can always be increased and while soonest is best, it should never be thought too late to invest in some financial security for the future.

Prosperous Generation

The over-fifties, with more money to spend and freedom to enjoy leisure time, are an important economic group, able to plan for years of retirement with more security than they have had in the past.

Currently, the over-sixties represent just about a quarter of the electorate in the UK, large enough to campaign effectively on issues of concern. They are also, however, a group which will become acutely aware of the potential problems and difficulties falling upon a country with a smaller working population having to support a larger retired sector. There will be many jobs with fewer people to fill them. It is estimated that by the twenty-first century, more than half of the population will be in the fifty-plus age band, holding some 60 per cent of private assets in the country.

Birthrate Bulges in the Past

Why is the sector of retired expected to expand in the next ten or so years? The explanation lies partly in the birthrate bulges which occurred during this century and partly in the rise in life expectancy. At the turn of the century, life expectancy was forty-eight years for men and fifty for women. Half a century on, this had increased to sixty-six and seventy-one, respectively. For the 1990s it is forecast that more people can expect to reach eighty, ninety or even 100 years of age.

Recently, I enquired in a local newsagent shop as to whether they had any birthday cards for someone of 100 and they produced a selection. The Queen's telegram of congratulations to those who have reached their century goes out from Buckingham Palace more often these days.

Attitudes make a Difference

Society tends to label the aged in a way that not only undervalues them but is derogatory. Partly this is the fault of the elderly themselves and their own negative attitudes. Any group which contains even a small proportion of senile elderly, those unfit to work or whose quality of life is poor may be seen in its entirety as a liability to the nation. The healthy, happy and useful majority are too often discounted.

The elderly, as a group, have a wealth of knowledge with which to enrich society. They can contribute to their own health and well-being and to that of others and, as the proportion of elderly grows, so must that contribution of self-help grow. Not only is the continued independence of ageing people essential but practical use must be made of their experience and capabilities.

Provided that they retain their health and strength and live their lives usefully and enjoyably, the aged will be respected as a group. Younger generations will then view their own forthcoming years of retirement with a measure of pleasurable anticipation.

It is no more correct to dismiss all old as elderly than it is to say that all young are youthful. Many young are less modern in their thinking and outlook than some of their elders. It is not possible to hang a collective label upon a sector of the population which is so varied. Too often it is the inclination of the younger members of society to say of older generations that they are 'stupid old codgers' or 'funny old dears' who should stick with their television or bingo. Or worse, that they are ready for the scrap-heap.

Ageing may be accompanied by corresponding impairment but much support is available which can conserve good standards of ability, certainly far beyond that which is presently achieved for many of us. The pursuits of the elderly can be as varied as in any other age group. Provided only that we take good care of our health, then the variety of hobbies, occupations and exercise can remain almost unlimited. Some of the most respected of our judges, ministers, professors, experts in every field are past the age of normal retirement but still making a valued contribution to the community. Age is often rightly identified with wisdom.

Reagan was a popular president of America in his seventies; Adenauer remained prime minister of West Germany until he was over eighty; Golda Meir became prime minister of Israel when she was in her seventy-third year and, in her sixties, Mrs Thatcher continues as prime minister of the United Kingdom with undiminished energy. Many High Court judges did some of their finest work in their seventies.

Moderation in all Things

We should be capable of doing much in our later years that we did in our youth and many of our problems are caused by an immoderate style of living. We can still enjoy ourselves while adopting a sensible life-style, then, as the birthdays go by we should feel very little different. We should not decline at fifty or sixty and only slowly at seventy or eighty. In our nineties, when our genetic life-spans approach their full term and our cells are no longer able to regenerate, we may continue to be mentally alert, bright and active as many 100-year-olds prove to be.

Anne is a lively acquaintance and we had a date for lunch. The weather was humid and I certainly felt a bit weary. I had to smile as she sat down and said, 'Phew, I feel 100 today'. Anne is ninety-two.

We should expect to continue active life no matter how many years we clock up, keeping youthful deportment, retaining vitality and a zest for living. It is often a question of mind over matter and our subconscious thinking plays an important part in our behaviour.

The 'New Look' Older Generation

The early twentieth century produced a generation which does not conform to a pattern or allow age to limit either style of dress or behaviour. Freedom of expression once thought unseemly in senior citizens is quite acceptable today.

Age and experience breed a confidence which may well produce pleasant changes. Maturity can work wonders, transforming shy, reserved or dull young people into interesting older ones. From every walk of life there are countless examples which show that older men and women have the energy and ability to enjoy the opportunities which many young believe are limited to themselves. Older people are not necessarily less capable than other age groups, either mentally or physically. They are often resilient and energetic and can appreciate new as well as old friends and enjoy their hobbies, holidays and leisure at least as much and quite likely more than they ever did. In fact, they often find it hard to believe that they are not young any more.

The Years Catch Us Out

The period we call 'middle age' catches most of us unaware. It may be a chance look in a shop window when we notice our reflection with incredulity. Or a youthful shop assistant may address us with a friendly wink and cheery, 'Hullo there, Ma'. Can we really be looking old enough to be their parents? It comes as a bit of a shock. Not only are we forty something, but we look it!

Grandchildren are candid creatures. Their observations can throw you. They ask dismaying questions. 'Why is your neck wrinkly, Grandma?', or, 'Why haven't you any hair on top, Grandpa?'. Do we think that no one has noticed? Hang on to your sense of humour.

Age creeps on us imperceptibly, without anyone remarking any change for years and inside we may never feel any different. The inevitable alterations in appearance may not be welcome as youthful looks fade, but there are compensations. With age comes wisdom, experience and, hopefully, that invaluable quality, tolerance. Remember, we can counter the years by straightening our shoulders, putting the spring back in our steps and wearing a happier and more pleasant expression.

Staying Youthful

The search for ways of keeping young in looks and mind is not new. Youthfulness is a desirable concept, sought from early time, long before medicines and beauty aids were on the market. If we are to become the youthful elderly rather than the querulous old we must take sensible precautions to avoid sickness and early ageing. We can all promote normal healthy and active life by following simple dietary rules and taking sufficient physical and mental exercise.

Yesterday's Elders

How was it for yesterday's elders? Fewer people lived to a great age and to have known one's grandparents was more rare than now. When people became ill, even as early as in their fifties, it was considered to be part of ageing and accepted as normal. Such negative thinking contributed to ill-health and early deterioration, but those who did attain great age with undiminished and good physical and mental health were generally respected, considered wise and able to pass on skills.

Keeping a warm seat by the fireside for the older members of the family was regarded as a familial duty and responsibility. The enfeebled old were more often than not regarded as a social problem whose families had an inescapable obligation to care for them. Only rarely were relationships such that young people bore them with real love and compassion. The duty of care when thrust upon relatives was often regarded as a bitter burden, borne with resentment and suffered without any relief or respite from the daily arduous and frequently distasteful routine.

Care for Carers

Today there is concern for carers and an appreciation for the value of the duties which they undertake. Caring for someone at home relieves the State of a considerable responsibility. It will often mean financial sacrifice when someone has to give up a job to provide 'round-the-clock' care for a bedridden or housebound relative.

Today's planners and developers must accurately forecast needs so that there is sufficient housing of the right kind to permit independent and comfortable living for retired people. Housing must be thoughtfully designed and constructed so as to postpone the time when help becomes a necessity for the disabled or older band of the population. There must be proper community support with an adequate number of GPs together with their teams of nurses, occupational, speech and physiotherapists, chiropodists and counsellors as well as social workers and home-help services.

Carers, themselves often in their sixties and seventies, merit relief from the total responsibility and care of their own elders. Dependence by the very elderly sector on the close or extended family has decreased and attention has focused far more on support from statutory and voluntary sources. But families may recognize responsibilities and be more willing to undertake filial duties if they can depend upon back-up support and regular respite care.

Prolonging Independent Living

The number of residential homes for the elderly and infirm continues to rise and these make special demands on the National Health Service (NHS). Doctors in close proximity to such homes can find their workloads increased with numbers of dependent elderly constituting as much as 30 per cent of their practices.

It is for today's middle-aged themselves to consider the future and prepare to become the youthful elderly, not by a process of disengagement from work but by considering a change of direction, creating a pattern of living after retirement that encourages self-reliance and a feeling of self-worth.

Retirement does come as an emotional shock to many of us, even when we believe that we are prepared for it. There is natural apprehension as the actual time approaches, a feeling that we have fallen off a cliff and life has stopped. It can prove overwhelming, bringing despondency and a cycle of ill-health. This can reduce activity and start a winding down process which can actually reduce the life-span. A good quality of life entails positive thinking at every age and never more so than when retirement looms. A seventy-two year old said, 'When retirement came I thought, "That dreaded time is here." But in fact these past years have been the best of my life.'

Being Positive Helps

Many people in their eighties and nineties, who have led active and absorbing lives following retirement, continue to remain involved in whatever is going on, showing a lively interest in friends and community affairs. The life force remains dynamic and they are proof that ability for enjoyment need not be reduced by age.

At any stage it takes courage to live life to the full. It helps to maintain a contented outlook and good health. Even for people aged seventy-five it has been shown that there are discernible benefits when health promotional advice is followed.

The eighty year old who swims and cycles regularly may be far more youthful than the fifty year old who never walks a yard more than necessary, who smokes and drinks too much and eats the wrong food. Changing to a more healthy life-style is worthwhile at any age, paying dividends in performance and looks and making the effort itself enjoyable. People are liked more and like themselves more, for good health is visible and attractive.

We should continue to look well-groomed and personable regardless of age, but there are many disorders which cause our personal standards to drop and among them might be depression or a physical disorder. The advice of the practice nurse or doctor should be sought in order to determine what the problem is. Their recommendations could well improve mental outlook and greatly reduce the risk of heart attacks, strokes and diabetes.

Class Distinctions

A relevant factor to retirement, as well as to health, is the local environment which often determines social status. Industrial areas or districts of high-density housing do not provide such ideal places to live in as those more sparsely occupied. However hard people may try for themselves, when the environment, social class background and poor housing militate against them and ill-health adds another burden, they need extra help. Where lower social ratings apply, resources should be increased to provide what people need.

There is a rising expectation that everyone should have a good life following retirement. Television and other forces have gone some way to levelling classes, but there are still wide differences. Lower social groups work on for more years and for poorer people there continues to be a lower standard of health and comfort. For example, recent research has shown that some women do resist cervical smear tests and breast screening, even though this could reduce their chances of contracting cancer.

A Role for the Retired

Thinking about retirement means one is looking for a future. This future may be in finding some worthwhile occupation suitable to personal tastes and capabilities, perhaps taking part in community affairs or seeking a voluntary commitment to help others; any of these would be helpful in making the years ahead meaningful.

What the young and old often miss these days is the extended family; the aunt, uncle, grandmother or cousin who could stand by when there was need for support. The 'Family' used to be reliably counted on to help the weaker or needy members; money might be short but at the very least good and practical advice was plentiful.

Peace of mind is essential to good health but life today is so complex that there are few of us without problems of one kind or another. When these get out of proportion, we may need help, especially as we come to retirement age. We can all cope better and with more understanding when we are able to discuss worries with a counsellor, someone sensible, discreet and impartial, who is a sympathetic listener. Often, retired people fill this role.

The Survivors

Most of us will have good reason to count our blessings when the 'golden years' are reached. We are a specially interesting group, representing a complete mix of all types of people who have in common one factor – we have attained senior citizenship.

2 When to Retire?

The Right Time to Prepare

As we reach the mid-forties we should begin to consider when might be the right time to retire, because if early preparation is made then many problems can be avoided.

If we are prudent enough to think about retirement well before it is due, we can make plans to suit ourselves regarding pensions, housing, occupation, hobbies and so on. It takes discipline when we are fairly young to take a mental leap forward to our fifties and sixties with happy anticipation and we may not want to think about growing old. But these future years have much to commend them. The day when we will give up work seems so far away to the majority of the younger population that any idea of planning for it simply doesn't occur.

We consider retirement for a variety of reasons and at different stages in life. Some will recognize that it is financially advantageous to make decisions about pensions when young, for the earlier preparation is made, the better the terms that can be obtained. Others will put it out of their thoughts until the last possible moment. It is not wise to put off all preparatory measures; it is much better to look positively toward retirement as a time for relaxation and enjoyment, a time when many ambitions may be realized. It is more sensible to make considered decisions which will enable those dreams to come true.

Apart from the usual reason of age for retirement from the main occupation, there may be other causes which are prompted by personal feelings. These may result from sudden desires or long nurtured ambitions. They can impel immediate decisions to change, or slow and careful planning towards the new aims.

Do You Like Where You Live?

Some people live and work all their lives in a district which they do not care for, looking forward to the day when they can retire and move to a place they prefer. Work and the need to make a living may keep us tied and it is often only retirement which provides the freedom to make the break. Sometimes, however, things work out in a surprising way as they did for Hugh and his wife, Isobel.

They were of the same age, just on fifty and had lived for many years in a pleasant apartment close to the centre of London. He had a well-paid job in banking when he unexpectedly inherited an interest in a smallholding deep in the Lake District. Hugh and the other legatees met there one blustery December day. None of them was interested in taking it over and it was agreed that they should either find a manager to run it or else sell it. A man was engaged and all went well. But Hugh found his thoughts often straying from his busy City office and crowded London streets to the peaceful quiet and green world of the Lake District.

The following May, he and Isobel went there for a long weekend, ostensibly to take a break but in his heart Hugh had determined that he would leave his job and take over the little farm. When Isobel remarked that it was a shame to leave the tranquil beauty of such a place, he told her of his hopes and ambitions. She was concerned about the financial insecurity they would face but agreed that they should make the move. Now, six years later, they are part and parcel of the local community; in addition to their busy farm life, Isobel serves on the council and Hugh does voluntary work for a charity. They are financially stable and have not only paid off their co-legatees but also enlarged their holding to take in more land. They visit London rarely, reluctant to leave their new home and thankful that at least part of their lives is to be spent in a place they have both come to love so much.

It is an added bonus that their only child, a daughter who is divorced, has decided to look for a job in their area. She likes their present life-style and wants to be part of the same sort of community.

Work should be Interesting

One real incentive to take early retirement is because of boredom at work. Unless there is interest and satisfaction in the daily tasks to be done, unless it is felt that there is a sense of appreciation for a job well done, long-term employees tend to feel demotivated, dejected and jaded. It is a feeling which stifles all initiative and takes much of the joy out of living.

Today's youngsters want much more from a job than just a wage packet. They expect to enjoy work and to be appreciated for their efforts. In the past, young men and women took a job and remained there for years, sometimes for their whole working lives. They were disciplined by the need to make a living and the fear that they might not get another job.

One woman talked to me about her life since she had left school. It had been hard and the years of retirement were proving the best. Ruby had held only one job continuously from the age of fourteen, apart from a break of a few months when her only child was born. Her husband had developed tuberculosis shortly after leaving the army and subsequently had never kept a job for long. He died when their child was six-years-old and Ruby continued working at the laundry. She enjoyed the friendship of her workmates but found the work repetitive as well as hot, steamy and tiring. Nevertheless, it gave her a measure of security and she had too little self-confidence to think that she could ever do anything else, so she stayed on while other people came and went.

When Ruby was sixty she gladly took retirement although she would have warranted a larger pension by staying on. She said: 'To me it seemed that I had worked there for ever. It was such a relief to stop and I never thought that I would live to see the day. When the manageress asked if I could stay on a few years more, I went speechless. I don't believe that I could have stayed a single hour I didn't have to.'

Ruby moved to a smaller flat which was closer to her

daughter and grandchildren and where she is happier than she has ever been. 'The days are full', she said. 'And I'm never bored.' Although she has only her State pension, and money must be very tight for her, she manages quite well. She feels intensely proud that her eldest grandson wants to be a scientist and is to go to university. 'He has escaped from my social class, somehow that makes up for a lot.'

If children move away on marriage, settling where they have found work, they may welcome the idea of retired parents moving near, particularly if there are grandchildren. There must be no intrusion of privacy. Parents are not always welcome, nor do they themselves always want to be near their adult children, but when relationships are loving and close they provide comfort and support for all concerned.

Work Satisfaction

Levels of work satisfaction tend to decrease towards the final years of employment. This is natural, given that there will have been changes in staff with younger people coming in with more up-to-date training. Technological developments are less well received by older people, some of whom may believe themselves to be unable to adapt and find the very idea of coping with the changes discouraging. This lack of confidence can result in a diminishing ability to keep up with workloads, changing conditions or a combination of the two. Even when the job does not suffer it may be recognized that a greater effort is needed to equate with previous performance.

Recognizing the Time to Retire

Too much pressure and stress escalate anxiety. Everyone associated with the person concerned, at work and at home, suffers and this can lead to a breakdown in health. It is never easy to reduce tension or switch off stress. The more tired and ill people feel, the more difficult it is for them to keep things in perspective and to relax.

Perhaps this is the time to say enough is enough, retirement time is here and it might be better to find some less stressful occupation. It is not surprising to find that energy comes pouring back once pressures are off. If one can re-establish self-confidence and interest, other work, either voluntary or paid may often be found which will help to recover self-esteem. With his new-found attitude comes contentment and more often than not, better health.

Travel Problems

John, at sixty-one, was the office manager of an engineering firm. He had always worked industriously with rarely a day off and his office was well organized and ran smoothly. But times had changed. Driving to work in heavy traffic had become increasingly frustrating, often taking more than an hour.

Due to expansion, younger staff with training in computers were being recruited for the office. They had very different ideas from John's about work methods and targets and all this added to his worries. When retirement was offered he decided that it would be right to accept, although his wife worried about what he would do. But he then told her that he was going to take a computer course. His wife was amazed since she felt that it was the arrival of computers in his office which had contributed largely to his problems.

Once retired, John took the course, buying a small word processor for himself and joined a local computer club. He soon became proficient and in demand for advice. With the pressure off, he had no difficulty in assimilating the knowledge required for that very technology which had previously so dismayed him. The commitments he has taken on since retirement keep him fully occupied. But he goes at his own pace, feeling much fitter today than he did on leaving his job. When working, he knows how much he is appreciated for the service that he offers. He also readily agrees that he is more relaxed and happy now than he ever was during the past ten or so years and is particularly thankful that he no longer faces the frustration of daily commuting.

Relocation of Companies

The relocation of factories and offices to other areas is a problem for older employees who feel that they cannot face a move of house away from friends and a district they are familiar with. Even though the move may offer them the opportunity of continuity of employment with the same firm, they feel the ties with home have a higher priority.

Robert, at fifty-nine, is a reserved and conscientious man who was very popular with his colleagues and enjoyed his job in an accounting department. When his company's factory was re-sited some eighty miles away, he and his wife decided reluctantly that they could not face moving from their home and garden. They knew that it meant retirement earlier than they had wanted or expected but the factory move precipitated Robert's decision. Following retirement, Robert accepted the position as honorary treasurer at his bowling club and this, together with his keen interest in gardening and walking, was sufficient to keep him occupied. His wife was already retired from her office job and the couple contentedly came to terms with their reduced income in the knowledge that outgoings were also less. They enjoy and appreciate each other's company and say that they are really glad that the company moved. He would otherwise not have realised how ready he was for retirement.

New methods and sophisticated electronic equipment in offices and factories can seem threatening to those accustomed to less up-to-date methods of working. However, if older people give themselves time to learn new skills, practise them and gain confidence, they can compete with any age group.

Competition from Younger Employees

The competition from younger and often more highly qualified people may not be easy to deal with. As one gets older and feels the strain of competing, the notion of retirement becomes more attractive and is a very acceptable option.

To have a younger person put in charge can come as a shock. The idea that education might be more valuable than long experience can prove difficult to live with.

Not Like the Old Days

Being an older person in charge of younger staff can be frustrating. The older generation is more often accustomed to being disciplined and to working longer and harder. Older people may expect today's young work-force to do as they do, keeping nose to grindstone. But there are quite different expectations today of more time off, easier working conditions together with self-certification for absence due to sickness.

The older ones often say that they worked through colds and sickness and it did them no harm, so why should today's younger employees not do the same? Those who cannot accept the new customs may find it easier to retire than try to manage a work-force demanding a completely different set of standards.

A Brief Step into Retirement

The introduction of new office equipment does not always mean an immediate lessening of need for staff, even though it is likely to do this in the long term. Reductions in staff often means that pressure is increased for those remaining.

Marion worked for many years in the office of a large nursing home. Computers were introduced and she was told that with changing needs everything had to be updated and the office would be run quite differently. She knew that she would be quite unable to cope with the 'new-fangled machines' and felt it best to retire. She was fifty-eight years old.

Over the next days and weeks she missed the work intensely, missed the routine and bustle of the nursing home. Occupied with the care of her mother until the old lady's death the previous year, Marion had never taken up any kind of hobby or indeed any kind of activity, other than her job.

She had busied herself wholly with that and keeping her flat in order. As a result, there was little social activity in her life. She lacked the nerve to try for another job and really felt that her life was now pointless.

The office missed her too, the other staff feeling hard pressed, trying to carry on while the problems relating to the new technology were sorted out. When it was realized that switching to modern systems was going to take longer than expected, she was asked to return and was thankful to do so.

Marion had always felt shy and insecure and this had prevented her from seeking and finding friends. But the brief step into retirement had been frightening and lonely. Spurred by the experience, she now decided to join a club where, under the wing of an understanding person, she is encouraged to take part in joint ventures, going to the theatre, visiting great houses and taking holidays together with new friends. Permanent retirement, whenever it comes, will find her less vulnerable.

Overtime is offered as an option in some jobs but may be virtually compulsory in others. Unless the job is enjoyable as well as financially rewarding, it is often not thought worthwhile to put in more time than is necessary. Where older people feel uncomfortable about refusing to do overtime, they may well determine to retire early rather than reluctantly work longer hours.

Be Happy in Your Work

It is worth finding an occupation where one is content. Feeling happy at work often results in being happier in every other sphere of life. The highest paid of jobs is not seen as satisfactory unless it is also a job one enjoys and can feel glad to do. Unhappiness at work can provide a valid excuse to take early retirement. People do not all have a primary interest in money.

By the time that a career is recognized as unsuitable it may be a complicated matter to train for, and find, an alternative occupation. Personal ambitions develop more slowly in some people than in others and success can be stifled when a personality is poorly matched to a job. If this is recognized late, it should never be regarded as too late. A change can still be made.

Challenging Work Preferred

People do not easily bring the right commitment and enthusiasm to employment when they feel discontented. Work must not only be interesting and worthwhile but also challenging. When people feel like square pegs in round holes they become stressed and sooner or later health will suffer. Happy people are far less likely to suffer ill-health.

Changing Careers

The only child of an ambitious mother, Harold became a surgeon because that was what she wanted. But he never got over his distaste at the sight of blood. Despite his qualification he felt at last that he simply could not cope with his work. Had he continued, his health would have been at risk and he may have had to take early retirement. Although he did not give up medicine he changed direction and became a psychiatrist. No doubt his sensitivity gave him an extra intuitive insight into the problems of his patients. He is now prepared to work on as long as possible.

Exploitation by Colleagues

Stuart is a widower. He misses his wife and his home feels too lonely, so after retirement he got a job in a café. It did not work out well. Working alongside a colleague who habitually takes excessive time off can be frustrating. Stuart did not mind the long hours in the café but the manager frequently came in late, took time off and generally failed to pull his weight. Stuart said: 'I had enough of that. One day I just told him that he could get on with it and I left. He was taking too many liberties'.

No one likes to feel that they are being taken advantage of and constant aggravation is wearing. If retirement is an option it could well be preferred. Stuart, with modest needs and a pension from work in addition to his State pension, did not need the money. What he did need was some occupation in order to combat the loneliness that he had felt since his bereavement. But he was not prepared to be exploited.

Feeling Unwanted

Four years ago, Teresa retired unexpectedly early. She had worked for one firm all her life and at fourteen she had been among the youngest of the machinists in a factory making ladies' dresses. At fifty-nine, she was the eldest in her section, with many of her younger colleagues frequently taking time off from work, for one reason or another. A conscientious worker herself, Teresa was rarely absent.

In a rare mood of rebellion, she took a few days off and on her return was made to feel so uncomfortable that she thought that she had better retire. It was clear that the management wanted younger employees. While she felt that her work was up to standard and that their attitude was unfair, she was not prepared to take the hassle and so she left.

She had enough for her modest needs and her spirits rose as she thought about the days of freedom stretching ahead. The unhappiness and vexation had been making her ill. Lightheartedly, she worked out the days of notice. 'They'd never seen me so happy at work. I left on quite good terms and go in and see them now and again. I tell them that they should think of retiring as early as possible, it's wonderful. I've learned to swim and go twice a week to the local pool. I go to the library and read all the papers and I travel about on the buses to places I never knew existed. I go to a lunch club and a friendly circle where they have speakers about subjects that I had previously never even heard of. We go in a coach to the theatre. Oh, I tell you, I'm out of the house every day by ten and there isn't a minute wasted.'

When next I saw Teresa she had been tempted by the offer

of a job as a part-time alteration and counter hand at a local dry-cleaners. She took the job for three days a week and enjoyed the change of working environment and the daily contact with the public. 'It's knowing that I don't *have* to work, that's what I like, that and meeting the customers. They tell you all their troubles and I was always a good listener. The extra money means that I can have holidays abroad which I never thought I'd be able to do.'

Anyone thinking of retirement will still need continuity, a link with all that they are used to. They should be able to take part in community life, remaining in contact with their own families and valued friends.

Preparing for retirement must not mean that an end has come or that one is to do nothing. On the contrary, it means a new beginning, a fresh start, possibly a use of knowledge in a different way. All the years of experience represent a storehouse, a wealth of valuable know-how which should not be wasted. The older generation has so much to offer.

Retirement is certainly going to mean change and some of us do not welcome that. But it is inevitable and provided that we make the most of what we have, life can be good, we can be serene, content and able to take pleasure in phase three of our lives.

3 Making the Best of the Rest

Being Positive

At no time in life is it so important to keep all your options open as when you reach the age of retirement and consider how to make the most of the next thirty or so years. Priorities at this time will be different, perhaps more selfishly orientated, but we have to think of ourselves and our partners, our own hopes and wishes as we plan the years ahead.

It is reassuring to find that most of those concerns and fears about our sixties are groundless. In our thirties we heard that life began at forty. But in our forties, we came to realise that the fifties, with the children off our hands, might be best of all. But isn't it at sixty, when we retire that we really savour freedom, feeling little different from the way we used to?

Still feeling Sixteen

Lena began her working life as a young girl training to be a maid in the kitchens of Buckingham Palace. She was a frequent visitor to our Citizens Advice Bureau and on this occasion she had some difficulties with household bills which we sorted out for her. Before leaving, she said, 'That's such a relief. I feel sixteen again'. Picking up her shopping bags she went on, 'I wish you could do something about my son. He is not a bit helpful. I do all the shopping and cooking and he will not do a thing'. 'How old is your son?' I asked. 'Eighty-two', she answered.

My client did not seem to have changed her views about her son. She was his mother and she expected help from him, just as she probably did some seventy years or so before.

Learning with each Decade

As we arrive at each new decade, our expectations and ambitions alter. We should expect and hope that at each age we will be reasonably happy and successful. Maturity brings its compensations, as we learn some lessons and know ourselves better, not only our capabilities but our limitations. How many of us take full account of our potential, only realizing in our later years how much more we could have achieved.

Early Psychological Damage

We set up mental blocks for ourselves and whilst they may not be easy to undo it is worth having a try. The process of learning is influenced by many factors, some of which relate to the characteristics of the learner. These may be due to personality, background experience, motivation or self-perception. By the time we are mature adults we may feel that we are set in our ways and nothing can change us. But if we understand that we have been conditioned by some circumstance or other we may be able to change. We may succeed in overcoming the responses of fear, anger, anxiety or doubt. On retirement, when we should no longer feel worried about whatever any one thinks, we are often able to successfully tackle projects we previously felt were beyond us.

For instance, most people have a fear of examinations. Robert believed that he could never pass the exams which would give him promotion in the Civil Service. All his working life, he remained in a minor clerical post. A year after retirement, he went to night school and took an 'O' level, passing with good marks. 'I was still nervous, dreading to fail, thinking that everyone would know how stupid I was, but now that I have had a small success, I don't feel so worried any more and I'm going to go on and do more, maybe even an Open University course.'

Realizing Ambitions

Throughout her life, Dorothy had been stage struck but lacked any confidence that she could possibly succeed as an actress. When she was sixty and retired from her job as a factory supervisor she decided to satisfy her long felt desire to act. She went along to the local amateur dramatic society and asked if she could join. It was some months before there was a play she could read for but she did well and impressed everyone with her natural ability and clear voice. No one can imagine her pleasure at having realized her ambition. It was early discouragement from her father at her attempts to act which had dissuaded her from trying her luck on the stage.

Age no Bar

Recently a woman of seventy set a new record for motor racing and it is commonplace to hear of sixty and seventy year olds who take part in unusual projects; parachute jumps for charity, gliding, learning to fly. Many are people achieving long-felt ambitions. The retired generation does not lack for courage, taking to sports they have never previously had the opportunity to try. They learn to sail, to ski, entering competitions and races and even if they do not stand a chance of winning, they certainly have as good a time as any of the other competitors.

Each year marathon races are run by numbers of fit retirees who enjoy participating in the day, along with people who are considerably younger. They run not to win but to prove to themselves and to the world that they can do it and that age does not bar one from these activities.

We need no longer worry about wearing the right sort of clothes. We can be casually clad in easy wear sweaters and slacks, dressing up only when we really want to or have special occasions to go to. We no longer have to fit into the role pattern that is expected of people who fill certain jobs.

Role Playing

We can fill other roles than those we are used to, sharing jobs like house care, shopping and cooking. Man or woman, we can try decorating, plumbing, dressmaking or painting. Anyone, male or female, can be good at fishing, or carpentry, photography or cookery. Retired, we can ignore the artificial limitations and barriers.

A hundred years ago people were confined by their sex to conform to a pattern. This was particularly restrictive for women who were not encouraged to do anything which required extensive study in case it was alleged, they might do themselves some damage. Lord Byron's only legitimate child, Ada, grew into a young woman whose outstanding mathematical ability was acknowledged, yet she found difficulty in pursuing her studies. It was thought that as a female, she must be too weak physically for the strain that study would impose. Fortunately for her, she married a man who did not hold this view and who acknowledged her intellectual superiority and encouraged her in her work. When she wrote analytical papers, they were praised but described as being like the work of a man, not at all like those of a woman!

Dr Anne Walton, a Fellow of the Royal Society of Chemistry, was commissioned to write a book entitled, *It's A Woman's World Too*, describing the outstanding achievements of some of today's women. It was frequently the case that not only did the work of these women fail to receive acknowledgement, but their male colleagues got the accolades for their results. No one can deny that such women are at least equal to men and suffered much injustice.

Equal Opportunity for Men

By the time of retirement any idea of role playing can be forgotten as people do any job that needs to be done or which they wish to do, regardless of sex. Men can undertake any of the jobs traditionally done by women and therefore often given a lower status. And women, without loss of femininity, can take up any work they would like to do. We have had a lifetime in which to prove ourselves and we know our own value. We have reached the time of life when we can stand firm by our own personal tastes, think for a change only of what pleases us and choose what to do and when to do it without bothering about what views may be held by anyone else.

Mature Students

Perhaps we have had interests or ambitions in the past that regretfully we could not pursue because there was not time. Now, there is time and we should never say, 'Ah, but it's too late'.

Alison was seventy-one, retired and living in the Bahamas when she began a correspondence course to study Greek. Her father had thought it was not worthwhile to let girls continue studies or attend university and, as a busy secretary, Alison had always been too occupied to consider additional projects. But, an ardent reader, she had always had an ambition to read original works by Greek philosophers. She knew the utmost satisfaction when she qualified and says that the years of study gave her much happiness. Now, she coaches students and says that she has no intention of ever retiring.

Henry was in his final years as a practising solicitor and beginning to think of retirement. Articled in 1936, he had to register for military duty two years later and was unable to take his degree because of the liability for call-up into the army. He did take his solicitors' final qualification in 1941 but within a few days was called up.

With the war over, Henry went into private practice until 1980. In all those years, despite a very successful career, he had often wondered whether he would be capable of further study in order to gain a law degree. He debated in his mind whether he was up to it. His wife, Edna, always supportive, encouraged him to make the attempt and, at sixty, he enrolled for a course, studied hard and at last gained a

Bachelor of Law degree. As a result, he felt equal to those of his colleagues who had earlier gained the qualification.

Retired people should not feel deterred by their age to undertake new work or studies. Those in the sixty and seventy age group can do anything that they set their minds to. Younger students as well as teachers have said that they find mature students a real challenge and stimulating to work with.

Tasting Freedom

The freedom that comes with retirement is heady. We can feel relaxed about time, move in a more leisurely fashion, doing what we want to do when we want to do it. We may read for as long as we want to, saunter out for walks or drive wherever we fancy going. We can if we wish, sit up and watch television until the cows come home and then sleep the morning away without feeling guilty. While we do not want to make a regular practice of lazy behaviour, it is pleasant to be self-indulgent for a while. We do not have to consider what other people think of what we are doing, saying or wearing. Our time, our money, our views are ours alone.

We may feel a little uncertain about our future objectives, needing to give some thought to what will suit us best. If we have not prepared ourselves for the ways to keep busy in the years ahead, then we need to look around, join clubs where there are activities which sound attractive to us and decide what to do with these lovely, leisure years.

Now is the time to seek out old friends, make new ones with whom we have mutual interests, meeting for tea or for lunch to talk together about future plans. We should try to become good listeners, joining in social chatter, which so few of us have the time to do as long as we are engaged in the hurly-burly of working life. We should question whether we concentrate on what other people are saying, whether we hear out their thoughts and ideas. It is so easy to get out of the habit of careful listening.

Research has shown that many people, especially when

they are older, interrupt each other continually without apparent attention to what is being said. This is not a good habit to get into. We should have the courtesy to consider other people's ideas, whether we agree with them or not. There are the dogmatic ones amongst us who automatically disapprove of other people's views.

Coming out of the world of paid employment, whether by choice or not, leaves us with a wealth of valuable knowledge which it is a crying shame to waste. Much of that experience can be used in so many different ways. Once the long holidays have been taken and all the jobs which we kept putting off are out of the way, we can be more successfully retired, more content, by becoming usefully occupied.

Whether we possess high academic qualifications or have gained our expertise in the work-place, once we give up employment the problems are the same. We have to decide what we can do, what we would like to do, with our time.

The First Days

The early days following retirement may be deservedly spent in idle relaxation. But this must not continue for long. We do not want to become habitually indolent, listless or to wind ourselves down too far. We must soon begin to tackle the question of occupation in the coming months in a definite way.

The future can be interesting and exciting and that is how we should perceive it. Provided we do respond in this way we will not be short of energy and there is plenty to feel zestful about.

Provided that we do not needlessly limit ourselves or close the doors on ambitions, however unattainable they may at first appear to be, we have a wide range open to us. All kinds of activities are possible even for those who have physical limitations – sports, education, jobs, hobbies, holidays.

The Odd Jobs

Home may be the first place to look and there is likely to be plenty to do. Are there jobs that we have put aside for some time, things that we felt we simply could not face? Are there matters that are tiresome or unpleasant to think about that need decisions? Try making a determined start with just one of them, perhaps the paper filing or organizing photos, or clearing out such items as we all accumulate that are unlikely ever to be used. Keep at it until something has been achieved, by which time any tiredness and boredom may well have disappeared.

We can all look back on those times when, regardless of our age, we felt full of life and never seemed to get tired. Remember how the days were never long enough to fit in all the things we wanted to do? How much of that energy was due to excitement and interest?

What about the other times when you felt too tired to keep going and wanted the day to end, when enthusiasm flagged and you needed matchsticks to keep your eyes open? How much of that fatigue was due to boredom and not to lack of energy?

Do we delude ourselves that because we have reached the fifties or sixties we have less gusto than we used to have? Few of us tap into those resources that we all have within us and consequently accomplish less and lower our feelings of self-worth.

Activity Promotes Energy

We must recognize our potential, form a positive view and take steps to increase our activity. The more we undertake, the easier it becomes to do more and the power to accomplish any objective flows in. How often is it said that if you want to get something done you ask a busy person? Someone who is occupied and interested has more energy flow yet feels less tired than another who is always relaxing or resting. We do need rest but too much of it saps strength.

Physical and mental activities complement each other, maintaining optimum strength if we stretch our brain and body. We must seek to employ these powers continually if we are not to lose or weaken them.

Today in hospitals patients are required to get up as soon as possible following treatment or an operation, because inactivity is weakening. We actually lose bone mass in quite a short time unless we keep going and keep well-exercised. We could lose height and strength and our bones might fracture more easily.

It doesn't make sense to lead a busy life up until the time we stop work and then switch right off. It can be dangerous. Too many examples exist of the busy executive or worker who took retirement too literally and did nothing, only to become despondent and chairbound. This pattern leads on to illness and such a person could even die within a few months of stopping work.

Getting into a Fit Condition

We need to have sensible life-styles and see to it that we have enough to occupy our minds with, as well as plenty of the right sort of physical exercise. Ask yourself whether you are getting out and about, bending and stretching, walking briskly in the fresh air. We are like complex machines and we must give ourselves the care we would give to a machine.

How often do people say that they feel too tired to go out, yet when they make the effort they actually return home feeling livelier? We should organize our time, set a plan of action and see that we keep to it.

Becoming fitter through activity and exercise results in an increase in self-esteem; when you feel good about yourself you naturally have more energy, more capability. Once you have this positive outlook, you have increased power, not only to do additional tasks, but also to withstand infection, illness and to resist the onset of ageing and its attendant problems. Positive people say, 'I don't get colds', or, 'I have no time to be ill', and they stay fit.

Try something Different

Whatever activity we undertake, whether it is familiar or something entirely new we should only take it on after consideration. Phoebe thought that she would like to undertake an educational art course and having almost reached a decision, suddenly changed her mind. 'I am going to try and get some voluntary work with a veterinary surgeon', she said. 'I love animals more than I like people and I want to give my time in this way.' She had reached this decision almost subconsciously, but having made it, she felt quite certain that she was right. She soon found something to suit her and settled contentedly to work.

There are many voluntary posts to fill, and we may be adequately experienced to tackle some of them, others we may need training for. These voluntary occupations can take one into a world quite different from that which was familiar to us during working life and they provide work which can be both rewarding and fulfilling. Some will be on an expenses paid basis so that we will be covered for any travel costs incurred.

Why is Seventy Different?

The age of seventy provides a landmark. It is when society says, 'Well, of course they are seventy, you know'. Or, 'How on earth do they do these things at their age'. It is as though people are thought to have crossed a bridge, suddenly becoming different. Of course there is no reason to be altered at all by achieving a seventieth birthday. The reason that people do what they do, whatever that may be and whatever the age, is because they maintain vitality and a sense of fun . . . in a word, they retain a zest for living.

The negative attitude towards people in their seventies is overdue for a change. What about all those in public life who are achievers in their late sixties and seventies and who are successful, healthy and happy?

In fact, getting to be fifty, sixty, seventy, eighty or more is just a celebration of birthdays. What matters is how you feel and act. A youthful friend, Henry, said to me recently: 'I can still feel thrilled and excited at the thought of a treat, just as I did when I had my first haircut or my first date. Some days I walk down the street all excited and still feel as though my feet don't touch the ground'. And he won't see seventy again. It helps of course that his wife Clare is such a delightful and understanding seventy year old herself. If you want to speak to him on the 'phone, make sure that it is before eight o'clock in the morning. After that he could be out of his flat and on his way.

The emphasis has to be on what we can achieve in a new period of our lives, regardless of age. The only problem is going to be in determining just what we want to do. We can get tired when we are young and tired when we are old. These are not new feelings. We are more natural, less conventional and we are more attracted by tranquillity. If we have been lucky and clever enough to have had a secure and happy marriage and good health then we will also have a contented spirit and we will feel our age far less. Contentment is like a beacon, it attracts people to us.

As the years go by and we have time to look back over different decades, each one allows us a deeper recognition of the more valuable things in life. Time to ponder on the mysteries of the universe, on religion, on humanity and to note sometimes how a few of the jigsaw pieces of life fit into place.

No one ever said that ageing was easy – and growing old is not for cissies. What we must do is to make the third part of our lives as rewarding, as much fun and as worthwhile as it is possible to do.

4 Education – No One is Too Old

An exciting new world of knowledge awaits anyone who is willing to stretch their mind and learn. Even those now retired, who left school at an early age, perhaps at thirteen or fourteen, and who have possibly never thought themselves capable of further education, should know that there is much that they can achieve.

They will be surprised at the wide availability and range of courses these days for mature adults. Education is a great way to broaden interests and everyone can choose something valuable to learn from such a range of subjects.

Districts will vary in what they can offer and you may have to look around to find the particular class you wish to join. What would you like to do? Something practical, where you use your hands, such as upholstery, embroidery, or woodwork? Or perhaps you prefer something academic offering mental stimulation, subjects like genealogy, world religions or Sanskrit. When you find that you have time on your hands, do try something new.

Among the long lists of interesting, practical subjects you can study, there are classes for plumbing, electrical wiring and other skills which can be invaluable in household maintenance. How useful it is to learn how to tackle home repairs. A course in basic plumbing would solve the mystery of the water system, teaching one how to change washers or taps or deal with a leak. Even clearing the drains can be attempted with every chance of success if we have the know-how and the right equipment. A set of cleaning brushes would cost about a tenth of the price a repair man might charge for a single visit. You don't have to buy the expensive items any more; hire shops have a comprehensive selection of most tools you might need.

A few lessons on electrical wiring and there would be no more doubt about how to change plugs or fit wall sockets and re-wiring a bedside lamp becomes a doddle. We would no longer have to hunt through Yellow Pages for emergency services in the event of a minor 'disaster' and then be shocked by the bill. We could be getting on with repair jobs with confidence in our own capability. Even when employing someone to do a job, it is better to know something about how it should be done, recognizing if it is done correctly. One can then comment with assurance.

With a background of a course in car maintenance, one can save a small fortune as well as wear and tear on the car. It is surprising how few know how to change a tyre or a gasket or recognize the more common reasons why cars fail to start.

What about mastering the right way to cover a divan, make curtains and bedspreads or those attractive cushions which add so much to the appeal and comfort of a room? French polishing is not all that difficult to learn and can make all the difference to the appearance of furniture. Learn something about the interior decorator's use of colour co-ordination, the professional way to paper walls and tiling a bathroom.

If none of these tempt the would-be student then find something to keep fingers busy, for example making toys for young relatives or charity bazaars and, of course, dressmaking skills would make one very popular. Anyone can learn how to knit, to crochet, make patchwork, do quilting or embroider, even if they have never picked up a knitting or sewing needle in their lives.

Men or women should not feel they are restricted by their sex or be too inhibited to join any one of these classes. Men, for instance, are among the finest couturiers in the country and colleges turn out successful male as well as female graduates, who can all design and produce beautiful clothes.

It was the sailors of old who brought the craft of knitting to British shores, but few men knit today. It is not only a rewarding occupation but since this craft keeps fingers constantly moving it is also a good means of improving circulation. Knitters rarely feel the cold.

Cookery

Whilst there will always be one or two favourite foods which we never seem to tire of, we can all get a little jaded faced with a diet of the same old recipes. A course in the preparation of varied menus can stimulate the desire to cook the unusual. It is often the quite simple but delicious and healthy recipes which are most popular in cookery classes. Many retired couples go together to such classes, finding it fun to share the lessons and taste the food. I do not know why people should express surprise that these lessons are of equal interest to men and women. Certainly, most of the cooking at home is done by women but the majority of the great chefs of the world are men.

Learn about specialized subjects, perhaps baking with yeast to produce delicious home-made bread and buns. Some will be attracted by the creations possible with cake decoration or sugarcraft. Specialist cake-makers are in demand for celebration occasions like weddings and birthdays.

After a course in cookery, eight retired friends decided to hold dinner parties in rotation in each other's houses, vying with each other to produce new dishes. They found it a lot of fun, providing a weekly, inexpensive evening of interest, following the meal with some music or a video film. They went on to organize charity evenings, demonstrating how to cook different courses and raising funds for local charitable projects.

Meat-eaters seem to imagine that vegetarian diets are boring and repetitive, not realising how appetising and varied their recipes can be. Attending classes to learn how to prepare meatless meals would doubtless be of benefit, not only to individuals but also to their families. Such meals may take more thought and time and it seems easier to put a roast in the oven or chops under the grill. But for a variety of reasons a great many people today are opting for vegetarian food and need to know about the use of soya, lentils, beans and other pulses which are adequate substitutes for meat.

Photography

A popular course with all age groups is photography. Modern cameras are 'idiot proof' and it is easy to get satisfactory results. However, to produce first-class photographs one needs a certain amount of expertise and the ability to appreciate the difference between mediocre and superb photographs. Achieving the best balance of subject and background, knowing how to use light to the best advantage are skills which can be acquired by anyone with the patience to listen and practise. Learning from past efforts and mistakes is one way to achieve steady improvement but getting the help of a professional is a more satisfactory short cut.

Exercising Body and Mind

There are a number of systems of philosophic meditation and asceticism, beneficial to physical and mental health and which can be learned in group or individual classes. Among the most highly regarded of these is yoga and most areas offer courses in this subject. Anyone who feels troubled in mind and spirit or thinks that they would benefit from learning how to relax, should try a course. It can become a way of life and weekends of study are often arranged. Here is one way of finding new friends.

There are many other systems, each having the result of generally improved health. They have in common their aims of attaining by natural methods a better mental and physical state. The students of the Alexander Method, for example, will say that they can recognize in the street or across the room another student of their method. The way they walk and hold themselves is said to be characteristic and basic to the teachings of Alexander. Good deportment and correct balance are regarded as all-important.

Karate has become well known as a defensive art. It is

fascinating to watch and is a Japanese system of unarmed combat where one uses one's hands and feet as weapons. Performed by an expert it can be a dangerous and deadly science. The student of karate must be in superb condition with every muscle under control and only the fittest of retirees could think of studying this subject.

Ketama is another less strenuous method, specifically aimed at reducing stress and helping people to cope calmly with the everyday problems of life, whilst also teaching the art of self-defence.

There are many different forms of defence, relaxation, breathing and exercise techniques. Whichever method one decides to learn, it is important to go to an accredited teacher who can demonstrate the proper way to practise. Incorrect and unsupervised exercises could be harmful.

The claims for all these methods are impressive, making the five senses more alert, improving circulation and breath control as well as reducing high blood pressure.

Art Appreciation

A course in antique or modern art appreciation would not only give one a better understanding and a deeper insight into the work produced by great artists, but could result in a trip to Paris, Florence or Venice to look at some of the magnificent galleries found there. Travelling abroad in the company of other students and guided by teachers, the study of art can be given quite a different perspective, broadening the vision and giving fresh insight into the artist's mind. There really is no telling where education might take one.

Education while on Holiday

Taking classes while on vacation is an increasingly popular option, particularly for those who are retired and who seek to broaden their interests. It may be the study of Scottish poetry in Edinburgh, architecture in Paris, classical music in Toronto, or basic Spanish in Alicante. The goal is not to get any kind of qualification but simply to satisfy or re-awaken a love of learning. There is an international programme of study vacations geared to people of sixty or more.

The interest in this kind of holiday is increasing as the number of student retirees grows each year. The English-speaking group numbers more than a quarter of a million, the majority of whom attend courses abroad each year. Some stay at the great or smaller universities in simple student rooms, others in guesthouses or hotels.

The non-profit making organization, Elderhostal, has now expanded to forty-four countries and more than 1,000 institutions. The range of interest varies so enormously as to be able to satisfy just about any taste and a glance at the list of what is available shows anything from Indian mythology to archaeology, from all languages and literature to various handicrafts.

One of the major advantages in taking further education is to develop and raise self-awareness, allowing individuals to broaden and develop their personality. They so often find qualities and levels in themselves that they either did not know existed, or only half suspected.

Other Subjects

Those not tempted to become practical handymen or women might join drama classes, choral societies, or take lessons in playing a musical instrument. Others might wish to study psychology or philosophy. Creative writing is popular with all age groups and an ever-increasing proportion of students go on to have their work published. With so many journals there is an enormous market for articles on all kinds of subjects and it is satisfying to get into print.

Learning to Grow Things

Lessons in gardening might arouse a latent enthusiasm for horticultural pursuits. People could find that they have green fingers after all as they learn how to solve some of the problems encountered locally with soil or in growing particular flowers, vegetables or plants. Working with plants and close to the earth can have a marked therapeutic effect.

Feeling Academic

The more academically inclined could study a familiar subject, perhaps taking a higher qualification. Or something totally new might appeal to them, history, a language, even accountancy or the law. A course in dealing in stocks, shares and investments could prove of interest as well as sometimes being of financial benefit. For example, at sixty-four Arthur unwillingly had to retire when his business failed. He and his wife were living in reduced circumstances on income support. Tentatively, he took a small gamble on the Stock Exchange. One success led to another and while he never recovered his previous financial standing, the couple had sufficient money to take frequent holidays which they very much enjoyed.

Not everyone can read the markets so successfully and the first lesson to learn would be that shares go down as well as up, as most of the promotional finance advertisements are now obliged to tell us. And always remember the City adage – do not gamble unless you can afford to lose.

New Technology

The keyboard skills which the young pick up with such ease, using them so matter-of-factly at school and at home, are not beyond our understanding. Learning to use word processors enables us to write effortlessly and to print error-free work. Understanding fax machines allows us to exchange letters and documents of any length almost instantaneously. This new technology opens up a magical world and there is no reason why grandparents should not become as competent as their grandchildren. All it needs is a few months of disciplined application and we can be as good at it as anyone else.

Wendy and Bill were two of a group of clerks who thought they would have to retire when their office filing system was computerized. But they and their colleagues were persuaded to take a college course which enabled them to understand the visual display unit system and every single one mastered it in a few weeks. This group of men and women were in their fifties and sixties. They retained their jobs and have great pride in their newly-found skills.

Mature Students Welcome

Local authority colleges offer courses to mature adults on these and other subjects, often supplemented by flexible lessons designed to suit the pace of the student's progress.

Colleges have excellent facilities, and give a particularly warm welcome to mature newcomers. Since such students are regarded as committed and rewarding to work with, they are good examples to their less mature classmates. Older people are proving that they can keep up with younger students, contributing an interesting dimension to the class.

Among the tempting amenities to be found in colleges are warm and well-equipped classrooms and libraries. Canteen prices are modest and well-balanced meals are served. There is a great opportunity for different age groups to meet and discuss not only their classroom subjects but topics of the day and social matters of mutual interest.

Some of the subjects may be studied off the main site but students can still take advantage of all college facilities, which in some of the more modern buildings include well-equipped gymnasia and swimming pools.

It is easy for the older generation to believe that with their greater experience they can monopolize a conversation. This must be resisted for it could damage future relationships. There are many things we can learn from the young.

Colleges, schools and polytechnics distribute leaflets and brochures listing the part-time and full-time courses they offer, covering just about all of the recognized needs of the particular area, including those of ethnic minorities. The modest charges incurred are generally well within the range of most pockets. In some areas courses are either free or offered at much reduced cost to pensioners or those on low income. Courses are graded and no one need fear that they will be out of their depth or that they will be made to feel inadequate. Beginners' classes assume that one knows nothing of a particular subject.

Initial courses last just a few weeks, allowing students a closer look at the subject while they decide if they really like it and feel comfortable with the work involved. If they do enjoy it, they can make a bigger commitment and go on to an intermediate stage. It is stressed that no one has to take exams, though it is rewarding to do so and a stimulant to students to continue the work.

Some courses include students who are of mixed ability and who work at different levels. Beginners might find that there are special arrangements to allow them to integrate well into such classes.

Could you Teach?

You might be good at one of the subjects and find yourself in demand as a part-time teacher, all set to enjoy a new career in your retirement. This happened to Fred who was bought out of his kitchen-manufacturing business but given a five-year contract as a consultant. When this concluded he was only sixty and wondered what he might do. He applied for a post at the local college as a teacher of carpentry where his skills were much appreciated.

University of the Third Age (U3A)

This national network provides the kind of education which suits local taste and demand. U3A caters largely for the retired and its brochures give details of local groups and the courses it runs. (See Useful Addresses.)

U3A is an association of men and women in the 'third age' or retirement phase; there are no age limits or any tests for admission. Fees are kept low because it is a self-help organization, a learning community and the central concept is that members shall participate in an educational experience to which they may all contribute.

Schemes have been developed to suit people who are home-based because they have limited mobility. Current outline programmes are sent to enquirers and members are sent full and updated programmes during each year.

The wide range of subjects includes languages, politics and philosophy, art, psychology and religion. There are study tours abroad, residential weekend courses and all-in-all there is much on offer. Members themselves provide the administrative support, sending out information about activities as well as runing the important social events.

U3A has affiliated with various educational institutions and while the London group is independent and self-governing it is aligned to the Third Age Trust which brings together the U3A groups of the UK. The Trust is itself part of a movement which is rapidly spreading throughout the civilized world.

Planning your own Course

Whilst the range and choice of studies at our colleges for day or evening study is immense, any group of about ten or more wishing to study a particular subject not already available, might manage to interest the local authority in funding the course. Alternatively, such a group might itself be capable of raising the funding for a teacher.

Correspondence Courses

Some companies offer a variety of courses by post and as long as a student has the determination and commitment to complete the work within a reasonable time, the correspondence course can be a successful way of acquiring knowledge. But there is usually less personal contact with teachers or opportunity to meet other students so the value of such courses is limited. Some find such courses ideal, preferring the privacy of working at home. Whatever the form of study, the keen student will find it stimulating.

Correspondence courses can be ideal for students who cannot easily get out, who are shy or who do not have a college within convenient reach. Examinations up to full degree levels are available and offer an added and enjoyable stimulus and challenge for those who wish to take them. Whatever course you decide on, use an accredited and recommended college.

Open University

The Open University (see Useful Addresses) has given thousands of mature students the opportunity to take degrees in a variety of subjects. Students meet their tutors and occasionally put in a week at summer school. They work from radio and television programmes and some of the lessons are in cassette form. Students go along at the pace suited to their own individual capabilities.

Jonathan became disabled following a fall from a ladder and retired early from his job as a school caretaker. He decided to obtain the education that he had never acquired as a young man. He was a plodder who worked slowly and methodically and although it took eight years he gained a degree in social science. Not everyone wishes to take education to this high level, many will be quite happy to sign on for a year at a time, or for short vocational or general interest courses.

Learning from TV and Radio

Further education provides not only a means to stretch the mind but a link with other people, an opportunity to make friends, form lasting relationships, taking one out into a wonderful world, brimful of interest. A number of programmes are arranged on both TV and radio which are backed up by books or cassettes. They are popular and a pleasant way to learn.

The Value of Study

There are even courses on planning for retirement which look full of interesting material and could be just what retirees might need. No doubt Alfred, who knows the value of education and who does not believe in retirement, will be studying one of these when he gives up his present occupation.

Alfred's schooling was abruptly interrupted by the war when he was thirteen and since his school was evacuated to the country, far from his home in London, he got a job in a factory. Now this young lad showed his mettle. He determined that the way ahead was to study and become an accountant and because he needed his wage of ten shillings a week, he took a correspondence course so that he could study in the evenings. This he doggedly followed all through the war, both when he worked in a coal-mine and later when he joined the Royal Air Force. Soon after the end of the war his perseverance paid off and he qualified, thereafter steadily rising in his profession to become a partner in a prestigious, international practice. At fifty-nine he retired, only to change course and become a financial consultant, busier than ever.

He plans to develop his interest in charitable trusts and institutions when he is sixty-five. In this he will be aided by his wife, Helen, who in her fifties is an attractive, vivacious and much sought after singer at charitable events. 'Retirement', he said, 'that's the wrong word. Change of direction is all it is.'

5 Hobbies and Pets

Enjoyable Activities

During our working lives when we are busy making a living and bringing up families there is precious little time during which we can do just as we please. So often we will have foregone involvement in something that would have given us pleasure, simply because there were so many other demands on us. We may have felt guilty at snatching hours for ourselves to join in sport or watch a favourite programme on television or even to read a book.

The commitment to things that have to be done takes over to such an extent that the hobbies or pleasurable activities which we enjoyed in our youth tend to get crowded out of our lives as we grow older. If we let this happen we are left with few interests outside of work and no ideas about what to do when we retire and suddenly find ourselves with this most valuable commodity, time, with nothing to fill it.

When the day comes that we no longer have a rush of activity, we will need some leisure interests. We will not have to think of 'spare time' or what is left over after work because all our time becomes our own.

You might, of course, be one of those organized people with full plans for retirement and all your leisure hours booked. In the course of writing this book I met several men and women who had reached their seventies and eighties and more. They fairly brimmed with ideas for leisure and while some asked questions about widening the range of their hobbies, most were absorbed in their day's activities and had hardly any time to spare. Could this be the secret of their healthy longevity?

A hobby which can be shared with the community is particularly worthwhile because it enlarges the circle of acquaintances. Find out what activities are booked for the next few weeks at the local community hall, civic centre or library. It is important to get out and about and see what is going on.

Having somewhere to go, occasions to dress up for, even though casually, give a sense of purpose to life. Sitting at home, hunched in front of a television set for several hours at a stretch is no good for anyone, nor is it healthy. Staying in quietly every night is alright for some of us but we also need the stimulation that comes from mixing with others.

It is sensible and comforting to have something put by for the inevitable rainy day, but we should not deny ourselves needlessly. When I suggested to a pensioner who had been ill that she once again start her hobby of taking days out to various parts of the country, she said that she could not afford it. But we both knew that she had a certain sum in the bank and when I asked what she was saving it for, she answered in all innocence, 'My old age'. 'Your old age is here', I replied, for she was eighty-five.

Changing Hobbies

With time to spend as we wish we may recall a pleasurable experience which we would like to repeat. Perhaps it was a concert, an evening at the theatre or a weekend away in a country hotel. Whatever it was we once enjoyed, we should do it again and re-live the experience.

There are some dreams we have which seem unattainable. Yet, if we really make up our minds, there may be a way to make the improbable become reality. Think of Grandma Moses who was well beyond retirement age when she began painting and despite the arthritis in her fingers produced astonishing work which brought her world fame and wealth.

Age did not prevent Francis Chichester from taking on the elements and sailing round the world. Their dreams came true. There is little doubt that many of us only lack confidence, some determination and willpower in order to succeed in our ambitions.

As we grow older, approaching retirement, we may prefer

to change some of our leisure pursuits and provided we are fit enough, it is worth having a go at anything we hanker after doing. Which reminds me that I promise myself to try abseiling and parachuting one of these days.

Sporting Hobbies

For those who have been occupied in sedentary work there is some danger in attempting too strenuous an activity. If we have been playing squash regularly and feel fit enough to continue, then there may be no reason to stop. But it is too physically demanding a game to start at a late age and something less arduous should be chosen. We can build up stamina at any age, but it has to be done slowly and without strain.

Bowls is one pleasant way of passing an afternoon in mild weather and is regarded as particularly suitable to older age groups. It offers enough exercise for those of us who do not want to put ourselves under too much physical stress.

Walking, cycling and swimming, camping and caravanning are all enjoyable hobbies, especially if they are undertaken in company with a group. Table tennis, billiards, darts, are each games with a large following. Not everyone can be a star player but they provide enjoyable ways of passing an afternoon or evening in friendly company. Golf can be a taxing game but if one is fit, it can be both beneficial and enjoyable.

The benefits of joining in one or other of these sports are considerable and go beyond the actual playing of the game. Groups of people form friendships and share many other activities, joining for social occasions, dances, dinners or visits to the theatre. There are many opportunities to take golfing holidays, either in the UK or on the Continent where the weather may be sunnier and warmer.

Almost everyone is pleased to learn to dance, even those with 'two left feet' can enjoy trying to sort the steps out in time to the music. There are all kinds of dancing to try: ballroom, folk, country, old time and – for those who are really fit –

tapdancing must be wonderful. These all provide healthy activities and a good excuse to get out regularly in congenial company.

Keeping up Appearances

Going out also makes us study appearance. We tend not to buy so many clothes after retirement but occasionally a purchase of some attractive item can be very cheering. An evening out also gives men or women an excuse, if one is needed, to go to the hairdresser or beautician. It's nice to put ourselves into the best shape possible so that we look and feel good when we are going to see old friends or perhaps make new ones.

A Relaxing Hobby

There may have been little opportunity or desire during our working lives to indulge ourselves with something like a regular steam bath and massage. Frequent visitors to saunas or Turkish baths say that they find these the high spot of their week and you may find it an enjoyable experience. But before going, you should get approval from your doctor, particularly if there is a history of high blood pressure. We should all be careful not to get over-heated and whilst massage will improve circulation, it can also raise blood pressure, so use some caution. No one who has had spells of dizziness or feels faint at any time, should consider these steam baths and in any case should be sure to get checked over by their GP.

I was interviewing a group of retired people and one of them, Emily, said that her favourite hobby was taking a Turkish bath and that it was a very friendly, social occasion. I had to admit that it had never occurred to me in that light. The rest of the group had never been and Emily explained the procedure and how one wraps in a towel and relaxes in the warm atmosphere, taking a brief steam bath if desired and following this with a massage. You may never before have considered taking a sauna or a Turkish bath, but it's not too late provided only that you are fit enough. It is a particularly pleasant experience, refreshing and making one feel thoroughly spoiled.

Many men and women go to these baths regularly on a weekly basis, believing it to be beneficial to health. Not every district has a Turkish bath but most will have a sauna. It need not be expensive; some baths are run by the local council and are very moderately priced. Find out whether there are separate days for men and women.

Music as a Hobby and Therapy

Music has long been recognized as a form of therapy and it provides soothing relief for anyone who is stressed or worried. We all get worked up on occasion and listening to music either alone or in company can be relaxing and soothing, allowing us to put everyday problems in perspective.

Those who do not go to concerts cannot appreciate how beneficial an effect music can have. It can be a powerful influence, uplifting and stimulating, as well as being entertaining. People do not always recognize stress in themselves or admit that they are tense and need to unwind and they might refuse to go to hear music. But override objections in a stressed friend or partner and insist on taking them. They will have cause to thank you.

One enterprising lady has made arrangements for groups or individuals to benefit from music when they are stressed. She is Mrs Pixie Holland, a registered music therapist, and her address as well as that of The Association of Professional Music Therapists is given in a later section.

'Quiet' Hobbies

Hobbies requiring less physical energy may be preferred and the choice is wide. Photography is one diversion which provides a never-ending source of pleasure, whether one is out walking, birdwatching, travelling or whatever. Things of curiosity or appeal can be recorded and so recalled later.

Modern cameras are 'idiot proof', but you still have to think to get good results. It is more ambitious to set up a dark room and do one's own developing and printing, but those who are really keen can do it at reasonable cost. Many districts have clubs where members can use the facilities and get advice.

Collecting as a Hobby

The whole object of collecting should be that you enjoy finding and buying something that you take pleasure in looking at. You are entitled to spoil yourself sometimes, you deserve a treat and should feel no remorse whatsoever in spending money in this way. It is perhaps not surprising that people who grew up in the more spartan 1920s and 1930s do have this feeling of guilt when they spend their money on an unessential object. But if it gives pleasure it is worth buying and if it turns out to be a good financial investment then that is a bonus.

If you are interested in the idea of collecting, start by picking up some information in the library. Browse through some books on art, on furniture, silver or china.

Take the latter. Plates, for example, can be very attractive, useful and decorative. They can commemorate some interesting event and they can also be valuable. Learn about various limited editions and the importance of dates and certificates. Interested collectors can soon acquire sufficient knowledge and confidence to set off to visit flea-markets, car-boot sales, charity bazaars, auction sales and antique shops, where they might pick up precious objects for little cost.

Carrying home a prize bought at bargain price is a joy. Don't do as I once did, arriving home carefully nursing a gorgeous set of old green Wedgwood ivy plates only to slip over, crashing them all to the floor.

Being a collector can be an absorbing pastime and sometimes a remunerative one. Following retirement, a cousin of mine developed his interest in collecting china animals, which he bought in various jumble sales, secondhand shops and markets. In ten years he amassed quite a valuable collection, becoming an acknowledged expert in this field and was in demand as a speaker on the subject.

Stamps are merely 'adhesive labels, printed with a distinctive device'. So says the Oxford Dictionary, but to the collector they are fascinating, brilliantly designed and colourful, taking one in imagination to all parts of the world. Stamp collecting takes mental energy and it intrigues and delights some folk who can spend hours poring over their collections, oblivious to the passage of time.

Keeping Pets

Pets of all sorts can be good company, responsive to their owners, loving them whether they are rich or poor. If you have never kept a dog, it is difficult to understand the closeness which such an association brings. As with all pets, you have to make a commitment; dogs have to be cared for, needing exercise and regular attention. But in exchange you get a wonderful return of love and affection. Ask any dog owner.

Breeding animals and birds, or caring for other people's pets while their owners are on holiday can provide an absorbing as well as a profitable hobby, if there is space to accommodate them. Be sure that you know where to get the advice of a vet in case problems arise.

Tropical and cold-water fish are fascinating in their variety of types and colours. If you don't already have one, try installing an indoor tank or dig a pond in the garden. A small fibreglass tank is not expensive and cold-water fish need little attention but they are lovely creatures to watch. The cost of installing aquaria with tropical fish can be modest or very costly.

We have one friend who has covered a wall in his home with tanks holding examples of the most exotic and colourful fish imaginable. He is an enthusiast who, having retired, spends all his spare time on his hobby and it is remarkably soothing to sit and watch these beautiful creatures. Our son, when young, had a tank with a few precious tropical fish until our cat learned one day how to remove the lid. She had an expensive meal.

Would you like to get interested in radio transmitting and communicate with people around the world? Numerous friendships have been struck up in this way and, who knows, you may be persuaded to visit the 'ham' in Australia that you have been speaking to.

A widower was very depressed following the loss of his wife. His children bought him a telescope, delighting him with this gift which cheered him up considerably. With this new interest, he now awaits clear and starry nights and spends them studying the heavens in company with two friends who are equally fascinated.

Card playing is not only an excuse for a social get together, but provides mental stimulation. Bridge players are very serious about their hobby and tournaments are held nationally and internationally. Specimen games are illustrated in newspapers and journals and there are many books on the subject. If you like card playing, take some lessons and join a local bridge club.

Scrabble Clubs

Does Scrabble fascinate you and is there a club nearby offering regular sessions that you can join? Arm yourself with a Scrabble dictionary and join in the fun. The time can simply fly by and with practice anyone can put in a creditable performance, finding partners to match their own standards.

Turning Hobbies into Cash

If we wish to develop a hobby which could bring in money we must consider what skills we have and put them to good use. Practise by making things for charity bazaars and sales and then progress to craft fairs where goods can be offered for sale at competitive and realistic prices. If they are snapped up quickly then you know that you can ask a little more next time.

Hobbies and Pets

Was there something that you were especially good at during your schooldays? I admired some beautifully handwritten and illustrated Christmas cards in a craft shop and out of interest I asked where they came from. They were made by a local woman of seventy who had learned script writing at school and after retirement had taken it up again as her hobby. Another pensioner showed me the old volumes which he had rebound for a bookshop. They were simply lovely. He had turned a hobby into a profitable little business, although he really didn't do it for the money, just for the sheer pleasure it gave him to restore those tattered books almost to their pristine state.

A youthful widow of sixty-four, Norah, who even as a child had loved making dolls' clothes, was short of cash. Now she set about making and repairing dolls and bears which she bought at jumble sales. Her customers were so pleased with their nicely-made purchases that Norah found her goods were quickly snapped up. She began to take orders and soon dolls were brought from far afield for repair and she became so busy that she took on a trainee in her little workshop. Now she is on a regular circuit, visiting craft fairs around the country, enjoying her occupation and supplementing her income.

The distinction between work and play, hobby or leisure reduces after we retire. We have to please ourselves, to enjoy whatever we choose to occupy ourselves with. It matters less whether or not we are expert, the important thing is that we are having some fun doing it.

6 Gardening is Good for You

Would you believe that flowers and plants have feelings? Or that they have auras which alter under some conditions and which can be measured and photographed? There are few plant growers who do not accept that their plants have understanding and senses.

Do you laugh at the idea that plants do better when they are spoken to nicely? Can you credit that this form of life has a sort of intelligence we know nothing about? Whatever the answers to those questions are, it is certain that working with the earth and with growing things has a pronounced beneficial effect on us, healing to the spirit and mind.

We do not all have the same tastes in occupation and I dare say that there will be some readers who do not care for gardening. However, as a recreation it offers outstanding benefits and I am hopeful of persuading some among my readers who have not tried it, that they should lose no time in discovering for themselves how rewarding and therapeutic it can be.

Gardening can provide us with all we need to keep us busy, interested and fit. It gives on-going pleasure all through the year, there being no beginning or ending for gardeners. Each month can provide a different sort of activity and excitement, an anticipation of the riches nature can provide in such abundance. Whatever sort of gardening we preoccupy ourselves with, the gardener can never be bored.

Among the many hobbies suitable to us as we grow older, and one of the most rewarding, is the cultivation of flowers, fruit or vegetables in whatever space can be afforded. With the right preparation, there are abundant returns for very little outlay.

One woman I have known for many years is a widow of

modest means. She has a small garden well stocked with unusual plants, some of which are rare and valuable but which have not cost her a penny. For years she has never gone out without a pair of nail scissors and a plastic bag. Whenever she sees an attractive plant she gets permission to do a little judicious pruning and knows how to nurture a tiny cutting into a healthy bush or tree. She is generous in her turn as she sends plants for sale at church bazaars to raise funds for charity.

A garden I never fail to visit in the height of summer is a glory of blazing colour and scents. It is certainly no great size, occupying a few square yards and is the back garden of a row of terraced houses. But I never saw more contented looking flowers and bushes anywhere. Every inch of ground is used and every wall, as well as the porch, is covered or hung with baskets of seasonal plants of brilliant or delicate colours, all flourishing and looking healthy.

The Lazy Gardener

Quite a lot of people regard any outdoor work as a bore and something to be got over as quickly as possible. Their experience of gardening may have been limited to a tidy up, a desultory mow of the lawn and an unambitious effort at weeding when strictly necessary. But it is really worth putting in more energy and the results show so quickly. Everyone likes to admire even a simple but cared for garden with neat beds of plants and flowers.

As an exercise, gardening provides all the bending and stretching movement needed to keep us in fit condition. While we have to be careful not to overdo things or carry heavy goods about, we can use lawnmowing, digging, planting, weeding and tree-pruning to keep ourselves in shape. You don't meet many obese gardeners.

The Choice is Yours

There are plants of different temperaments, suitable to every kind of soil and all kinds of wind and weather. Choose from those sturdy and independent varieties which grow tidily without the need for care, to the wild ones which romp everywhere they can and which need to be curbed. Some will give pleasure from their first flowering, steadily improving year by year. Who could not appreciate a tree which lights up the lawn or a garden corner, like the mock *Robinia acacia*, nick-named 'shower of gold'. Its radiant leaves last from May until October, looking all the time as though the sun is upon them. It needs only to be planted in an enriched soil and will reward its owner with years of beauty. The *Robinia acacia* can be grown as a bush or a tree and is a great favourite of mine.

There are thousands of flowers, plants and trees to choose from. Every park, every nursery garden, every florist will have a variety on show and it is up to each of us to make our own selection, something to please our own taste. If you have never done so, do take the trouble to visit some of the great gardens which advertise their special seasons of interest and beauty. If you find something unfamiliar which you would like to have in your garden, photograph it and have it identified at a local plant shop or the library. You can then order it and grow it yourself.

Save your Back

We do have to take care in our older years not to lift weighty objects, push heavy mowers or stay bent in one position for too long. There is no sense in setting up or aggravating back problems.

Some gardeners have flower beds raised on brickwork, so that they may work without the bending that is ordinarily involved. This is particularly useful for anyone who is confined to a wheelchair or is limited in movement. Hanging baskets of flowers and leaves can be lowered within easy reach of a seated gardener and raised again when they have had the necessary attention. People who have never really gardened and who determine that they will try are likely to be in for the most pleasant surprise as the results of their efforts literally blossom.

Helpful Gadgets

There is a wide selection of lawnmowers on the market and choice must be governed by pocket and the size of lawn to be covered. If you have an old mower, don't put up with poor performance, be sure that it is in good order since that will make it easier to use and will certainly produce better results. Look at the range of useful gardening gadgets and consider which you should invest in, because they can take some of the strain out of gardening. Long-handled lawn shears save bending as one goes around the lawn, but electric edge trimmers do a neat job and provide an effective way of getting around paths, borders and flowerbeds in the least possible time.

Exercise Caution

Always use a circuit breaker with any outdoor electrical tools. They should be available at hardware shops or department stores. Whatever job we are doing, it is worth exercising particular caution if we use electrically operated tools, eliminating any risks that could lead to accidents. Mishaps occur each year which are avoidable and it is worth the small expense involved in order to be safe. Consider buying trimmers with an automatic line feed, as trailing cords are an added danger. One can either trip over them or cut through them.

Watch out for flying pebbles and twigs thrown up by the trimmer. It is safer to wear goggles to protect eyes from such hazards. Sensible too, to wear strong shoes and thick trousers because the nylon cutting thread can be spiteful if it catches a leg.

There are cordless hedge trimmers available giving power lasting for about half-an-hour and having the advantage that they can be used at a distance from the house or plug.

Mental and Physical Benefits

Whether one tends a lawn, grows flowers, fruit or vegetables, one can feel an affinity with the earth. It doesn't have to be a big or even a little garden. An outdoor tub, window box or hanging basket, even a row of bottles and jars can be reward enough as cuttings thrive with a little tender and loving care. It is contact with Nature which is important and which has such a soothing and healing effect.

Because the earth is such a rewarding medium to work with, time can fly when one is intent upon the job in hand. There are few things more gratifying than to look at the results of a day's work in the garden, feel the benefit of the fresh air and a glow of satisfaction in the knowledge of a good job well done.

If you believe that your plants benefit from a few words of encouragement, go ahead and talk to them. You are not alone in this belief and you might be surprised to find how many people share it with you. In fact, if you hearten your plants in this way you are in good company. Prince Charles is an ardent gardener and is said to have found that his plants respond to a few kindly words. I say my first good-morning of the day to our indoor rubber tree plant. I like to think that the message is received; the plant is certainly a splendid specimen, having grown within the well of a staircase to a height of fourteen feet.

One friend wondered who her daily help was speaking to in the kitchen and finding it was the African violets, asked if it was improving their condition. 'Of course', the woman remarked. 'Have you not noticed? There are several buds now.' My friend said that she had to admit that the plant had been green enough, but had not flowered in years.

The most impressive story came from a report of someone who invited her plants to influence the fortune of her Premium Bonds. She had twenty-one wins which has so impressed her neighbours that they are to try out her methods.

Photographic experiments by interested scientists in various parts of the world have shown that plants not only appear to respond to kindly attention but also to a little chat and sympathetic company. They suffer in the presence of violence, whether oral or physical, whether to their own leaves and blossom or others in the vicinity. Plants and flowers, it has been claimed, have an electrical field which registers changes and an 'aura' which can be photographed.

Needs of the Garden

There are some vital requirements of any garden. Plenty of light, some warmth at appropriate times of the year, oxygen, carbon dioxide, all of which are usually naturally available. One element is sometimes in short supply and an interruption in the quantity needed can spell disaster to the most carefully nurtured gardens. That is water. Hoses should be kept at the ready so that during dry spells regular watering can be easily continued. It is possible to overdo it, but this is unlikely unless there is insufficient drainage. It is underwatering in the garden that is likely to be more damaging, especially to newly-planted trees and bushes. The roots of established trees and plants reach well down into the earth and find the water they need. Garden compost and mulch of some kind will help to prevent too much drying out during hot spells as well as assisting in discouraging weeds. One should mulch the right sort of materials in so that the correct nutrients for soil are supplied. Have you noticed how much more dry plants can be when they are planted next to walls? If too close, they are protected from rainfall and need watering so always try to plant several inches away from the wall.

During spells of drought we face real difficulties. We had sympathy with Bernard, whose treasured garden was suffering during a drought when hosing had been forbidden. He defied the authorities and hosed away. Despite the steep fine he said that he had saved his garden and it was worth it. However, we cannot all go around breaking the law even if we could afford it. Water is a very precious commodity which will become more costly in the future. It will be a sad day for us if we lose amenities like trees and gardens because we lack water. How dull the country would be without its marvellous abundance of green.

Specialized knowledge about gardening is always useful and pays dividends and knowing the right tips can save a lot of effort. There are local colleges which run courses designed to improve technique and to demonstrate in a practical way how to achieve good results. These courses also recognize local problems relating to earth quality and content and know which plants will do well in the area.

All libraries and book shops have gardening books to engross and interest every kind of gardener. It is worth finding out, for example, what kind of soil one is dealing with since it may be quite a simple matter to make up for deficiencies. Basic soil additions act as a tonic, enabling certain plants to do well, perhaps to flower where they have never previously done so.

Getting the Right Advice

Roses, hydrangeas, rhododendrons, azaleas, these are examples of potentially magnificent flora which often fail to reach their attainable beauty because they lack some chemical ingredient or other to balance the soil they dwell in. Sometimes, however, they need a change of venue or some exercise, perhaps an occasional jolt of encouragement, just as we do.

My librarian friend, Edith, has a rhododendron which had glossy leaves but failed to blossom. She asked her botanist son if he had some advice. 'Yes, Mum', he answered. 'Dig it out, put it in a wheelbarrow and run it round the garden, then put it back.' She looked at him in astonishment and then laughed at herself for being taken in. Next year, the hydrangea was a mass of blooms. 'Look at that', she told her son, 'and I didn't ride it round the garden.' 'No, Mum', he replied, 'But I did!'

Tips from Wise Old Gardeners

Over the years we have been given many an intriguing tip on how to use materials or substances to be found in the house. We had one gardener in his mid-sixties who looked older than he was because in his early youth he had suffered from severe scoliosis (a rounding of the back). He had never married and had worked all his life as a gravedigger. Following retirement, and despite his hunched back, he took up gardening and was capable of a prodigious amount of work. He helped to keep our garden and those of several neighbours in attractive order.

He had advice for every problem. 'Worms in your radishes?' he said to one neighbour. 'Just you take some wood-ashes and add them to the earth as you plant the seeds out.' For healthy marrows he advised a comfy bed of cut grass to go in with the seeds. Slugs were tempted away from plants into tiny pots of beer. Replenishing the lawn meant problems from birds who ate the seeds until he had us criss-cross cotton thread on stakes across them.

He had no use for tobacco other than as an insecticide. 'Boil an ounce in half a pint of water, brush on insect infected plants. Deadly poisonous', he'd say. He had no doubt that his plants had a language and that they shared a mutual understanding. 'More intelligent than lots of folk', he would tell us.

He solved our gardening problems but his own problem and sadness was his lifelong loneliness. He said if it were not for his deep love of plants he would have ended up in the loony bin. He had never thought himself good enough for any girl because of his physical deformity. He finally resolved things in a way that we thought would doom him to disaster but strangely, it worked out well. He became attracted to a young Spanish woman who worked as a domestic nearby and who was about to be married. When she set up home with her husband, the gardener moved in as their lodger. 'I know that there is no hope for me, even if I were younger', he said, 'but at least I shall be able to see her and be near her.'

When the couple had a child he took on the role of grandfather and the little family benefited from his generosity. He knew family life for the first time, and positively glowed when he spoke of his adopted status.

Gardening Clubs

Local gardening clubs will always have members who are more than willing to assist enquirers with problems. Both local and national radio stations offer relevant, seasonal advice and there are regular television series which demonstrate what can be achieved in gardens. It could be worth recording such programmes so that they can be listened to again and the maximum benefit be acquired from the advice and ideas offered. A fruitful garden, producing vegetables and soft and hard fruits cannot be achieved without a commitment of time and of work, but it can be something one grows to love. Who doesn't enjoy giving or receiving some home-grown produce? I have friends whose carefully nurtured garden has been the main reason that they have stayed on in their home.

A garden which has been cared for and which has turned into a mass of living colour is a warming sight and a joy to behold. Be persuaded by a flower catalogue to be extravagant. Follow all the good advice on offer and as you put in the work think of it as necessary, healthful exercise. Then in all the seasons, winter, spring, summer and autumn, reap the rich rewards.

Miniature Trees and Bushes

In recent times, there has been a developing interest in those miniature trees which have for long been popular in Japan. There is a comprehensive selection with leaves in every hue of green and some of them flower. There are, for example, tiny rose trees which bloom in yellow, peachy and pinky tones. Friends and relatives have no problem in finding gifts for anyone with such an interest. A miniature tree or bush makes a long lasting and pleasing present.

Planting Trees

Many trees have been destroyed in recent years, either by disease, poor environment or bad weather. We need our trees, they are lovely to look at, provide shade and give out oxygen.

We use up the trees of the world at a great rate as timber for furniture and for the vast quantities of paper that is used for books, newspapers, journals, advertising and for office work.

It should be the responsibility of us all, perhaps especially for those of us who are older and have time to spare, to plant as many trees as possible for the next generation to enjoy. Many local authorities have programmes for tree planting to which the public is invited to take part in special weekends, set aside for this valuable enterprise.

The Greenhouse Effect

There is wider concern felt for issues which affect not only our trees, plants and animals but also ourselves. The Greenhouse Effect is a potential disaster which could threaten all plant and animal life. Greenpeace is an international environmental pressure group which is concerned to protect nature. The group campaigns tirelessly and has accomplished a great deal throughout the world. Anyone wishing to support or join this organization should write to them. (See Useful Addresses.)

Legal Responsibilities

Planting trees in parks, schools, streets or squares is one way of benefiting the community of the future, those generations who will follow us. Trees can also, of course, be planted in private gardens. But it must be done with thought and consideration as to whether they suit the surrounding environment. A twig of sticky-budded chestnut could grow into a massive tree of grand proportions, not only dwarfing houses but stretching beneath them with roots that can reach at least as far as their spreading branches, damaging drains and sub-structures.

We have a legal responsibility to neighbours whose property we may damage in this way, so tree planting must be done with due caution and attention to future growth, perhaps in ten, twenty or forty years.

The owners of the great houses of old, who had used the

timbers of their estates for building their stately homes, regarded it their bounden duty to consider the future and anticipate their descendants' needs. They regularly planted the trees which would one day, perhaps as much as 400 years on, be needed to replace those timbers.

Saving Plants from Extinction

It is a cheering fact that many of the plants which could disappear from the face of the earth are being saved. There is a National Council for the Conservation of Plants and Gardens and they are keen for as many people as possible who have the time and the interest to help in preserving some 20,000 garden plants which are faced with extinction. Write for details to the Council. (See Useful Addresses.)

It was the habit of Victorians with time on their hands to collect and exchange rare and unusual plants and this resulted in a rich heritage for present generations to enjoy. We who are retired should accept the responsibility to do the same for the next generation. We have to look out for these endangered species and then to grow them.

The Council issues 'pink sheets' which list the names of endangered plants. Members can then begin by looking in their own and their friends' gardens, moving on to a study of hedges, meadows and parks or anywhere that plants grow. No one need be excluded from this fascinating hobby, even the newest of gardeners can turn out to be the one who makes a lucky find. The Council will also provide samples of threatened plants to be grown.

The lack of a garden is no reason to deny yourself the pleasure of joining this Council. Even a windowbox will do and the enthusiast will enable young plants to be tended until ready for setting out of doors.

Glasshouses

In a glasshouse the possibilities for the type and variety of growth are almost limitless. The question is what to choose.

One medical doctor's relaxation and favourite pastime was his forty foot greenhouse where he indulged in his love for growing (and singing to) rare orchids. He has found a profitable sideline since there is a ready market for his produce and the waxy, long lasting blooms are much in demand at weddings and celebrations.

Greenhouses do not have to be big to be quite productive. In fact, many gardens do now have small ones in which their owners can potter in all weathers, out of the wind and rain, nursing plants along for planting out later, when the season is right and weather improves.

Insecticides

It used to be the case that one felt safe from DDT and other sprays if one washed fruit or vegetables or peeled them. Nowadays products are used which are absorbed into the sap stream of the plant. It is all very well for manufacturers to claim that when these chemicals are used in accordance with instructions and not close to harvest time, the consumer is quite safe. But there is room for doubt.

If we put together all those additives that might be present on this or that food, we could be imbibing altogether too much undesirable chemical material and storing up future health problems. It is not just ourselves we should be concerned for but the future generations, perhaps our own grandchildren. The government and food industries share this concern and sponsor research to try to determine what levels of chemicals can be safely recommended.

It would be nice if everyone could grow their own fruits and vegetables, free of sprays, or at least subject to the least possible taint of them. For most people, it seems a totally impractical idea. Not everyone has a garden big enough to grow a great deal, although the smallest of patches can produce a surprising variety. Even a gro-bag, which contains earth and seeds, for example, can give a fine quantity of tomatoes or mushrooms.

It is enjoyable to experiment with seeds and different plants and little preparation is needed to grow numbers of fruits and vegetables, including cabbages, lettuces, tomatoes and blackberries, pears and apples.

We have tried several, mostly to give our town-bred grandchildren the surprise and pleasure of watching the produce grow but we did enjoy eating them too.

Cook with Fresh Herbs

Herbs can be grown in the kitchen, handy for the cook-pot and quickly produced from seed. Parsley is indispensable, taking only fourteen days or so to germinate in a warm cupboard and then flourishing on the window sill. It likes to be kept mist-sprayed and watered when dry. Chives grow just like grass and add piquant taste to salads. You can experiment with different herbs, growing what you prefer; remember, they need feeding too. It is a pleasure just to get the fragrant scent of a mint, thyme or sage leaf and to tell your dinner guests that your fresh herbs are home-grown.

Water Gardens

If there is a water feature in the garden, people seem to gravitate towards it, fascinated by the look, sound and content. It is not difficult to put water interest in somewhere. The prettiest look is achieved when a stream is directed down, over or through a rockery into a pool of some kind. It doesn't have to be large but will need quite a bit of preparation as well as some looking after in the future to keep it fresh and clear.

Pools should be of the easy-to-care-for variety and must either be lined with a strong plastic material or come ready made in fibreglass which is tough and long lasting.

Fibreglass pools come in many shapes and sizes and there is always a good selection on show in those nursery gardens which have sections for the water enthusiast. Never rush into a purchase of this kind but be discriminating. If carefully chosen, a pool can provide fairly trouble-free pleasure for years to come.

If you are ambitious and energetic enough you can dig a hole in the ground to the size and shape which appeals to you, line it with a suitable material and you have your own do-it-yourself unique fishpond. Most comprehensive gardening books give easy-to-follow, step-by-step instructions on preparation.

Remember that if you are going to have fish in your pond they will need a depth of about twenty inches so that they can go down to the warmer water below when the weather gets cold and the top freezes over. They will also need a fair area of water as they get bigger. Our fifteen-year-old fish have grown to be about eight inches long in quite a small pond, barely eight by four feet by eighteen inches deep.

There may not be room for a pool in your garden but don't be discouraged by that. Even a smallish receptacle, perhaps a stone trough or an old and deep butler's sink containing a few fish and some aquatic plants, provides interest. Put it in good light but where it can get some shade during the hottest part of the day and keep it clear of dead leaves which decay and turn the water murky.

A netting cover is a good idea over any pool, both to prevent debris from falling in and also to keep out cats or birds. I have seen a cat stay motionless for minutes on end, waiting by the pool, poised with paw extended, ready to flick out an unwary fish. Some birds, for example the heron, can spot the flash of water from miles away and will chance a visit to a garden in the hope of a snack, dipping a long beak into the water and robbing a pool of its live content.

Water Pumps and Lights

Adding a pump and then an underwater light are the next steps for an interesting pool, supplying a variety of movement and colour in the circulating water. These additions are not entirely trouble-free but the effort is so rewarding as you sit in your deckchair on a summer's day, soothed by the unmistakeable sound of trickling water. Time flies pleasantly by as you relax and unwind, sipping a drink, watching a family of frogs and listening to the soft plop of fish in the water, searching for food and cavorting in the environment you have created for them.

7 Leisure, Recreation and Holidays

Leisure Activities

On the brink of retirement we have more than 2,000 hours of leisure time to look forward to each year. Apart from education, hobbies and part-time paid or voluntary work, which should all be enjoyable activities, we must also think about devoting some of those hours to sheer pleasure, leisure and holidays.

Whether you elect for something soothing, relaxing and quiet or a pursuit more exciting and tiring, it has to be something you want for yourself, so that you can say when you are doing it that you are having the time of your life.

If we are going to try anything new and demanding we will need health and stamina. Get heart, lungs and general health checked out by your doctor before you start making any ambitious plans and consider whether you should have special insurance.

Adventurous Pursuits

Anything is possible. You may be among the more cautious individuals who think it would be madness to consider parachuting as a suitable activity for anyone of pensionable age, but equally, many of today's retired are not averse to such exciting activities. I envied a woman in her fifties who said that she would never regret the fraught moments she spent before launching herself from a plane on a parachute jump. I, too, felt fraught when shooting the rapids in Canada, but it was worth the exhilaration that followed.

Do you feel that you would like to have a go when you read about such ventures or see someone hang-gliding from a cliff or racing a wind surfer over the waves? We are an adventurous generation on the whole but could you be drawn away from your snug fireside to do something exciting? Might you be tempted by the idea of ballooning beneath a blue sky? It would certainly be a sensation to treasure, something you could never forget. Could you tempt your contemporaries to join you in a flight in a hot-air balloon? They could think it well worth the cost of around £100 for each person. I have listed details of a few addresses later in the book from where you can find out about some of the more adventurous pursuits.

Gliding is a sport which appeals to young and old. If you can drive, they say, then you should have no problem learning to qualify as a glider pilot. That would give them back at the office something to draw their breath about. You could take an introductory flight for about £25.

Hang-gliding takes more courage as well as considerable stamina and suppleness and would only suit someone in superb condition, but no doubt there are older people who can qualify. A four or five day training session would cost around £80 to £100.

Land-yachting keeps you on the ground, quite safely they say and it is meant to be an easy sport, attracting many in their sixties and seventies. Make it an outing for half-a-dozen friends to watch and see if you are not tempted to have a go. It is rather like go-karting or dinghy sailing and clubs provide crash helmets while costs are moderate, under £50 for four half-day courses to enable one to qualify as proficient.

Getting about can be a problem as we age, especially if we don't have a car and few of us would consider a motorbike or moped. These have always seemed to me a hazardous means of travel and I give riders a full car width when I overtake them, but one woman I know who uses a moped without fear is a familiar sight as she whizzes around. Doris learned to ride so that she could visit the places and people she wanted to see, using her leisure hours profitably. Because her arthritis had worsened she could not easily get about and instead of accepting this situation she went out at the age of sixty-six, bought herself a moped and some lessons in how to ride it. That was ten years ago, but even now she still goes wherever the fancy takes her. In fact, just riding about provides her with great enjoyment and her grandchildren have titled her 'The Whiz-Kid'. She does not lack enterprise and recently tried out gliding, finding it 'a beautiful experience'. What will she do to celebrate her eightieth birthday?

Parascending might look dangerous and difficult but it is neither, somewhat akin to parachuting, but you take off from the ground, ascending while being towed by a boat or a car. I tried it from a beach, wishing I could have gone higher and for longer, it was a super experience. The British Association of Parascending Clubs will provide an information pack and a one day course will cost around £50. No stamina is required but you need to have a healthy heart and wear ankle support boots.

You could never get me to pothole but for some it is the ultimate action. You could probably get a free trip just to make sure that you do actually enjoy it and the cost would be about £50 for a one day course. Contact the National Caving Association; they say you need not only to be fit but also to have your wits about you. The way I feel about it is that my wits would have had to desert me before I tried it.

Nothing could keep anyone fitter than regularly rowing a boat. Even if you have never tried it, if you are in robust condition you could begin, taking a few minutes at a time until you have the knack. Once this is acquired you can go out on a pleasant stretch of water with a companion to share the rowing. Pulling a boat through quiet water soon warms you up on a bright and chilly morning and it's a lovely way to unwind. Or take a picnic and a book one sunny afternoon and row to a quiet backwater, very soothing to the spirit.

If you have never sailed you may think it is too late to start. Nothing is too late. I was sixty-plus when my son-in-law gave me an hour of instruction and then left me on a breezy stretch of water to put into practise what I had learned. I have since taken two days of sailing instruction to reach Level 1 of the Royal Yachting Association dinghy proficiency scheme. Next time we are away together I shall amaze him. The cost is about £55. You need to like messing about with boats.

Scuba-diving can take you into the fascinating world under the sea, but you have to start training at a swimming pool and ought to be a proficient swimmer. You will need to have a mask, snorkel and flippers as well as self-contained underwater breathing apparatus, then three months instruction and you should be prepared for the open sea.

If you have never tried you may think that down-hill skiing would be too strenuous and difficult but cross-country skiing might be suitable. The latter is hard work but such a pleasure when you have learned the knack and can skim along paths over crunchy snow under the winter sun.

Water-skiing attracts all ages but it is a strenuous sport, better if you have done it before. Eric is a busy GP in his sixties who practises this sport twice a week and has the lean and muscular shape he had at eighteen. He says that if one is fit, age should not be a deterrent. Apart from the cost of membership of a club, the fees are modest, bearing in mind that you are hiring a boat and crew member.

Perhaps you will be able to fulfil an early ambition by trying out one or other of these adventurous sports. We might meet up land-yachting or gliding. If so, happy landings, take care, take medical advice, take insurance and enjoy yourself.

Think about Holidays

The nice thing about being retired is that we can take our holidays when we please, no longer thinking about school holidays or fitting in with other people's arrangements. Senior citizens have become a holiday market well worth attracting since they spend twice as much on holidays as the younger groups. We can take advantage of off-peak travel offers, special concessionary fares and the reduced rates offered by many hotels, out of season either in this country or abroad.

Holidays Abroad

One of the benefits of age can be to escape bone-chilling winters and go off to a milder climate. Ice, snow and freezing winds are hard on older bones and it is sensible to miss out the worst weeks by spending them in kinder climes where we can walk outdoors in comfort instead of huddling indoors trying to avoid draughts.

There are house-owners, both in this country and abroad, who will pay reliable people to caretake for them while they are away. The pay is usually modest but a change of surroundings can be stimulating and variation provides interest. The care of a family pet may be part of the deal. In this way holidays are gained which might otherwise be unaffordable.

Long holidays are within financial reach for many of us and it has become feasible, even for those on reduced funds, to take time in the sun for as long as from one to six months. Long-stay holidays are available in a number of European resorts such as Spain, Italy, Portugal and Majorca where prices are temptingly low and often include in-house entertainment.

Great bargains are available everywhere out of season and the retirement years can be a particularly good time to go abroad in order to miss the worst of the winter. Apart from the Christmas period, hotel charges, apartment rentals and airfares are at their lowest. Staying for a month or more works out cheaply in the long run since the airfare is usually the biggest item, occurring once. Back at home, heating would be costly and food in winter is generally more expensive.

Hoteliers are glad to have guests during out of season periods, are anxious to please and hopeful that visitors will return another year. Many retirees return year after year to the places they are familiar with, for there is comfort in knowing the area and the people one is going to. Entertainment out of season is different too, set in the days of the youth of visitors, so there is plenty of 1930s and 1940s music.

Choosing Accommodation
Hotels are not the only choice, although a good one can make you feel pampered, providing room service and breakfast in bed. But the immediacy of self-service and the convenience of having things to hand as well as privacy and independence often make rented accommodation a favoured choice.

Depending on what country you visit, the quality of apartments, villas or cottages will vary. But today, most will come with modern amenities and many will have TV, video recorder and use of a whirlpool bath, swimming pool, squash or tennis courts and so on. Kitchens, too may vary from basic to those of a standard equipped for the gourmet cook.

Whether we go on holiday to some of the villages, mountains, cities or coastal resorts of our own country or elsewhere in the world, we need to plan with care to get the best out of what can be a major investment. Get all the brochures and take time to choose the right kind of holiday, don't just dash off somewhere without forethought.

What do you Want?
The choice is so wide these days; any travel agent can provide a dozen or more brochures to browse through. The major companies specialize in lengthier stays abroad for the older groups. Determine what it is you are looking for, consider temperature, beaches, mountains, scenery, sightseeing, certain amenities in accommodation and, of course, price.

Learn a Language
No one should jib at learning a little of the local language. Knowing how to ask for certain things, or to say hello, good-bye and thank you is pleasing to local people who probably know quite a lot of English. If they have tried to learn, so should you.

It is rewarding to be able to speak to fellow guests from other countries and useful, too, in aiding our enjoyment of foreign television programmes. Age stops no one from learning and a little perseverance pays dividends.

Finding Plenty to Do
There should be no worry about being bored in a mixed company of retired folk, sharing amusements like card playing, scrabble, table-tennis, reading, walking or just talking and exchanging experiences. Meals become an important break in the day and menus in hotels can be adequate but repetitive. Local restaurants and cafés are usually modestly priced and welcome customers, so finding alternative places to eat is rarely a problem. It may feel a bit wasteful to have an all-in rate and then eat out but the age of retirement is the time to spoil ourselves. The cheap, all-in price which tempted us in the first place does not allow extravagance on the part of the hoteliers, so prepare to spend a little extra in this way.

Camping and Caravanning

If you have never camped by the time you reach retirement age you are unlikely to wish to consider this as an option, which is a pity. A well-prepared camping holiday can be a lot of fun.

Enthusiasts say that for privacy and comfort nothing can beat the camping or caravanning holiday. With a good tent, snug sleeping bag and cooking gear, little compares with sleeping under the stars. Caravans or mobile homes provide privacy, comfortable sleeping quarters, cooking and bathing facilities and you can stop to sightsee or shop anywhere you please in this country or abroad.

Luxury Cruises

Those people who like the special relaxation of life on a liner can enjoy any one of a variety of luxury cruises. They are more expensive than most other types of holiday but they do offer something special. The larger cruise ship is quite a spectacular sight offering a wide range of facilities to several hundred passengers. The food is generally superb, there is daily entertainment and well-organized trips ashore at places of special interest.

Cargo Cruises

Two friends looked forward to their retirement, when they planned to take an extended holiday of several weeks on a cargo boat. They were not attracted by what they saw as the rather frantic life of a big liner with lots of entertainment, much changing of clothes, discos and a huge menu. They wanted to feel part of the real life of a cargo boat, one with deliveries to make and a crew whose jobs were other than just taking care of passengers.

These trips are in great demand and must be booked many months in advance. The number of passengers is limited, though accommodation is usually very comfortable. The passengers' steward has the responsibility to care for the needs of travellers who must be prepared to be resourceful about their own entertainment. Spending several weeks in close company with unknown fellow travellers can be chancy. But normally everyone is relaxed and people soon learn to respect each other's privacy.

A cargo boat may make unscheduled stops so one never knows quite when and where one will land. However, inland trips, such as can be arranged on a cruise liner, are not always possible, which could be a little frustrating if one wanted to visit the town centre. But on the whole, a cargo cruise provides a diverting, worthwhile and unusual experience, informal and less constrained than the luxury cruise.

Information about cargo boat trips from the ABC of Travelling, Freighter World Cruises or British Blue Star.

Travelling Far

Look farther to the west or right over to the other side of the world to Australia or New Zealand. The great trees of Perth, the spectacular harbour of Sydney, the stretches of silver beaches and magnificent flora of New Zealand, we should like to see them all. But it is a long way to go and it does take about twenty-four hours flying time to get there. One usually find that people who travel that far have relatives or friends to visit.

The USA
No language problem, good weather, beaches or mountains, the choice is wide and whether one goes to rest in Florida, sightsee in New York, gamble in Las Vegas, or find somewhere in between, good food, superb hotels and a pleasant reception are virtually guaranteed.

Sun-Seekers
There is a small place in the USA called Quartzsite, too small to be a town, with neither piped water nor sewer system. But it has become an annual popular holiday home to almost a quarter of a million people, mostly retired. They winter there in caravans and mobile homes, including in their number shopkeepers who bring in sufficient stores to cater to these large numbers. The sunny weather, blue skies and clear air are good enough reasons for this migration. Little more is asked for than escape from wintry weather and the camaraderie of other like-minded people.

Travel to Canada
Among the main cities are Vancouver, Toronto, Montreal and Ottawa each having individual character and beauty, but I can best give a flavour of this spacious country by telling of a city I know well.

The capital, Ottawa, is set in a uniquely attractive location. The Rideau Canal runs through the city, providing recreational facilities all the year round. In the winter, when it is frozen over, it becomes the route into the centre of Ottawa as colourfully dressed commuters skate to work.

The Rideau and Ottawa rivers wind through the city, the water borders providing beaches for all to enjoy. Within easy reach lies a sportsman's delight, with choice wide enough to please everyone, fishing, boating, canoeing, sailing, or skiing. Or you can visit towns preserved as in the past.

In Ottawa itself there are all kinds of restaurants, while in the market centres one finds exotic food from all nations, with street vendors and musicians providing arts, crafts and entertainment in an all-year round buzz of activity. In pedestrian-only shopping malls there are chic and unusual boutiques.

There is a French flavour to most Canadian cities and all signs are given in French and English. Cross a bridge from Ottawa to Hull and you find another world where Canadian is spoken with a French accent.

The green tinted copper roof-tops of Parliament, smartly red-jacketed Canadian Mounties, an immense Glass Museum housing international art collections, all fascinate the visitor. Anyone could have a lovely holiday here, we love to visit and hate to leave.

Exploring Surroundings

If you prefer self-drive holidays you can take your own car to most destinations in Europe, either driving all the way once across the Channel or putting the car on the train for part of the journey. It is very pleasant to stop in villages, to shop at will and to experience the countryside as it is impossible to do when flying.

Check with the motoring organisations for up-to-the-minute advice. Cars can be hired in advance so that one awaits you if you prefer to take a fly and drive holiday.

Self-drive in the USA and Canada, where the roads between towns are very good, can make for an interesting holiday and some very exciting scenery. Motels offer excellent accommodation and food is of a high standard.

Taxis are, generally, reasonably priced abroad but it is a good idea to use buses and explore the surrounding towns and villages. One could bus into a mountain region enjoying a relaxed drive amidst splendid scenery. Discover a pleasant café and sit awhile over coffee or a beer.

Insurance is Essential

So many things can go wrong either before going, en route or during the holiday itself that insurance cover is a must. Consider this when you book, in case you have to cancel for the reasons specified, like ill-health or that of a close relative.

Most holiday brochures describe a form of insurance cover which may be included in their package offers, but this is an option and does not have to be accepted. Many have all-in policies which might include health and travel cover, so travellers have no need of additional insurance. Comprehensive policies cover most risks but note any exclusion clauses which leave you with small bills to pay.

It could spoil a holiday if you lose valuables, particularly if you are in strange territory. Take precautions and behave as if there might be a thief around. Never put bags and carriers down where you cannot keep an eye on them. You could easily be distracted while someone snatches your property and makes off, perhaps with an accomplice on a motorbike. Be careful to keep handbags on your arm, away from the roadway where they are out of reach of the thief on a cycle.

It is best not to take expensive jewellery on holiday. There is so much fashion jewellery about and it is better to risk losing something inexpensive rather than something you value. Back trouser pockets are not the place to keep wallets. The front or deep trouser pocket is safer.

Leave your valuables in the hotel safe. Rosemary left her credit card in a drawer by day, checking that it was safely there each evening. What she did not realise was that it was being 'borrowed' during the day, and she found herself with a bill of several hundred pounds. Luckily, she was covered by an insurance policy.

Should the unexpected happen and you become a victim of theft, do not panic. There is no sense in making yourself ill, although it is difficult not to feel a sense of outrage when a sneak thief strikes or a burglar goes through your belongings. Provided you are insured, it is not too bad. It would be far worse if there had been personal injury.

Medical Cover
During a period of weeks away, we may catch flu' or get a tummy bug so anticipate sickness by being prepared. Medical treatment may not be entirely free in the destination country, even in Common Market countries and certainly not in the USA. The provision of health care at any holiday resort may prove expensive.

Insurance premiums may seem high but they are small compared to the costly bills which can arise for hospital procedures or doctors' visits and medication. Do remember the importance of taking full courses of prescribed antibiotics or they can be ineffective. Ask the travel agent to explain the general and medical insurance cover so that you have peace of mind.

Lost Luggage
It can ruin a holiday to have a carefully planned wardrobe of clothes disappear. Some air companies will provide cash to cover essential purchases while they locate the missing suitcases. The latter usually turn up in a day or two but never leave money or valuables in unaccompanied luggage.

Make Travel Easy

A large wardrobe can be a nuisance but it is essential to some and suitcases with wheels are best so that in an emergency, luggage can be handled personally. Most people travel with too many clothes. One hears of people taking a dozen pairs of trousers, eight pairs of shoes plus different accessories for a two-week vacation, which seems somewhat excessive. The best way is to travel with the minimum of luggage.

In our family we each limit ourselves to the least possible luggage, usually about ten to twelve kilograms. Male or female, one can have a varied wardrobe within this limit, including lightweight day or evening wear, swimwear, cardigans, shoes for walking as well as dress wear, washable underwear and toilet essentials. Only one suitcase each is needed, the heaviest outfit can be worn and a light raincoat carried.

Travelling Alone

With the increase in longevity more of us reach retirement in tandem with our partners so that we go on holidays together. But not always. Divorce and bereavement take their toll.

The loneliness of travelling as a single person makes many people regard holidays with horror, unthinkable or not worth the effort, perhaps something they will never do again. When one has been accustomed to travelling with a partner on pleasurable holidays the sadness of being alone is compounded, for the time away becomes a trial. Life during most of the year for older, single people may be reasonably happy – they have adjusted to their independent state and grown accustomed to it as a way of life. Yet when holiday times come around, they find the idea of travelling alone distasteful. For example, going out to eat on one's own abroad is not much fun, particularly for women who tend to get offered the worst of tables and the least of attention. And single rooms in hotels are more expensive per head than double ones as well as less attractively placed.

Travelling as part of a group which is made up mostly of couples, tends to emphasize the loneliness of a single traveller. It is worth trying to find a companion, in like circumstances, with whom to plan and go away. Find someone of a suitable age bracket and with common likes and dislikes. Tolerance and flexibility are qualities well worth developing, otherwise it may not be possible to cope with idiosyncrasies. If banishing loneliness is more important than treasured independence there may have to be some sacrifices. Set a balance, admit and recognize your own limitations and aim at a give-and-take relationship. The rewards of shared experiences, fun and laughter are considerable.

Sharing is Best

The main pleasure for most people in going on holiday is sharing the experience, the journey, the shopping trips, the evening strolls. It is companionable to watch out for a partner who is having a swim or playing a game, nice to talk to someone about what to wear for dinner and hear them say, 'You look nice'. Minor things but they are important.

Two women who themselves experienced the misery of lone travel after their husbands died, met up and decided to share a holiday. For Vera Coppard, a Citizens' Advice Bureau organizer and Lisa Harrison, a teacher, this was such a success that not only did they determine to repeat the experience, but also agreed to set up a venture called Travel Companions.

The purpose was not to organize the holidays, although Vera and Lisa do have considerable travel experience and are prepared to offer such advice, but to match up compatible people who could go away together. The service is for people over forty and those interested are required to fill in a questionnaire which enables interests to be determined. It has been a successful venture and Travel Companions has been the answer to lonely holidays for many. (See Useful Addresses.)

Cashless Abroad

Consuls in embassies hear problem stories every year from holidaymakers. Some concern the loss of credit cards or cash and the person involved will be in difficulties. How does one go about getting emergency cash?

There is no legal obligation on the part of a consul to provide or lend money but they can telex a message home, on your behalf, requesting that money be wired to a bank.

Ask your bank, before travelling, for a leaflet which details how one can get money in an emergency. Make a separate list of all account and card numbers as well as any emergency twenty-four hour telephone numbers of banks and card companies. When there is any trouble, such as lost or stolen cash or cards, it is a relief not to have to worry about getting hold of the vital telephone numbers. Help is needed quickly and it is available on the end of a phone, so it is wise to keep such numbers handy.

Take at least two credit cards with you, leaving the spare in a safe place. That way, there can be rapid access to money should one card get mislaid or stolen.

There are a number of card protection schemes and the major banks will be able to recommend one. They incur a modest fee for which most will forward interest-free money to help out at times of urgent need following loss of cards.

Traveller's Cheques

Most tourists are knowledgeable about traveller's cheques which are a convenient way of carrying money. They must be signed when they are bought and counter-signed when they are presented for payment. Banks charge a small commission fee for traveller's cheques but, if lost, the bank or travel firm which issues them will usually be able to arrange for immediate replacement. To ensure this prompt action, keep the receipt in a safe place, separate from the cheques themselves.

Credit Cards

Certain credit cards can be used in many countries, others only in a few. Some can be used in cash dispensers, whilst others are limited to banks. Obtain from issuing banks the locations of dispensing machines available in the destination area. These machines can only be used if you know your Personal Identification Number. Double-check that you can use your cards in the country you are visiting.

Rates of Exchange

Money can be changed at hotels, banks and cash-exchange bureaux. Rates of exchange fluctuate but usually quite minimally. Expect a better rate of exchange for traveller's cheques than for currency. There are modest charges for transactions.

Transferring Pensions

Anyone staying abroad for more than three months and who is entitled to a pension should advise their own Social Security Office of their plans. Arrangements can then be made for the cash to be sent either to the holiday address or to a local bank account. Sending money abroad does take some time and it is wise to send it well in advance of the date it will be needed. Your bank manager will give advice about these transfers and can also change British currency to local currency if given notice.

Misrepresentation

The misery of a holiday which has been ruined by unsatisfactory accommodation or misrepresentation of facilities can be compounded when attempts to get damages fail.

It is often an uphill struggle to get recompense but the aggrieved traveller who is determined can usually succeed. An independent conciliation service should be set up by the Association of British Travel Agents (ABTA). People with complaints should write as soon as possible to the firm with which the holiday was booked. Include all the relevant details such as dates, holiday address, cost and the reason for complaint. Send a copy of the letter to ABTA. Gerry Fernback, a past-president of ABTA, advises that the reputable companies do their best to please their customers and will write to apologize, offering redress. If there is no satisfactory outcome, take the dispute to the small claims court. A court official or the Citizens Advice Bureau will explain the procedure.

Tips on Flying

One problem when travelling long distance by air is swollen ankles and feet. Exercise your feet and press your toes and heels alternatively against the floor at regular intervals. Rotate your ankles and try to walk about every hour or so.

Don't exert pressure on your veins by crossing your legs and always wear easy-fitting shoes. Clothing too, should be loose and comfortable. Drinking wine and spirits is dehydrating, so be sure to drink plenty of non-alcoholic liquid.

Last-Minute Check
Check in good time that your passport is current, that you have the necessary inoculations and that your tickets are correct as to date and time. A valid air ticket does not absolutely guarantee you a seat on the plane. Should you turn up late, you may well find that the plane was over-booked and no seat is available for you.

Take with you some local currency to cover the cost of incidental expenses on arrival, such as taxi fares, gratuities or buying a cup of coffee.

It is all Worthwhile

It may all sound a hassle. But sitting outdoors on a warm evening, watching the sun set over the horizon or lunching in a hillside café amidst leafy lemon and orange groves makes it worthwhile. Especially if you are reading about blizzards and icy conditions back home.

8 It Pays to Keep Busy

How about we forget 'retired' and think 'change of occupation'? What are you going to do with the rest of your life? A sudden cessation of activity, the change from a busy work-centred life to a potentially aimless existence can be demoralizing and depressing. Some alternative occupation must be found and the difficulty will be choosing which because today there has never been so much call for experience. It doesn't have to be the same kind of work that we have been used to; we may even re-train for something quite different to occupy our time, choosing the type of work to undertake and possibly becoming 'freelancers'.

Work is like meat and drink to most of us. We dislike the idea of having nothing to do, lamenting that without occupation we will become dull-witted, have little purpose in life and be needed by no one. If we became idle, that could be uncomfortably close to the truth. But we have to find a way to bridge the years ahead successfully, probably making some of the most valuable contributions to our families and communities that we have ever done and extending our usefulness far into our old age. We certainly do not want to fall into the trap of having everything done for us while we do nothing for anyone.

Regular Part-Time Job

If you are handy about the house you may be able to advertise and earn extra funds with your decorating or carpentry skills. There is a good deal of scope for this, especially in or close to towns where it is generally harder to get help. Women can be just as good as men at all of these jobs, but are more hesitant to use their talents outside their own homes.

Nursery gardens frequently offer part-time jobs to reliable people who can help care for plants, deal with customers and keep greenhouses, young trees and bushes tidy and shipshape.

Sheila and Bill have retired from their administrative jobs in a hospital and hire themselves out as a house-cleaning service. They find it interesting and remunerative and are treated with the greatest respect by their clients whose homes they keep in immaculate order.

Norma had her own boutique but after her husband died she gave it up. She felt that she wanted an undemanding job which would keep her occupied and bring in a little cash. She advertised a garment alteration service and is busy for three afternoons a week, which is as much as she wants. It gets her out meeting people too, which is important for her.

Dorothy revived her typing skills when she wanted something to occupy her as well as to earn her a little money. She now works regularly three days a week for an author who likes the old-fashioned sound of a typewriter tapping away and won't hear of using a word processor. That suits them both for Dorothy cannot abide new-fangled machines either and resolutely refuses to have anything to do with them.

Learn New Skills

Reaching the sixties does not mean that we are going to change overnight. We will have the same intelligence, the same knowledge and experience. We can use our existing ability or learn new skills because age is no bar to education and any difficulties or slowness are more than likely to be just an expression of our apprehension. Mature students may at first be regarded with deference to their age but they are soon accepted with respect for their learning ability.

There is a huge reservoir of resources among active retired citizens, far too valuable to be ignored and which can enrich the community and the government. One hears of trained people, teachers, doctors, engineers, plumbers, accountants, retiring at fifty-five or sixty. If this expertise is not used it is wasted and should at least be harnessed to train younger people.

Effect of Inflation

Inflation and its erosion of savings is an important consideration for anyone who looks forward to retirement. It may be that the value of savings is so reduced each year that some way must be found of raising income to maintain standards they had thought would be assured. The return on savings accounts may seem generous until it is set against the inflation rate, when it could look pathetically small. And you cannot always rely on property values to behave as you expect they will.

Early retirement was a high priority for George and Beatrice. They intended to sell their house and buy a bungalow on the South Coast. Anticipating that there would be a large sum left over from the property transaction to invest and so boost their income, they made the decision to go ahead. They were unexpectedly frustrated in their plans. First, they found that South Coast prices had risen and there was little financial advantage to be gained by selling their town home and moving to the seaside. Second, the return on any such capital was not as high as they had hoped and would be annually eroded by inflation. However, they were determined not to be thwarted in their plans and eventually they moved to a bungalow, but in order to maintain their income and standard of living, they took in house guests for part of the year. They have always been interested in helping handicapped people, particularly those with mobility problems and since their bungalow and its two bathrooms and toilets are accessible to wheelchairs, their accommodation has been in demand. They made many new friends and they feel financially secure enough to employ all the help they need.

Retired but Needing Income

When retirement comes earlier than expected or wanted, or there is an enforced change of direction, it helps to find some positive aspect in the situation. There may be an opportunity for a career change and development in a different way. Finance may be of major relevance and so fundamental that it often overrides other considerations. Whether the enforced change will bring about income equal to that previously enjoyed may be questionable, but it can and does happen that an increased remuneration is the result.

When John's printing business failed he tried all sorts of jobs. He thought he would never again be able to earn the sort of living he had been able to provide for his wife. This additional problem helped end what had been an unsatisfactory marriage but a new life was ahead for him. He went into selling insurance, was very successful, re-married and at sixty-two is the proud father of twin daughters.

Getting Paid Part-Time

Before answering any ads or accepting offers, consider what you would best like to be doing. What are you interested in and what are you good at? Are you good with people or do you like bringing order into an office? Your qualifications and age may not look good on paper but you may do well in person. Call at bureaux and offices, let your friends know what you are looking for, that you are prepared to give two, three or more days per week. Read the cards in shop windows and put one in yourself. The attraction of a paid job can be a temptation, especially if standards have had to be reduced because of a drop in income.

The manager of a computer office retired from his position with a pension, needing to earn some money but wanting a job with less responsibility. He obtained a clerical job, works three days a week and feels the benefit of both the work and his time off. He is certainly appreciated in the office where under his mature guidance there is an added stability and everything runs smoothly.

There are people who can never accept life without employment and who are constantly interested in advertised jobs. They may wish to take the opportunity to increase income or make use of their abilities. Geoffrey is one such man. Retiring at sixty-five from a demanding job as manager of a clothing factory where he was responsible for a staff of 200 people, he found himself at a loose end, wondering what he should do with his time. All the odd jobs were done, he had put up shelving, lagged the roof space, tidied the little garden and he and his wife Shirley had made trips abroad and visited family and friends. He now felt despondent and redundant and Shirley was understandably concerned. He saw an advertisement for a part-time alteration hand. 'I could do that', he said. 'I designed and made clothes all those years.' Shirley cheerfully encouraged him. 'Go on and try. Part-time only mind.'

Geoffrey got the job and worked for two days a week, enjoying the commitment and his new employers much appreciated his excellent work. He was invited to take a bigger interest and even to manage the shop. But Shirley insisted that he should remain a part-timer and he knew that she was right. He had not been ready for full retirement but neither did he want a full-time commitment.

Working for Free

The choice of voluntary work is immense. There is something of a problem in suiting volunteers to occupation, although willing hands and minds can usually be found something useful to do. The decision has to be made as to whether we would prefer to be engaged actively in helping people or to work on the administrative side. Is it important for us to be busy on just one or two days a week or more? Do we need some occupation close to where we live or can we put up with travelling? Will we need to be paid expenses or can we afford incidental costs? Do we just want to find a way of extending our life of useful service or give ourselves a good reason for getting up in the morning?

Whatever the answers may be, there is one thing we can be perfectly sure of – somewhere, someone needs and will appreciate our help.

Value of Work

Too often, unpaid work is viewed as valueless. But a job which attracts expenses only, providing for a passing on of expertise can be a most rewarding experience, allowing plenty of free time for holidays and leisure to be planned. However, a degree of commitment has to be made to any job that is worthwhile. We cannot undertake a job, paid or not, and then leave to suit a whim, putting other people to inconvenience.

The Charity Digest

This is an annual digest of charities which is published by the Family Welfare Association and it can be found in every library. In this fascinating book are details of some of the more important of the 170,000 charities which are now officially registered by the Charity Commission, the government-approved regulatory body.

To qualify as a charity, an organization must be set up for the benefit of the community in some way. This could be to provide some kind of relief for those in distress, to advance religion or education, or to alleviate poverty. The aim may be to help those who are disadvantaged in some special way: the blind, deaf, physically or mentally disabled, either old or young.

Bona Fide Charities

Each year many applications are received by the Charity Commissioners from various bodies who want to become registered charities. There are distinct advantages to this and the Charity Commission jealously guards entry to its list. It has to consider each application on its merits and grants the coveted official charity status to comparatively few. Even so, some charities use methods of fund-raising or spending which raise doubts in the minds of would-be donors. Anyone who wishes to give money to, or work for, a charity should establish that it is in fact bona fide and operates in a manner which the donor or worker could approve of.

Charities recruit all manner of employees, paid and unpaid, so a wide range of skills is sought and often some training is provided. Some of the work requires abilities which must be paid for. It would be unlikely for example that physio or occupational therapists could be drawn from volunteers. Professional medical people such as these must be paid for from the charity income.

In Demand

Secretarial ability is constantly in demand – there are always letters to be written, case work to be kept up to date and papers to be filed in order. It is important in any office to have someone with a good telephone manner who can be relied upon to give information and to take messages accurately.

Older Drivers

There are many older drivers who are good, reliable, careful and courteous and these are valuable qualities in today's difficult and crowded road conditions. Drivers are always needed to transport people such as the handicapped to clubs or on outings. Senior citizen volunteers are generally welcome although it is recognized that older drivers tend to have certain limitations.

A study conducted by the Automobile Association (AA) in the UK looked at the driving habits of 1,000 drivers between the ages of fifty-five and seventy-five. The study showed that one in six does not drive at night, because they are so bothered by the glare of headlamps. One in four has made an insurance claim in the past five years. It was also found that busy junctions represent a particular driving hazard for older groups.

The AA found that although numbers of older people take some kind of medication regularly, few say that they have been warned by their GP that side-effects might be hazardous to driving. If you offer yourself as a driver, be sure that you are fit and capable of undertaking the responsibility and care of passengers.

'Contact'

'Contact' is a charity that it must be a real pleasure to work for. Its main asset is its force of over 4,000 drivers, helpers and hosts. Throughout the country they collaborate to provide Sunday afternoon outings each year for 2,500 elderly people. Many of the organizers are themselves the youthful elderly who bring together the young and the very old. Both age groups enjoy each other, especially the children who are fascinated by people who started life so long ago, many of whom have excellent recall with interesting memories to relate.

There are lists of lonely old people waiting to join, some recommended by local hospitals, GPs, social workers and home-helps. The leading members of the charity meet regularly to discuss future outings and there is much warmth and friendliness among them and their elderly friends. Get in touch if you know of someone who could benefit, or if you wish to offer your own services. You may be good at making the sandwiches, cakes or biscuits, you may be a good listener or talker. You may have a talent for entertaining guests or be content just to drive people between home and venue. If this idea attracts you, a telephone call will bring you more information.

Beauty Care Services

The British Red Cross and St John's Ambulance services both seek volunteers. The familiar uniforms of these organizations can be seen at many public events and members are trained to render first-aid to anyone in need until a doctor can be found or the person taken to hospital. (See Useful Addresses.)

A less well-known service provided by the Red Cross is for beauty care. Volunteers serve in hospitals and homes, working for the disabled, the mentally ill and long-term and geriatric patients. They have a Hand Care service for the elderly who welcome such attention. Qualifications needed are little more than a kindly manner, pleasant personality and supple hands. Training is thorough, although necessarily limited, and covers elementary massage, hand and beauty care, depilatory work and cosmetic camouflage. Anyone with a background of this kind of work would be particularly welcome. If you do not mind the hospital atmosphere, can face treating sick people with compassion but remain impersonal you could find this work rewarding.

General Hospital Work

There are many jobs in hospitals which volunteers can undertake. Some will need to have been trained in first-aid, others need only be willing to help with all kinds of simple duties. Receptionists are required at main ward entrances helping visitors with enquiries; they cover rotas for duties such as taking patients from wards to chapel services or the shopping precincts to be found in many hospitals. They can help the play assistants in children's wards, serve in the shops or restaurants or act as drivers and escorts.

In one hospital a volunteer was needed to sit and cuddle a long-stay patient, a little boy of twenty months with a very weak chest problem. His relatives could not visit and although the nurses gave him what hugging time they could, they were very busy. He did not have the single person who could give him the loving, individual care and attention that he needed every day in order to flourish. I am sure someone was soon found.

Volunteers without specialist knowledge but who have general life experience can be found useful slots in many areas. They can assist in the distribution of library books in homes as well as hospitals, run trolley shops, collect shopping lists and call on neighbours to check that they are OK. A telephone call to any of the various disability groups catering for either children or for adults will reveal an ongoing need for a pair of hands, a ready listener or someone to give common-sense advice.

A Holiday Camp

In a radio broadcast I heard of an unusual charity. In the USA, the film actor Paul Newman had set up a holiday camp for children who are terminally ill with cancer. The aim of the charity is to give these children the holiday of a lifetime. It is proving extremely popular and there are candidates on waiting lists from around the world, including the UK, for children to visit the camp. The fact that they can meet so many others who are in like circumstances has proved to be a big morale booster to these youngsters.

Interestingly, the money to support the charity comes from a food business which Paul Newman began just a few years ago. This started almost as a joke when he bottled some of his home-made salad dressing for friends. There was some dressing left over, so he sent it to the local grocery store. Demand exceeded the supply and so a business was born which now raises over 40 million dollars annually. Every penny of profit is devoted to the camp.

The broadcast ended with an appeal for someone to start a similar camp in the UK, since there are so many applications from children here that cannot be satisfied. This is a wonderful idea and no doubt someone will start it off and there will be another successful charity which will be able to relieve distress for many youngsters. Volunteers will be wanted both to raise the money needed and to serve the children at the camp. Paul Newman himself is in his mid-sixties and regularly helps in the American camp despite a busy programme of film making. In such a place age is no bar for many of the jobs which need to be done.

Helping Handicapped Children

Many residential schools for handicapped children offer respite care so that parents can get a break. The schools welcome assistants who can help regular staff by feeding the children or teaching them simple skills such as reading, writing or even walking.

Advising Families

'Homestart' is an association which provides walk-in centres where young families with urgent problems can attend. Volunteers from all kinds of backgrounds are needed to undergo training and visit these families on a regular basis, perhaps weekly, to offer the comfort and support of friendship and practical advice. Families are also encouraged to meet regularly at the headquarters so that they see other people in similar situations and can talk through their problems over a cup of tea.

This kind of back-up can often prevent baby battering, abuse and the mental or physical breakdown of the mother or father. Problems are identified before they reach unmanageable proportions. There is no upper age limit for volunteer workers, only the desire to help and some training is necessary.

Volunteer Bureaux

There are volunteer bureaux in many areas which run a type of umbrella service, receiving both requests for help as well as offers to help. One need which never seems to be filled is for assistance in keeping gardens tidy. So many people who can manage to continue residing within their own homes find that they can no longer cope with the garden as well.

If they do not have helpful relatives or neighbours they are saddened by unkempt lawns and weedy flower beds. There is the danger too, that these signs of neglect disclose the abode of a lonely and vulnerable person. Confidence tricksters and thieves watch out for such clues when selecting their next victim.

Counsellors Needed

In many parts of the country Citizens Advice Bureaux, known familiarly as CABs, suffer from a chronic shortage of bureau workers. They urgently need younger retirees, male or female of the right background who can train as counsellors. They also need those who are prepared to contribute their office expertise, perhaps with typing, filing or word processor skills.

There are more than 800 CAB offices in the country whose local communities look to them for friendly, confidential advice and assistance about every conceivable kind of problem. More than a third of the questions asked are concerned with housing difficulties and a large proportion of others relate to marital and other family problems. Getting into debt causes grave difficulties for many of the younger families whose mortgage or credit has run out, leaving them to face possible homelessness and ruin.

I have worked in bureaux which always had queues of people waiting to put their problems in the hands of someone they could trust. The government has for years expressed its confidence in the national CAB organisation by making large grants to help to keep the service going. But CABs never have enough money and are always short of suitable workers. One difficulty for the bureaux is that as soon as they have trained a person to be capable, he or she becomes eminently suitable for the job market. That is not a bad thing but it leaves a gap and replacements will always be needed, particularly in the cities. Enquire at a local bureau or write to the national headquarters in London. (See Useful Addresses.)

Passing on Handicrafts

If you have a particular skill, especially in a handicraft, there may be an opportunity for you to teach. It is worth letting the head of your local technical college know of your ability and that you are available. There may be small clubs or associations who would like such aptitudes demonstrated or even taught to their members. Specialist craft clubs with talented members have frequent requests for teachers for one or other of the training schemes for the young.

Age Concern

This charity provides extra services for the very old and it is the newly retired who form the backbone of the organization, offering their new-found time. They visit people in their areas, bringing understanding and kindliness to the problems they find. All kinds of events are organized, outings of interest, shopping expeditions, days away and so on. Escorts are provided for trips to hospitals and clinics and all is done with such goodwill that the people involved find that they really enjoy the work. They also run classes of various kinds and one is always struck by the good humour and laughter, evidence of the enjoyment of these activities by everyone concerned.

Sometimes we fail to recognize our own potential for helping others, nor do we appreciate how much pleasure this will bring into our own lives. Volunteers get a great deal of satisfaction out of helping others in this way. (See Useful Addresses.)

Teach a Craft

The Crafts-at-Home scheme has a great demand for visitors who will call on the very old and teach them to make things. Subjects range from needlework, jewellery making, macrame, painting, to toymaking, mosaic designing, picture framing – all kinds of interests are covered. If you are good at any of these, do offer your time.

On the other hand, one housebound woman in her seventies held classes in her home, teaching how to crochet. She enjoyed her pupil visitors and the opportunity to feel useful and to see people regularly, which she otherwise could not do.

Reach

REACH is an organization which has expanded in the last few years. Its full name is Retired Executives Action Clearing House and it sets out to match retired executive people to positions where their expertise can be used. The association has been enormously successful, providing opportunities for people with energy and know-how to use their invaluable experience. So many executives, dreading the loss of the keen satisfaction they always felt in doing a good job successfully, find a whole new reason for living opening up to them. (See Useful Addresses.)

A self-employed builder retired when his doctor advised that he should take things a bit easier. At sixty-two, Patrick missed his active life and said that he had never before looked at his hands in his lap, wondering what to do with them. REACH put him in touch with a charity which was about to begin the building of a sports hall. He has taken a keen interest in the project and his ideas and experience gained him the respect of the young people he has worked with. 'I have shown them where you can take short cuts to save money, and where you must be careful to avoid mistakes. I brought in a solicitor friend who had also retired and he sorted out their legal problems. In fact, he got so involved that he became chairman of their charity committee. Between us, we saved them a lot of money. I have already told REACH that I am ready to look at anything else they have on offer.'

Young people wanting to set up in business often lack the knowledge which experience can provide. An intelligent person with a sound business background can guide a 'young' company, steering it into safe waters, demonstrating how to operate and what pitfalls to avoid.

Retired experts are able to provide the kind of sound advice and judgement that could cost a fortune if sought from a professional consultant. There is a need to exercise caution however and anyone setting themselves up to offer expert advice must be aware that their advice could end up costing a client money and, therefore, they might find themselves liable to be sued. Advisory charities do have to insure themselves against such an eventuality. But such cases are extremely rare and the large majority of client/adviser relationships turn out to prove satisfactory.

Charities must be Businesslike

Voluntary bodies are no more proof against failure than any other kind of operation. But they are often run by keen and enthusiastic people who simply do not have the kind of know-how which seems so basic to the experienced business person. Many a charity owes its survival to a little of the right kind of advice, others have foundered for lack of it.

Treasurers in Demand

Accounting skills in a treasurer are in great demand, for income must be carefully looked after and skilfully managed. Money can produce interest, careful budgeting can produce savings and prudent purchasing can result in getting more goods for a given cost. The partnership of entrepreneurism and goodwill can expand the value of slim and scarce resources. Good organization is usually at a premium and volunteers with a proven background should not feel dubious about the value of services they can offer.

Be Ready to Learn

It may not be easy to take criticism from someone running a voluntary organization, especially when you feel you have seen it all before. Be patient, persevere and everyone will come to recognize your value and respect you for it.

From the organizer's point of view it should be remembered that it may not be easy to deal with volunteers. They might well not take kindly to being told how to do a job for which they are not being paid. Paid or not, jobs have to be done properly and if there are differing views about which is the right or wrong way, problems will arise.

Fund-Raising

Some people feel they are more suited to organizations or tasks which only raise money. They may help with arranging flag days, coffee mornings, good-as-new sales, sponsored swims, walks or parachute drops. They can organize car boot or garage sales, fashion shows or become ambitious and fill a large hall for a dinner dance or a grand ball.

People are really ingenious about fund-raising and there are few charitable projects of worth which do not succeed in raising the necessary money. Raising funds calls for a special ability which is much in demand, requiring energy, ideas and hard work.

We will Never Retire

We need to be needed. So we must indeed forget the words 'retire from work' and think only of what work we are going to change to.

9 Relationships

Our later years should be a bonus following the time spent working and if they are to be enjoyable, lively and full of interest, then they need to be shared with those we love, our families and our friends. There are few of us who are so self-dependent that we have no need of any other close person.

Mutual relationships can have many variations and some parts of these are bound to be negative. We may love people while recognizing that there are certain things about them that we do not particularly like, but we show forbearance and tolerance for any shortcomings. When there is love and a need for each other, then a happy, companionable and mutually rewarding relationship can be enjoyed. There must be give and take, acceptance with understanding of each other's idiosyncrasies.

By the age of retirement we have learned some valuable lessons. We know how to conduct ourselves in our relationships, developing good habits in time to make living graceful and comfortable. We can be positive about ageing, making it something pleasant to look forward to.

Where there is mutual respect there is a sound basis for partnerships to rest on. We do not want to do or say anything which causes unhappiness or resentment but, instead, show consideration of each other's needs. Discipline and restraint are essential in order to develop quiet and reasoned discussion between two people rather than dogmatic and peremptory orders from one. Screaming and shouting are defeating in the long run, rarely resolving matters satisfactorily. While they may be a way of letting off steam they can also be damaging.

Whatever their ages may be, partners must recognize each other's emotional needs. It is then easier to understand the self doubts and fears which are part of everyone's make-up. Each partner can naturally then want to satisfy the other and take joy in doing so.

We face new enigmas as we age but being old has its attractions. We have experience, wisdom, dependability, we develop patience and we have learned how to get along with people. We know too, the value of our own generation, the one we grew up and feel most comfortable with.

Patching up Quarrels

Where there has been a rift between friends or relatives which needs repairing, set about trying to mend it while there is still time. It is rewarding to look for the good in people rather than to recall the bitterness of the past. Be positive, take the initiative and you may wonder what you ever found to quarrel about in the first place.

Families which experience only sweetness and harmony, never knowing the bitterness of quarrels, are few and far between. Psychologists say that those families which scarcely speak have little feeling for each other whereas those which show strong emotion and argue are expressing passion and that the dissension is one way of showing it. When feelings are aired they often pave the way for deeper understanding and a renewal of affection.

There are some shared relationships which are not anything like as good as they could be. Perhaps there have been misunderstandings which never quite got cleared up, problems which were never talked through. Bitterness and anger may remain below the surface, spoiling everything. Emotional problems between two people or within families are not always capable of solution and there are times when certain relationships are best ended. Infidelity and brutality are hard to forgive and forget and they are just two causes of marital breakdown. But people must put things in perspective and then judge for themselves.

Counselling should be Sought

Anything which can release stress within families and produce a happier association must be of great value in the long term.

Counsellors are trained to discuss problems quietly in a relaxed atmosphere, taking into account the personality of the client. Simply talking about a situation can help people to understand more clearly how it has arisen. It then becomes feasible to assess how things can be improved, if indeed that is possible.

Men seem more reluctant to go to a counsellor than women. Some couples will go together but usually it is the woman who takes the initial step. We all have hang-ups and these may be the result of very early experiences. It could need extended psychological treatment to discover these and hopefully to correct them. Such treatment usually consists of confidential sessions with highly-trained therapists and could continue for months and possibly years.

A counsellor's job is not to make decisions for anyone. It is rather to clarify unresolved problems, to outline new approaches that are achievable and to suggest how to bring about changes which will be effective. It may take several visits to a counsellor before a troubled client can perceive things in a new way and come to a balanced conclusion. But once decisions are made it can bring real relief and an improvement in health, a new will to move out of an unacceptable situation and hopefully towards a better future for all concerned.

It might be imagined that counsellors find listening to problems at length a tedious business, but it is necessary if one is to be helpful. The knowledge that people can come in at the door burdened and go out feeling lighter-hearted can be rewarding and brings a sense of satisfaction and achicvement. When there are no solutions, as sometimes happens, the counsellor too, is left heavy-hearted.

Sons and Daughters

Relationships with one's own children seldom remain the same throughout life. Children may grow up and separate from their parents but, even as adults, they are sometimes unable to forget the emotions and pain they knew in their younger years and continue, sometimes unjustifiably, to resent the parents for it.

This may be one cause for them to refuse to assume the responsibility of ageing parents they do not feel close to, preferring to keep themselves at a distance, both physically and emotionally.

Some parents find it hard to give up the authority they once exerted, especially if they hold the purse strings to family wealth. But trying to retain control in this way does not make for the respect and love which most parents seek. Sometimes it divides the surviving family even after the parent's death.

Married children present many different problems. There is the classic one of difficulties between mother and daughter-in-law, unable to feel real love or respect for each other, each jealous of the love the man bears for the other.

Under some circumstances there can be the warmest of affection between the mother and daughter-in-law. When Luisa came to the UK to study and fell in love with a young Englishman neither set of parents felt it was going to work out well. The young couple married but although the girl missed her family deeply the English mother was very sensitive to these feelings and a deep affection grew between the two women. Having no daughter of their own, the English parents, so wary at first, have come to love Luisa dearly. She is devoted to them and welcomes them warmly.

A son who remains a bachelor in the parental home can at first be a source of pride as he gives priority to his parents. Where the mother has been a dominant personality she may have discouraged him from marrying. Then as he grows to be middle-aged the mother's attitude changes. She worries about what will happen to him. He has grown used to his independence and marriage may not seem a welcome alternative. Never becoming mature or fully self-reliant, he may fear a strange and new responsibility.

Jim adored his mother. When she was widowed he felt he would never be able to leave her and when she was disabled by arthritis he took the greatest care of her. She was grateful to him but possessive, always discouraging him from making any close friendships. When she was in her eighties he was sixty and considering his retirement. At last she faced the future and worried about what would become of him. She suggested he ought to marry and after she died he met and married a widow. But they were never happy as he knew too little of life to understand that the contentment he had shared with his mother was very unlikely to be repeated with a woman of his own age. There were different demands on him and he just could not cope with them.

Adopt a Grandparent

Where there has been estrangement from family there may well be less reason to retire. Acquaintances at work could be all a person has. In such cases it may be worth enquiring whether there is a local scheme which encourages lonely elders in a community to act as grandparent to a family. The benefit is two-way and to everyone's advantage. Children form close friendships with an older generation they may never otherwise have the chance to know, perhaps being introduced to museums, fishing expeditions or golf, experiences their own parents may not have time or inclination for. In return, the surrogate grandparents may be invited to an occasional meal or get their shopping done for them. Such friendships are good for the soul and can benefit all concerned.

Unwanted Ties

People are limited by their responsibilities and may resent this, wishing that they could feel free to make plans without having to consider anyone else. Regardless of such feelings most will protect their dependents as best they can, while a few will consider their own needs first. There is nothing new about deserting a family.

Not many, for example, could take off as the painter Gaugin did. His personal ambitions were so strong that he gave up a successful career, deserted his wife, children and all responsibilities and made off for a tropical island where he lived a simple life, allowing nothing to interrupt his painting.

It is certainly not unknown today for families to be left by either of their parents, more often than not the father. Fortunately most parents are committed and responsible, bound by natural love and devotion to their children. Many will try to make a go of an unsuitable marriage solely for the sake of the children. Couples split up too easily, wishing in later years that they had tried harder to make a success of their marriages. We do live at a more stressful pace today and inevitably a proportion of marriages will break down irrevocably. Fortunately there are still many couples who go on to enjoy retirement together.

Ten years ago, Derek and Teresa were in their late-forties, with two daughters aged seventeen and eighteen. It became clear that something was wrong when Derek changed, becoming uncharacteristically moody and withdrawn. It turned out that he had involved himself with a recently divorced neighbour, thinking himself in love with her. This came as a considerable shock to Teresa, who felt that their marriage had always been a very good one.

Meeting as students, they had married when young and had both worked hard to attain their present comfortable standards, he as a dentist and she as a librarian. Their ambitious plans for retirement were shelved while she fought for months to save the marriage. His practice suffered and he despaired over the emotional entanglements which had entered his life. The daughters were appalled by these events and deeply affected by the unhappiness in the household. They were all concerned too, about the prospect of a future loss of financial security.

There was great relief on the part of Teresa and the girls when it was decided that the family should not break up. Derek still loved his wife and she cared for him too much to give him up easily. His infidelity had arisen more out of pity for the neighbour than anything else. Nevertheless, months went by before this family regained a measure of their previous happiness. Today, some ten years later, they both agree that it would have been wrong to part, that their marriage was well worth preserving. Derek said, 'I felt guilty. I felt torn, but Teresa was so understanding. She must have been so hurt and angry but she put her own feelings aside. She saw me through it all and I can never thank her enough. In the end I knew that I would have lost something priceless if our marriage had ended.'

The best of relationships can need exclusive attention at times and it is certainly worth giving the partner in your life some special thought. A well-planned 'make my wife (or husband) happy' week, has saved many a marriage from slipping into the doldrums. Give some praise instead of criticism, take pains with your own appearance, plan a treat for your spouse. Resist giving the snappy retort or surly look, refrain from responding sharply to displays of temper. Work at being specially nice and see if it doesn't prove worthwhile. Be patient for at least the week, it can pay surprising dividends.

Grandchildren

Family links are extremely important to older folk and if grandchildren live nearby they can be a good reason to give up work. Time can be spent helping to care for the young ones. If family bonds are close but members live far apart, then it is worth considering moving near in order to become more involved.

Children greatly value leisure spent not only with parents but also with grandparents who may have much more time to give them. Youngsters' needs should be thoughtfully considered and it can be gratifying to satisfy them. Remember how fast children grow up and emotionally move away from relatives who do not give them enough of their time.

Mary, at fifty-two, taught in an infants' school. She loved her job and got along well with the colleagues she had known for many years. But she greatly missed her children. Her son lived abroad with his wife and child and her daughter was married with three children who were growing up in a distant county, scarcely knowing their grandmother. Mary grew thin and suffered frequent headaches and chest pains and although there seemed to be no physical reason for her condition she felt the cause was her separation from the children. Since she and her husband, Len, had a good relationship with their daughter and son-in-law she persuaded him that they should retire a few years early and move to be near the children. He was not at all sure that this was a good idea but agreed reluctantly.

They have found that communication between the adults in the family can occasionally get a little strained but they are all tactful and careful to nurse the relationship. On the whole, the help that the grandparents can provide for a household with three small and active grandchildren is welcome and appreciated by both parents. The young and old generations adore each other and that is very important to Mary. Her health has improved and that means more than anything to Len. They have both found plenty of activity in their new area and they are thoroughly enjoying the extra years of leisure due to their early retirement.

Baby-Sitting

There can hardly be more reliable baby-sitters than a child's grandparents who usually undertake this role with pleasure. But no one should be taken for granted. It can be fatiguing to be responsible for young children and to have to look after them, especially for extended periods. Even grandparents need time off and it should never be assumed that they will be there whenever they are wanted. If favours are requested too often and expected as a matter of course it can lead to ill-feeling.

Equally, grandparents must avoid being intrusive into the close family unit which comprises parents and their children. Young parents must be allowed to get on with their lives without interference or there will be conflict. Resentment may fester on both sides and no grandparent should consider it a right to move in with children and grandchildren. There is nothing so miserable as feeling in the way, unwanted and unwelcome, as can often happen. There are exceptions of course, particularly if, over the years, relationships have always been cordial and pleasant.

Elizabeth was widowed at the age of sixty, soon after the marriage of her only child, Sara. When a grandchild came along the young people searched for a larger house and Elizabeth looked with them. They were all attracted to a lovely, old and spacious cottage. Son-in-law Philip wished that they could afford something like it. Elizabeth, very diffidently, suggested that if they all moved in together, then they could. They thought it over and agreed to go ahead.

Sara said how much she longed to continue teaching and would welcome her mother's help. Philip liked his gentle mother-in-law and so it has all worked out well. The proof that it is a happy arrangement came when they insisted that she went on holiday with them.

Grandparents' Rights

At present, grandparents have no automatic independent right of access to their grandchildren after divorce of the parents, but check the latest legislation. This has led to some harrowing stories of children being separated from devoted grandparents who have no rights to see them at all.

The heartbreak which follows a divorce is not limited to the participating partners and their children. It also involves grandparents, many of whom face the loss of companionship or even visiting rights to their grandchildren. The bitterness between married couples at the time of separation and divorce may spill over in vindictiveness towards parents-in-law. The fact that this can cause additional heartbreak for children, even resulting in virtual cut-off from loving grandparents, seemingly has no effect in many cases. Sometimes the estranged parent moves abroad with the children and their whereabouts are not revealed.

Unless grandparents have the support and encouragement of one or other parent they have almost no legal standing in their claim to see their grandchildren. The loss is akin to a bereavement, dominating their thinking and ruining their peace of mind.

Even those with grandchildren who have been put in care, can be totally ignored by the authorities. Often it is found that there is no established local authority procedure for even discussing the future of the association. Grandparents are frequently described by social workers as 'too old to be responsible' or 'too close to the family'. There may even be a feeling that the grandparents were somehow linked with the problem which caused the family break-up in the first place. I often wish that social workers had more life experience rather than the formal training they undergo. They might make very different and wiser decisions. Whatever the reasons may be the facts are that agony and heartache are caused to innocent grandparents and children share in this suffering too.

Age Concern and The Grandparents Federation are among agencies which have been pressing for changes in the law affecting children in care. Hopefully, they will also obtain some recognition of the rights of grandparents to be allowed at least to see or communicate with their grandchildren occasionally. One can only feel great compassion for people in these tragic circumstances.

I knew of one grandmother whose later years were sadly blighted by separation from her granddaughter. Stella was a delightful woman who was thrilled when her son's first baby arrived. The birth had been difficult, and the mother could not feed the child. It was decided that the young couple should take a holiday and went away for a fortnight, leaving Stella in charge of the new infant. On return, the daughter-in-law expressed no gratitude but intense anger that she had been encouraged to leave her child. She vowed that Stella would have no contact with this child and she remained implacable. Her son was never able to persuade his wife to allow his mother to visit them or get to know her grandchild.

There are always going to be family problems. Therapy will help in some cases and be useless in others. There has to be mutual trust, sufficient liking, love and a wish for better understanding before a satisfactory result can be achieved.

Just talking things over with a concerned and attentive person who will respect confidentiality can be amazingly effective. But if not, then one has to accept and make the best of things as they are.

Making the Best of Things

We have achieved more anniversaries than our predecessors and so have greater experience. We have many advantages today with better homes, better diet and better health. We have more opportunity to live life to the full and to be happy and content. It is sad when we have to give up people we love dearly and hard to accept as inevitable that we cannot mend breaks, especially when we are not at fault. But if there are irreparable rifts in relationships, we can do nothing about them and we must simply make the best of all that we do have.

10 The Importance of Sex

One of the most powerful urges we have is our sexual drive which remains a compelling force however old we are. It achieves a maximum level in early adulthood, gradually declining as we grow older. As long as we can still feel excited, elated or aroused, age simply does not matter.

It is present for the whole of our lives, just as important in retirement as it ever was, except for one fact. Women of pensionable age no longer bear children, and men, although still capable, rarely wish to become elderly parents.

Sexual activity is not something that has to be learned, it should come naturally although this aptitude can be spoiled or inhibited by our experiences, unless we learn how to deal with them. Normally, sex develops gradually and flowers, reaching a stage in youth where it is fostered or smothered, tolerated or enjoyed according to the development and experience of the individual. There is a wide variation in the rate of decline, some people saying they feel no difference however old, others knowing just when a difference was felt.

Sexual relationships are important at every adult age and the vigorous sixty or seventy year old who has always enjoyed sex will actively seek to continue to enjoy it. And why ever not? An imaginative approach to sex can keep interest alive for both men and women, providing mental and physical stimulation at the right pace. No age group is excluded and tests show that ninety-year-old men are capable of an erection and ninety-year-old women capable of responding.

Sexual Problems

The range of sexual problems is wide, many needing medical expertise in their management, but no book of this kind would be complete that did not invite discussion on this subject. We think often about sexual activity because it is vital to almost every one of us and also because at every age it should be fun and enjoyable. And yet, while for many it is a simple and uncomplicated business, for others it is anything but that.

Individuals vary and so do their problems, some of which can be simple, others extremely complex. Psychotherapists are wary of identifying a difficulty for a client simply because the details are similar to some previously encountered. People who believe they have problems which they cannot solve, or who feel unable to respond sexually in what is considered the 'normal' way, should speak to their doctor. They will receive a sympathetic hearing, for doctors are familiar with the pain and suffering caused by supposed or real failings in this regard and will offer helpful advice.

Our hormones control our sex drive, being more active in some than in others. But we should all be physically and mentally able to maintain a balance which allows us to indulge our sexual appetites in a healthy way. This can be true even for those who have suffered unpleasant, sometimes cruel, encounters. But the result for some unfortunates is that their minds are disordered and they in turn, inflict brutality.

Effects of Abuse

It is known from the number of adults who say that they endured sexual abuse in childhood that this practice, so abhorrent to most of us, must be more widespread than is generally thought. In a recent inquiry, a woman in her sixties revealed that from an early age she had suffered sexual abuse at the hands of an uncle. She had never spoken of it but after she grew up was unable to form a happy relationship with any man and had always lived alone. Today, abused youngsters who are robbed of their innocence in this way can find sympathetic doctors or counsellors who can help them to recover and live happy and natural lives.

Finding Sexual Happiness

Leaving aside the great majority of people who can cope with their own problems, particularly when they are older and more experienced, there remain many individuals for whom there are obstacles to a worthwhile sex life. What happens to cause bars to sexual happiness? And should people, even in their later years, attempt to deal with these? My answer would be, 'Yes, most certainly'. The satisfaction and relief of understanding why we are as we are, makes it worth taking the trouble to seek professional help, possibly enabling one to find a rewarding, intimate life.

An early experience of being laughed at or found wanting in some personal way can result in a life time feeling of inadequacy or despair and can form a barrier to the enjoyment of sexual intercourse. The problem which affected Donald and Gwen arose out of an incident at the beginning of their married life thirty-two years previously. Gwen had been sadly disappointed to find herself unresponsive in their sexual relationship and for years she thought that Donald had 'looked elsewhere'. Before their marriage she had thought that she would be a passionate partner and had looked forward to married life, but an occurrence on the first night of their honeymoon had blighted the whole of their future. She had emerged from the bathroom wearing a lacy nightie and Donald was already in bed. 'He said, "That's gorgeous, but take it off." I was very shy, we had never made love, nor had he seen me undressed. I slipped out of my nightie and stood there smiling at him and he just laughed. "Oh, you're like a boy", he said, "No bust at all". Do you know, that memory still stings? I felt frozen and wanted to walk away from the marriage there and then. He was nice and kind in so many ways, but I think I fell out of love with him in that second. I never forgot it.'

For Gwen, her husband's laughter had served to turn her off sex. She thought that she did not look desirable and she resented the destruction of the blossoming feelings which she had experienced. He had certainly been insensitive, but he had also been a nervous young husband, perhaps worried about his own slight physique, inexperience and performance. They sought help only when their children had grown up and left home; they were on the verge of retirement and they had already decided to part. Many sessions with an experienced therapist were needed but these two did find a new understanding, tenderness and sexual joy in their life together. There had been a sad waste of years but happiness is better found late than never.

Feelings of Inadequacy

Individuals, male or female, may imagine that they have unattractive facial or bodily features, physical abnormalities, or are too small – or too large – in their genital areas. In fact, is is much more likely that they are well within the wide band of 'normality' and quite needlessly have wasted years in worry on matters of little or no concern. They may feel that some physical detail makes them unattractive to the opposite sex. Are they too small in the breast or chest, too gawky and tall or too short? And one only has to read some of the multitude of advertisements for cures for those supposedly overweight or undersized to appreciate the extent to which those factors are deeply worrying.

At seventeen, Justin heard someone say that his large mouth 'spoiled his face'. This chance comment made him feel so unattractive that it affected his confidence all his life, particularly with the opposite sex. Yet his mouth is really a nice, generous one. I spoke to him when he was sixty-seven and he became emotional on recalling the pain that this remark had caused.

Some think that they have a facial feature so unattractive that they could only feel desirable if it were to be changed. Margaret was a child with little confidence and as she grew she pictured herself as totally lacking in allure. She had inherited her father's large and rather misshapen nose, which much depressed her. Finally, her family took her to the doctor and it was decided that she should have the nose 'bobbed'.

Once this operation, known as rhinectomy, was completed, everyone was delighted with the result and it did make her into a pretty girl. But still she lacked confidence in herself. The feeling of inadequacy went deeper by far than a facial feature and she needed sensitive counselling.

Gertrude had an extremely large nose and heavy eyelids but she had such self-confidence, projecting such a cheerful personality that in a room full of people she was the centre of attraction. She married a man who adored her as did their two sons. All the same, she disliked her looks and, finally, in her forties and despite her husband's considerable reservations, she decided to have corrective surgery. The result was dramatic. We knew nothing of the operation, so when she asked us over one day I could barely suppress a gasp of surprise. Gertrude was quite beautiful. Her husband liked the result but still says he misses the face he married.

One needs to have confidence in one's normality and the belief that someone out there will love us just as we are. Character matters most, attracting others in age as well as youth, lasting right the way through life, much more dependable than mere physical beauty.

Psychological Dilemmas

A formidable problem to deal with is the deep-rooted fear or contempt felt by some for members of the opposite sex. Such difficulties as these may lie at the root of some of the cases of rape by mentally unbalanced men which unhappily occur with increasing frequency.

Psychologists have to unravel strange cases. One example revealed that a man had a deeply-rooted respect for the woman he loved, together with a belief that sex was 'dirty'. The man could not have intercourse with this woman, yet he committed several offences of rape.

Another man had a fear of young women and he sought much older women of more than seventy upon whom he forced himself. Such a man needs prolonged psychiatric treatment if he is ever to have normal relations.

It is not unusual to find men and women who are unable to have intercourse with the people they love. They may have married someone while they were seeking a parent figure who, while fulfilling a security need, did not attract them sexually. The problem may continue for years, worrying them but being accepted, while they feel it quite impossible to discuss it with anyone. In such a marriage the idea of sex may have become a secondary consideration. A feeling of shame, as though intercourse is wrong in the relationship, or an unshakeable conviction that attentions must be unwanted, will sometimes render any approach to their partner impossible. Help from a professional is needed when such beliefs have created an untenable situation.

Talking about Sex

Sexuality is not limited to those who enjoy physical good looks nor to those who are young. The myth of an upper age limit for sexual drive and interest is exploded as it becomes evident that the over-sixties have a very positive interest in social and physical relationships. We only need to be well and willing, to enjoy it all.

The sexuality of a person is what they are, not what they look like and has little to do with age. The scope of sexual expression is wide and our individual attitudes are based on our personal views, experience and education. Sexuality can be regarded as an emotional development naturally present from birth and an appetite which we can control or indulge at will. We may regard the act of love, actual sexual intercourse, as something casual to be found as we go on our way, or something that only goes with marriage – linked with falling in love. The value of monogamy and the sanctity of the single relationship are undeniable, more people wanting this than is recognized.

Society pays a great price when families break up. So many times I have heard from re-married individuals of how they wish that they had tried harder to preserve their first marriage. There should be more compassion, a greater attempt to reach mutual accord, to share and solve problems, many of which are based on sexual mismanagement or misunderstanding. More effort and consideration, as well as more education are needed.

'How was it for you?' is a question that could be asked following the sexual act, but which might not always get a truthful answer. At any age, it should be easy to talk about every aspect of sex to partners, saying what is pleasing and what is not, yet it seems to happen rarely. Some men and women, even when young, do not find sex a subject easy to talk about and so it is unlikely that they will be any different when older.

This reluctance may have its roots in a number of factors. It is bound up with an inhibiting shyness, the way a person was brought up, how they were taught to behave and what they were told they might expect. There is also the question of one's personal belief and how experiences have affected preferences. There is the important issue of religion and how strong an influence this has been and there is the aspect of law and what behaviour is regarded as correct, legally.

No one should feel forced into accepting unwelcome situations and one's sexuality should develop quite naturally in a relationship, according to one's tastes but only ever with mutual agreement. Sexual conflicts may mirror much deeper problems in a marriage and both partners should be aware of this possibility.

The need to express sexual desire generally conforms to ordinary methods of lovemaking but there are wide variations outside the accepted so-called norm. Sex should never feel dull or repetitive and everyone should be encouraged to experiment even if only to fantasize. A judge once remarked that having sat in the family courts for many years he was of the view that provided people could agree about how they should behave in bed, everything else was likely to prove tolerably acceptable in the marriage or partnership.

Buried Problems

Both William and Marion would agree on one thing at least – that their marriage was a mixture of attraction and dislike.

They had two children after which their sex life lacked interest for either of them. Small wonder, for during their quiet but intense quarrels they were cruel to each other, neither being willing to take the first step to make amends. They lived out years of this half-life before William decided to make the break. At fifty-five he learned to play bridge and found Wendy, ten years younger and a lonely divorcee. Their association flowered into something passionate and together they have had seven years of real happiness.

Marion on the other hand, remains bitter that the early love she knew withered so soon and she was helpless to find it again with William, the only man she ever wanted. Perhaps with counselling they might have reached an understanding, sharing a retirement based on mutual affection and satisfaction. On the other hand they may have realized earlier that they were incompatible, parted sooner and both found other partners.

Solving Problems

Today there is far more comprehension of sexuality. It is, after all, basic to each of us and not present merely for the purpose of having children. The practice of sex is healthy, beneficial to men and to women, an expression of natural desires.

It was once thought that women did not enjoy sex but tolerated it as a duty in marriage, for procreation and for the sake of their men. Men having this belief, performed hastily, leaving women no chance of pleasure. There are many retired people today whose marriages suffered and sometimes broke up because of this attitude. What a lot of misery this must have caused. Today, frank discussion on television and radio as well as articles in newspapers and magazines, educate and inform, so that there is little excuse for ignorance. For both sexes, a slow arousal with tender foreplay, ensuring pleasure for partners, is essential to the maximum satisfaction of each.

Couples with problems of a sexual nature may be introduced to a professional sex counsellor who will suggest ways of improving matters. It is essential that both partners attend and keep open minds for they must each be prepared to accept that either one may be at fault and be ready to discuss their relationship fully. It may require several sessions to resolve the issues but it is worthwhile if there is a successful outcome.

It does not necessarily follow that there will be no happy sexual relationship in the future just because one partnership has been a failure due to sexual incompatibility. At any age, before or after retirement, two lonely people whose friendship is deepening may find that sex will become an enjoyable and important element of their lives together, no matter what their past experience has been.

Different Sexual Tastes

The idea that some people indulge in so-called deviant sexual practices is abhorrent to many. But we should all be tolerant. If no harm is being done to anyone, if no child or young person is being drawn into an unwelcome situation, if adults are willing, then individuals should not have to feel guilty about practices which bring sexual relief and make them happy. For the sexual deviant, finding a partner is not a simple matter. They may not even realise that theirs is an unusual or unacceptable activity. It cannot be easy to find out whether someone else is going to comply with unusual tastes.

A Transvestite Experience

A good-looking divorcee of fifty-seven, Estelle held firm ideas about sex and marriage and had little notion of unusual practices. She was pleased to be dating an attractive man, Malcolm, who was about her own age and who came from a similar background. They had been going out together for several weeks when it was arranged that she should call for him. When he answered the door he greeted her with a big smile but he was wearing a maid's uniform. Bewildered, she walked into the house and sat down, lost for words. 'I've shocked you', he began, 'I should have waited or tried to explain.' Estelle could not comprehend that this gentle man, so 'normal' in other ways, actually felt satisfaction and pleasure when he was dressed in women's clothing. Malcolm was a widower whose wife had been tolerant of his desires and he was keen to find someone who was equally understanding.

Estelle simply could not accept that there was any excuse for a man to behave in this way. She left the house shortly after her arrival, ending the friendship. To her, such behaviour was incomprehensible, quite bizarre and certainly something she could never even countenance in a friend, let alone a husband. And yet many women can and do accept that their men feel happy when they dress up in women's clothing and no harm is done.

For the transvestite life can be complicated. How are they to acquire the clothing they wish to purchase? They can shop by post or ask female friends to shop for them. I know of a gown shop which has a good customer in a young man who is unidentified because he wears a motorbike helmet and visor when making his purchases. The shop assistants have overcome their initial surprise and treat him as they would any regular customer. The mail order houses are said to do a considerable trade with people who like to buy clothing of the opposite sex, privately and through catalogues.

Homosexuality

It is many years since a male homosexual couple came to me for advice on how they could be married. They had lived together for many years and wished to legalize their union. On investigation we found that in Holland and in some states of the USA, such marriages were possible.

Recently, in Denmark, there was international publicity when several pairs of men were married in a registry office; some were of advanced years, some young, but all were anxious to be married. Male or female homosexuals, like any other lovers may wish to show their commitment to each other. They may live good, useful lives, reach retirement age and have the same expectations as anyone else. Lesbian women co-habit, forming lifelong loving partnerships without exciting undue comment. Yet life for male or female homosexuals may be difficult since they are outside what is considered the accepted 'norm' by the greater majority.

People do not like behaviour which is unfamiliar nor do they readily accept what they cannot understand. Much needless suffering is caused for homosexuals through ignorance and innocent people who are merely living out their lives as they want and need to, go through agonies of rejection by society. A greater degree of tolerance is called for.

Age no Bar to Sex

I was concerned to find men and women of retirement age whose sexual relations had been marred for long periods, sometimes almost the whole of their married lives. Happiness is elusive and it is so often lost needlessly. Is it ever too late to reach understanding?

Feelings of guilt may pursue individuals all their lives, ruining sexual happiness. It is known that many women have such feelings following an abortion. In part this was imposed by the moral stands made by various bodies, although in the post-feminist world it is no longer seen as such a bad thing. Women do not have to accept pregnancies which they do not want.

Some retired folk say that they left sex behind many years ago. Even within a comfortable marriage it may have been allowed to flag for some reason. That is a pity and it should be revived at an early opportunity if at all possible. Getting out of the habit of regular intercourse happens at times of extra fatigue, occasionally at a young age and sadly sometimes never resumes its full potency.

Wives may have been tired out by young children or by a job, husbands may have been wearied by tiring work-routines. At such times, either spouse may have resented a partner who wished to impose attention, wanting satisfaction. This resentment may continue for years, in time successfully burying sexual urges. It can be very damaging to the relationship and harmful to personalities.

Maternal feelings at the time of a birth may have tended to take priority for a while, the man then feeling unwanted and jealous of the child. The woman may have worried about another pregnancy, refusing intercourse.

Stress and tiredness are not, of course, limited to women. Men find problems occur through all kinds of changes in circumstances. Business may prove so demanding that there is little time to talk together. Living with someone with whom there is only the barest communication means there will hardly be time for the essential warm and meaningful preliminaries which make the act of love so agreeable.

During the weeks or months of breast-feeding, women may have found a temporary dryness in the vagina area due to a shortage of oestrogen. If at that time there had been uncomfortable or even painful intercourse, the women, not unnaturally, might have resisted a repeat of the experience and so a temporary reason for cessation of sexual relations can turn into a long-term one.

Resentment on both sides may have built and damaged the marriage, spoiling the years ahead. Emotional ordeals can leave their mark for a long time, sometimes for the remainder of life unless they are sorted out at the time. Even appreciating years later why things happened as they did, can be helpful and may allow sexual relations of a fulfilling nature to recommence.

The loss of a business or a job, with all the consequent feelings of failure may reflect in poor sexual performance. It needs an understanding and supportive partner to help a person through such times.

Impotence

Advice about impotence should always be sought from a doctor, regardless of the age of the patient. Physical examination is necessary to exclude the possibility of any organic disease such as diabetes or hypertension. If medicines have been changed or recently prescribed they may have an undesired side-effect causing the problem and some alternative may be available.

For those people who have never been able to enter into a meaningful sexual relationship, merely dabbling in occasional affairs, a form of impotence may occur in older years as affairs become fewer with long periods of abstinence between.

Older women too, have problems, some of which should have been dealt with years before. Don't imagine that it is ever too late to get them sorted out. For example, dryness and discomfort during intercourse is common and easily corrected and there are often simple answers to other questions. Every older woman should take the opportunity now offered to have a smear test. Some do not understand that this is to detect the earliest forms of cancer and to prevent serious problems.

If there is a feeling of fatigue from real or pyschological causes or some vaginal pain then there is understandably less interest in sex. But there is no known reason why women should be less sexually potent as they grow older. Men may become impotent for physical reasons but provided they are in a happy and sympathetic relationships then there is a very good chance for their potency to return. The action may be at a slower pace, it may not mean ejaculation or orgasm every time, but it can still be a pleasurable and satisfying experience.

Sexually-Transmitted Infections

There are a variety of infections common to the genital area, some of which may be transmitted sexually. Treatment is available for almost all of these and in addition something will be provided to ease or remove discomfort.

Some infections have names which may produce alarm, but no one should anticipate that they have anything seriously wrong unless a doctor has confirmed that this is indeed the case. The chances are that any infections picked up are completely curable by simple and prompt treatment. But never delay in seeking advice.

Try not to feel embarrassment about seeking advice, doctors have heard it all before. They are accustomed to hearing problems which some of their patients find it difficult to speak about. It is better to be quite frank or to write down details, handing the doctor a note. He or she will not be embarrassed you may be sure, but will be sympathetic and helpful. Some women do not like to go to male doctors but there are now many more women doctors to whom the female patient may refer. Most practices now have partners and a choice of male or female doctor.

Sex Life in Retirement

The satisfaction of sexual appetite in a healthy way should be part of our everyday lives. The exchange of tenderness, the fun and goodness of sex makes people more caring in every way for their partners. However, whilst I maintain that sexual activity should continue always, or for as long as it is desired by the partners, there is considerable comfort to be derived from the emotional support offered by a caring companion, someone who can provide the affectionate cuddle and satisfy ordinary everyday needs and feelings. Sex is special but it is only one part of any whole relationship.

One couple had just retired and having always enjoyed their sex-life were distressed when the man became impotent. They went to their doctor who was kind but suggested that it wasn't important at their age. They were mortified and left feeling distressed but, fortunately, they later went to a marriage counsellor who was able to help them. The wife, Glynis, said that although they had enjoyed being close and cuddling it was wonderful to resume regular intercourse. 'Sex has always been important to us' Hugh said, 'It's life isn't it, we didn't want it to stop.' Glynis added, 'Now that we are retired and all is well, we really relish waking up early in the morning, having a cup of tea an a pleasant half hour of sex. Not every morning, but it's lovely when we do.'

Generations don't always see eye to eye. Even in her late-fifties, a woman could not understand how her father, Donald, could contemplate a new relationship. I could well understand it and it was a pleasure to see him, together with the new love of his life, Jessie. They are close to eighty and they love each other. Donald says how lucky he feels to have formed this sweet association in the late autumn years. His wife had been ill during the last ten years of her life and sex had ended for them some time before that. Several months after her death he had met Jessie. 'She is a warm woman' he said.

The fact that both men and women remain emotionally sexual whatever age they may be, was confirmed for me when I asked a man of 103 when sexual desire ceased. He gave me a smile and said, 'It's not the same from about ninety, but the interest never ends'.

11 It Runs in the Family

Upper Age Limit

If your brother John and your sister Martha each lived to be ninety and you, the youngest, are eighty-five and planning a holiday with your spouse of equal age to Florida or a trip to India, then your children have a very good chance of long life. You come from the kind of hardy stock that withstands disease and your genes are potentially long-term survivors. But if the reverse is true and your folk did not enjoy long life, can you beat statistics and make the century or near to it? Well you can certainly alter the odds in your favour.

What are our chances of living to enjoy years of vigorous old age? They are distinctly better than they were for our ancestors. There always were a few people who attained the century and some rare ones who went on a few years beyond that. But, the numbers of people who live longer are much greater as we approach the twenty-first century, although the maximum age to which we might live has not changed in hundreds of years.

Apart from the genetic gamble, our health is governed to some extent by the social class we were born into, the places we live in and the kind of work we undertake. We can choose where we live and work, but the one factor over which we have no control is our genetic inheritance. From conception, our facial and bodily features, colour of eyes and hair is already determined and we will resemble someone whose genes we have inherited. Those genes may come from either of our parents, grandparents, further back from our ancestors or a mix of any of these, so we are each completely individual. We also inherit other factors such as characteristics of personality and might, for example, be sweet-tempered or irascible; we may be fortunate and be born with a healthy constitution or less lucky and have a delicate one.

We could inherit the tendency to succumb to certain illnesses, you hear it said that 'it runs in the family'. People will say, 'Well, my mother went deaf early so I half expected that I would. Do you think that my grandchildren will be affected'? Or, 'His grandfather had diabetes so we knew that there was a risk for our children'.

The wife of a retired accountant, recognizing that he had difficulty in memorizing messages, worried that he might inherit the condition from which his mother had suffered for years. Furthermore, she fretted that perhaps their children and grandchildren might also have this sad inheritance to look forward to. She asked, 'We know now that what his mother had was Alzheimer's; can he avoid it and will our children get it'?

What are the Odds?

Insurance companies are interested in, and will request information about, the diseases and disabilities of all close relatives of applicants for life or health insurance. They will also inquire about the causes of death of close relatives because they know that there is an added risk if a parent or sibling has died at a young age or suffered from certain illnesses. An actuary must take all these factors into account when calculating for the insurance company what premiums should be.

Some ethnic minorities and workers in certain trades and professions have a predisposition to certain medical conditions. Several thousand years ago through a quirk of nature, the gene was evolved in white people, which, if present in two parents, may produce cystic fibrosis in a child. Today, there is a 1 in 22 chance of a person carrying this gene so that there are many more children being born with the disability.

Black people, indigenous to a hot country for many generations, have a high risk of inheriting sickle cell trait or disease. The reason for this is that Nature, attempting to compensate for the hazard of contracting a dangerous form of malaria gave immunity to it by developing a sickle-shaped blood cell. But this 'cure' has proved to be as harsh in many cases as the malaria iteslf.

Coal miners, and other workers in trades producing dust, sometimes develop chest problems, which can curtail the term of life. We cannot change our genes but greater care can be taken of health. We can, however, be protected as a worker in a dangerous industry or if we have a weakness we can change our occupation or where we live.

A geneticist could examine a new born baby, obtain all the details of its heredity, family longevity, social class and environment and make a fairly accurate prediction as to how long it will live. The way the child grows and develops, thinks and worries, will reveal more about its expected life-span. With so much knowledge, the parents and then the child when adult, can take precautions and increase the chances of making the future healthy and pleasurable. To some degree, so can we all.

It is important for people to know what their family histories mean to them because preventive and corrective measures taken early can be very helpful. We can advise our children how to avoid conditions which have occurred in our own families. The general environment and individual life-styles, including diet and exercise all have a bearing and play their part in influencing health. Diabetes might run in a family, occurring to members as they reach fifty and sixty caused by the high fatty content of the food they are used to. It might, however, be predisposed by our genes. And it is our genes, over which there is at present no known scientific control, which dictate our make-up down to the last detail.

We all begin life following the union of simple cells, microscopic in size. These contain, as it were, a kind of incredibly complicated blueprint having all the information necessary to produce a complex human being within nine months. Perhaps, in the future, it will be scientifically possible to alter genetic structure. It is an intriguing thought, offering many benefits, but also with alarming implications.

Present and future generations may be affected, not only by food and the additives they contain but also by the contaminated air we breathe. Stress too, is held to be an important element which can influence our health. We should advise our sons and daughters to consider all of these factors in advance of the time when they wish to become parents.

Preparing for the future health of an unborn child in a natural fashion is sensible and there are planned procedures for prospective parents to do this in a structured way. They undergo physical check-ups which include blood and cholesterol tests and determine the levels of minerals in the body. Advice is given on balanced nutrition and avoidance of stress. It is strongly recommended that smoking and alcohol be avoided and that no drugs, medicines or immunisation be given. Attempts to conceive a child should be delayed until this regime has been followed for at least three months.

This is good news for our grandchildren because the results have been promising. They show that health care prior to conception increases the chance of producing a baby who will be brighter and enjoy better health throughout life; someone who will survive into old age with a more youthful body and mind.

Consider the statistical likelihood of inheriting a medical problem in your family. As an example, the children of diabetics have a 1 in 4, and grandchildren a 1 in 8 chance that they will inherit diabetes. The likelihood increases if the grandparents from both sides have it.

Precautions for our Children

If you or a member of your family has heart disease and a high level of cholesterol then it is worth having other members of the family checked out. Special diet and controlled exercise may correct any problem found but doctors may think it necessary to prescribe some medication.

Women who are overweight, are without children and whose mothers have had breast cancer are shown to have a higher risk than others of inheriting the disease. They would be well advised to speak to their doctors about regular check-ups and preventive measures. Whilst it is recognized that some families tend to inherit certain cancers these tendencies can be checked by a change in life-style. Precautionary measures should always be adopted where family histories of illness dictate that this is prudent.

Our hearing may deteriorate as we grow older but some of us will have hearing as acute as ever throughout life. A tendency to rheumatism is likely to depend on environment; living in a damp climate can be hard on older bones and joints. But why do some suffer while others do not? Research is progressing at such a pace that is likely that for future generations tests will disclose far more than is presently known. Our descendants will know in advance what their tendencies will be and how they may secure better health for their own long and active future.

Happily, longevity and good health also seem to run in families. So if we can live to a good and robust old age, then our children are entitled to feel optimistic about their own outlook. Meanwhile, have regard to your own background, take steps to secure the best health you can for yourself. It does not necessarily follow that you have to conform to the pattern set by a parent or grandparent and although the age you can expect to live, statistically speaking, is the average age of both your parents plus two years, I am sure that if you live a healthy life-style you can add several years to this.

Take for example Jack, our friend of long standing. Ending a holiday on safari in Kenya, he congratulated the other members of the party for managing to keep up with him so well. It had been a strenuous nineteen days in Africa, driving across rough terrain, staying in primitive lodges and walking a great deal. He stopped in London on his way back home to Canada to see us and we reminisced. Twenty-three years ago, Jack and his wife Edith emigrated to Vancouver leaving behind a married daughter but joining two sons. Jack found work selling car-wash equipment, helping out at exhibitions, whatever he could turn his hand to. Always interested in working for children, he joined the Variety Club and over the next twenty-two years earned many awards for his work. He said, 'We had a second life, doing things we had never thought possible'. After Edith died a few years ago, Jack's enthusiasm for life remained undiminished and his new delight is a baby granddaughter. He recounted the fascinating details of this most recent trip to Africa before leaving to catch an early plane for Vancouver, telling us to stay well. What exuberance. Jack is eighty-five.

Whatever has been your line of work, whatever hobbies you have adopted, if you are feeling well, go on as you are. If not, remember that you can improve your health at any age by changing your diet and your habits. Keep your limbs as supple as you can, don't sit still for too long, even if you are in a restaurant you can quietly and unobtrusively move so that you don't get set. Take care, so that you can say, as you celebrate your ninetieth birthday with a five-mile run along the beach with some contemporaries, 'My folks died young in their seventies because they didn't know how to look after themselves. But I do'.

12 Age is Not the Problem

Old is not Elderly

Ageing itself is not an illness. To hear some people talk you would think that growing older itself is an affliction. A doctor said, 'In my surgery, I see elderly patients of eight and young patients of eighty'. Old age seems so far distant when we are young that we take liberties with our health. We want to be fit and well so of course we would not do anything that would have an immediate bad effect. Many think little of living life-styles which they know will eventually cause health problems and will reduce their chances of a healthy old age. Another serious drawback to longevity is attitude of mind. We expect old age to bring problems, forgetting that even in youth we were not always in perfect health. The trouble starts after retirement when we have more time to dwell on ourselves, noticing failings which may have been part of our make-up all our lives but which only bother us as we grow older. Did we really always have such a good memory? Did we never have twinges of rheumatism in our youth? Did we never have occasional feelings of weakness? You can safely bet that most of us did. We didn't have time to notice.

The young, too, may need spectacles, dentures, wigs even and some will suffer from disabilities. We should not make a great play about the ill-effects of ageing but rather accentuate the positive, making the most of what we have. And that is plenty.

Facing Changes

We are going to see alterations in ourselves. Hair changes in colour and texture, it grows white and we do not have so much of it. Our skins change, we lose the bloom of youth and that plump layer under the skin. But we take on character. We have laughter lines as well as worry frowns. If we spend time out in the open air we take on healthy skin-tones which make up to some extent for the loss of the sheen and flush of youth.

We lose a little height because there are changes in our spinal discs that we can do nothing about. But if we hold our posture, maintaining an erect stance, that shrinkage will be minimal. If we allow ourselves to slouch, our muscles get lazy and no longer offer the same support. As one result, we may lose our waist lines. We look droopy, shorter and dumpier, but that is not the fault of ageing. We do not have to let it happen and we can try to correct it if it has happened.

The Internal Systems

If we hold ourselves well we will breathe more deeply. Lungs become less efficient as we age and it takes more effort to empty and fill them properly, but we have to do this correctly if we are to maintain health and energy. Otherwise, we starve our brains and our bodies of oxygen, leaving behind the carbon dioxide to act as a poison, making us feel tired, head-achy, less able to think clearly and, dare I say, elderly.

Changes occur in the arteries, some almost certainly hurried along by our own behaviour. Older arteries are thickened and stiff, they are no longer so efficient and the blood passes through narrowed channels. This means that hearts must work harder in order to send sufficient supplies around and some of us get high blood pressure.

One thing leads to another. Irregular habits lead to constipation, piles, diverticulitis and worse. If we form good dietary and toilet habits then these problems are far less likely to occur.

We cope less well with heat and cold as we add years but we can compensate sensibly. We lose a lot of heat through our head, hands and feet and should keep hats, scarfs and gloves at the ready for colder weather. Sitting about at home does not help circulation and when relaxing we need to dress more warmly indoors than ever we used to.

Memory Recall

There is no proof that age itself produces a decline in mental thinking or ability. Why some of us should experience difficulties with remembering while others do not is a mystery that has been pondered through the years. No doubt research will produce some of the answers in the course of time. Meanwhile, we should recognize that some of us have good memories throughout our lives and others do not. Ageing alone does not mean memories must fail.

In 1989 I listened to Gwen Ffrangson Davies, the singer and actress, being interviewed on radio. It must be over forty years since I saw this accomplished performer as Lady Macbeth. Her voice over the radio was unmistakable and her memory was astonishing. At ninety-seven she recounted names and dates without hesitation.

My stepfather when in his eighties had exceptional recall, both distant and recent. He could give dates and details of events going back to his childhood and described episodes which occurred on the battlefields of the First World War in such interesting detail that we recorded them. He was a man who ate and drank sparingly, had a fine bearing, walked briskly and was always learning something new, ready to discuss and question. No one could think of him as old.

Illness in Age

People may be more prone to common illnesses as the birthdays pile up. The breakdown by one or other of our parts can put a strain on the whole of the body, which provides an added risk.

After being bedbound, following any kind of illness, pneumonia may develop, sometimes without warning of cough or fever. A mixture of medicines, supplied at the time with the best of intentions, may leave the patient confused. An accumulation of drugs may be found in homes, leftovers from repeat prescriptions, others bought over the counter in trials of self-medication. We should clear cupboards of old drugs since they are a potential danger at times of illness and temporary confusion.

Accident-Prone

Falls are responsible for some 5 per cent of deaths in the over sixty-fives, most of them happening at home. Potential causes of accidents should be dealt with straight away. Some common faults are bad lighting, lack of handrails on stairs, rugs on polished floors and worn slippers.

If someone trips over, establish the cause, so that it won't be repeated. Get along to the surgery and have the doctor check in case there has been a serious medical reason to cause the fall. Someone who is falling about a good deal may be suffering from occasional dizzy spells or there may be other contributory factors.

Temporary Immobility

It can hardly be emphasized too strongly how important it is to keep active. Immobility may start with a slight illness, feelings of weakness, pain, anxiety or depression. It leads to a loss of confidence, joint stiffness and to wastage of muscle. And it happens relatively fast. Each cause is itself a contributory factor to greater loss of movement and preventive measures must be taken to avoid a decline. A shock can provide a stimulus as happened to Sidney. He was independent, living alone but depressed, a miserable man, his family said. They called one day to find him cold and deeply asleep; the doctor pronounced him dead and he was taken to hospital. He awoke to find himself under a sheet with a label tied to his big toe. DOA it said, Dead On Arrival. His fury brought him to and following this fright, he recovered to enjoy a further six years of life, his depression quite gone.

If a partner, parent or friend should fall ill always encourage self-help and independence. It is not being kind to do everything for someone so that they end up just sitting about, immobile. Alfred and his wife, Miriam, had been married for over sixty years. He adored her and following a mild attack of flu', he would not allow her to do anything for herself, fussing and insisting that she rest. When her joints stiffened and she moved with obvious discomfort, he was concerned to save her pain and gradually she had less reason to move. He could not be persuaded that it was in her interest to keep herself mobile, even though she found it difficult. She became progressively weaker and within months, at the age of seventy-nine succumbed to an attack of pneumonia.

Once a pattern of immobility is established other problems speedily follow. Too much sitting may bring pressure sores, the danger of blood clotting in an artery and incontinence. If there is no underlying cause, the doctor will probably recommend physiotherapy and massage and gentle movement will be encouraged.

Rehabilitation of this kind can take a lot of effort on the part of everyone, including the patient but it brings rewards. No one should be isolated by immobility and advantage should be taken of day centres or visits out of the home where the patient can be interested in events and become involved in doing something which takes effort and movement, improving circulation.

Osteoporosis

The bones and muscles of a well-exercised old person remain strong enough to permit them to engage in most activities. But osteoporosis is common among older people and responsible for some of the fractures of old age. Because the bones grow more fragile and brittle and the joints stiffen, mobility tends to reduce, making it all worse. We must nurse our strength, not by saving it, but by using it.

Alzheimer's Disease

This disability is a form of premature senile dementia added to physical weakness, hitting a small proportion in their fifties and over. The earliest symptoms may be so slight as to cause little concern. Soon however, failing memory and functions become noticeable, everyone wonders what can have happened and it is left to the doctor to diagnose the disease.

Help is needed to keep the patient as fit as possible. The outlook is not good and it is distressing to members of the family to recognize that a person previously bright and alert is becoming mentally unsound, incapable of conducting their own lives or looking after their own personal needs. The Alzheimer's Disease Society offers helpful advice and local groups set themselves up to assist carers in their task of coping with sufferers. (See Useful Addresses.)

Whilst there is no scientific confirmation, because of the presence of aluminium in the brains of many of those afflicted, it is thought that this mineral may be a contributory factor. As a precaution it is proposed that it would be better to avoid cooking or drinking from any utensils containing aluminium. There are deodorants which have a percentage of aluminium in their composition and since this might be absorbed through the skin, this mineral is now to be omitted from toiletries.

The Medical Research Council's Unit in Southampton General Hospital did a survey of eighty-eight districts in England and Wales. Where aluminium is present in the water supply, we all take in betwen 5 to 10 milligrams daily but only a minute proportion is absorbed. The researchers have to determine whether some forms from certain sources are more easily retained and why these affect certain people but leave others unscathed. It was found that where the concentration of aluminium is higher than 0.11 milligrams per litre, the risk of Alzheimer's Disease is one and a half times higher than in areas where the concentration of aluminium is lower. While this provides a possible clue, there are other sources in foods. It may be that certain additives could also be factors contributing to the onset of Alzheimer's. Research continues and scientists are hopeful of finding the cause and a cure.

Diabetes

The pancreas, a small gland about the size of an almond, is located beneath the stomach. If this gland fails to produce insulin, glucose cannot be used as intended, continuing to circulate in the blood stream and getting into the bladder. It is easily detected in the urine and this condition is called diabetes. Symptoms include an unquenchable thirst, vomiting and passing excessive urine and there may be weight loss and a feeling of imminent collapse.

The older person who contracts diabetes does not necessarily need insulin injections (as most younger patients do). They generally manage very well if they keep to a special diet, low in fat and carbohydrates and are sensible about keeping their weight down. Urine must be tested daily by the patient who should keep a record which the doctor can look at so that adjustment to medication can be made if necessary. Provided exercise is regular and vigorous it helps to eliminate poisonous wastes and ensures a correct balance of the constituents of blood. There is a big stockpile of energy in the fats, starch and sugar we eat, so even with exercise, diets must be adhered to strictly.

The diabetic is liable to infections of all kinds and the feet must be cared for with special attention. A nick or a scratch could be dangerous and prove difficult to heal. Some patients refuse to believe they must diet and this was the case with Stanley who was only fifty when he was found to have diabetes. He ignored all advice to eat sensibly and to reduce his consumption of beer as he simply did not believe what might happen. Following a minor foot injury which would not heal, he had to have a leg amputated.

Heart Attacks and Strokes

In Finland, some thirty years ago, there was an alarming rate of death through heart attacks and strokes in the population, particularly in men in the age range of forty-seven to sixty. The government took action, bombarding the public with warning advice. The nation took the warnings seriously, cut down on their fat intake and soon the number of deaths and illnesses dropped dramatically. This was reported throughout the world and many countries adopted similar health-seeking campaigns, with successful results. Unfortunately, in the UK, we now hold the unenviable record for high mortality through heart attacks and strokes. Doctors have done a great deal to persuade their patients to adopt healthier life-styles and diets. Where health promotion programmes and opportunistic screening has taken place, there has been some improvement, but there is no room for complacency in this country. People still say that they like to eat and drink as they wish, wanting a short life and a merry one. But they could be ensuring lingering years of ill-health.

Anyone who loses the power of speech through a stroke must find it the most frustrating experience. The inability to speak or to find the right words to match thoughts are exasperating beyond measure. Speech and movement are important but the need to convey emotions, the need to talk, are paramount.

When Sam had a devastating stroke he suffered this inability to find words to say and sat with tears streaming down his face. His wife recognized and shared his feeling of loss and helplessness. She sat with him, holding his hand and crying too, not knowing how to help. Their niece was a nurse who noted that he could still read. She took an exercise book and divided it into sections, headed Family, Friends, Food, Drink, TV, etc. Then she entered under these headings a number of relevant names, details and adjectives. Sam used this book to express himself, turning the pages to point to the words he wanted to use.

Reducing Cancer Risk

Every man and woman should be familiar with regular self-examination techniques. Any lumps, bumps or unfamiliar symptoms should be checked out by the doctor without delay. The government has recently introduced cervical and breast cancer screening programmes for women in the most vulnerable age groups. It has been shown that in other countries where these measures have been taken, the rate of death from these cancers has been significantly reduced.

One surgeon returned to this country after working among people living on natural and fresh food containing high fibre. While there, he found not one case of stomach or bowel cancer. Yet on taking up work here he had case after case and felt that the food generally eaten was at fault.

Lung Cancer

There is no longer any argument, smoking can definitely cause lung cancer. I had five women friends in my youth who smoked and who all died prematurely, of one form of cancer or another. I see their grandchildren and think with bitterness of what these children and their grandmothers have missed. It is true that a few people will get cancer regardless of whether they smoke or not, but these numbers are small compared to those who do smoke and who will become ill because of it.

The Bonus Years

We all have a responsibility to be well. One woman told me, 'I take care of myself and I feel ashamed to be ill. The last time I visited the doctor I said I was tired and he said, "What do you expect at your age?" What I expect is to be well and able to be busy'. She is Kay Evans, a lecturer on health with a busy schedule and will be ninety on her next birthday. Long may she continue, she gave me some excellent advice on reducing stress.

13 Staying Mentally Well

Old does not mean Loony

Bright, perceptive and astute as ever, that is how the majority of people in the retired sector continue as they grow older. More than three-quarters of those over the age of sixty have no intellectual impairment. They can and they do remain creative, able to learn new subjects and hold sparkling conversations well on into their nineties. Others, who could do just as well, sit about expecting deterioration and behaving as though it had already happened. And sometimes, because it is expected, it happens. There is little point in fearing the worst, statistically, it is less, rather than more likely to occur.

There is no reason why age alone should bring about mental deterioration. A lot depends on how fit we are physically and how occupied we keep our minds, which is why I continually emphasize the importance of exercise for both mind and body. Read your daily and weekly newspapers, keep up with what is going on in the country and the world. Memorize the names of national and international leaders and local councillors. No matter what your political persuasion may be, you will find your local council meetings of interest and their decisions are likely to affect you. Write to your councillor about any local issues which you feel strongly about. Write to the letter column of your local paper if you feel moved to. This will help to keep your mind alert and aware of what is happening.

Conversations between people who are well versed in topical matters are much more diverting. They are more often sought as dinner companions and can bring a new and refreshing dimension to any discussion group. You don't have to be concerned only with political matters; know the background to your local football or cricket teams or any outstanding personalities.

It used to be accepted that all cases of mental illness in the elderly were grouped together under the collective title of senile dementia and this view was held until the beginning of this century. Now it is known that there are many different causes and different outcomes, some behaviour may be labelled strange, deviant or eccentric rather than mentally unbalanced.

Some elderly people may find that they are offered the comfort of care due to their aberrant behaviour and this gives them a reason for continuing to act strangely. Once they are correctly diagnosed and told that there is nothing wrong with them and that they are to be sent home, they become quite normal, reverting to unexceptional behaviour.

We all need the abilities to deal with life's stresses and some of us have to re-learn these at a late age when there are new problems to cope with. This is another reason why early preparation for growing older is essential. We cope better with the anticipated and expected dilemma than that which comes as a surprise or even as a shock.

Any significant setback such as the failure of a business, the loss of a dear one or the sudden reduction in the value of one's investments can age a person, physically as well as mentally, well beyond their chronological years. One man who had a responsible position for many years in an engineering company was made redundant at short notice when the firm was taken over. A youthful man of fifty, within a year his appearance had so changed that he looked more than sixty. He had been unable to find suitable employment, had become apathetic, unresponsive and his wife feared for his mental health.

This kind of misfortune can happen to almost anyone but it is up to individuals themselves whether they allow circumstances to change them and ruin their health. It is never easy to cope with a drastic change in status but a positive and challenging attitude can at least protect sanity.

It was once believed that people who became mentally

slow, forgetful or unbalanced were untreatable. The idea that the social environment, one's own experiences, the acquired habits of a lifetime or family influences could disturb mental function, came later. Today, it is recognized that most people who have a mental illness can be treated and restored to good mental health, possibly by counselling, perhaps by the omission of certain foods from their diet or by prescription of one of today's many powerful drugs.

During the last hundred years or so psychiatrists and researchers like Jung and Freud have thrown new light on the mysterious workings of the mind. It was realized how troubles can affect us, how stress and strain can unhinge us, how delicate is the balance between mental health and breakdown. What the experts said was that some people who were suffering from mental disorders could be helped to regain sanity and to re-develop healthy personalities. Some of us could be shown how to help ourselves whilst others would need specialized professional help.

Recognize Depression

Feelings of misery are common to us all at times. But when depression and anxiety exist together they can create a sense of hopeless despondency which can prove overwhelming. Feelings of alarm can progressively build up to become a serious illness and when this is happening, it needs to be recognized and discussed with the family doctor. Experiencing hopelessness for long periods can be quite dangerous and if it is not checked it can lead to a sense of the decreasing value of life and sometimes a desire for death to end it all.

It is often the loss of someone or something valued, the death of a partner, relative or close friend which can trigger depression. While sadness is perfectly natural, if it continues to be severe and is overly prolonged then it is known as clinical depression.

There are some common things which may cause one to feel dispirited, perhaps the change from a working life to one of retirement, a loss of self-esteem or possibly the devaluation of some achievement. These occurrences, whilst they may not be tangible, can yet be extremely disturbing.

The predisposition to worry does exist in some families. It is not only contagious but could be a genetic factor if there is a background of anxiety in other members of the family. People will say, 'Oh, we are great worriers in our family', and they seem unable to help becoming unduly alarmed for the least thing.

Anyone who is even mildly depressed takes less pleasure in life. They have a more shallow interest in the daily round and in what happens to them or their families and friends. The most minor task can be seen as a drudge, causing undue fatigue. The depressive person shows a marked lack of energy and enthusiasm and anything and everything can seem to be too much of an effort to be bothered about. There is little use in telling such an individual that they should pull themselves together for that is seemingly impossible for them to do. Necessity may force the person to carry out the essential daily routines, but perceptive family and colleagues will recognize the clues and realize that something is amiss.

Depression is not always easy to identify. It can occur without good reason in those who are apparently without any troubles. It can happen suddenly in someone who has seemed to be perfectly content, even happy. Depression and happiness occur like peaks and troughs in a volatile personality.

Changes in Behaviour

Some people tend to go on behaving as they always have done as they get older, but the traits of their character become more marked: the sweet-natured becoming more gentle and considerate, the ill-tempered becoming more cantankerous and demanding. Some just accept that they probably function less well mentally at retirement age than they did when they were young. But real differences in conduct, unusual irritability or irrational acts, may be signals of undue anxiety and the forerunners of depression. However obstreperous or aggravating a person may be, such behaviour does need to be correctly interpreted. An early chat with a doctor or practice nurse may reveal some worry that is removable at that stage but which could become deeply entrenched if left. Early detection is important.

Counselling Needed

Many doctors now have counsellors in the practice team. These may be trained psychiatric nurses or they may be people whose background enables them to listen sympathetically, to inject common-sense into thinking and to propose practical solutions to whatever is the worry. Often, this results in a better and more balanced appreciation of the problem by the patient and an ability to put things into perspective and come to a sensible decision. They may then wonder what they were so miserable and anxious about earlier.

Treatment may be simple, just a few sessions of counselling to alleviate stress. The services of a Citizen's Advice Bureau may be sought; often their recommendations can be helpful. For example, a retired widow incurred debts for heating after a cold winter, she could not pay the bill and spent disturbed and anxious nights. The CAB was able to arrange for the bill to be paid by instalments and also advised a more economical form of heating. This comparatively modest help relieved her apprehension and put her back onto a level keel again.

The situation, however, may be very much more complex, so that it will be debated whether to use longer term psychotherapy. It could be determined to try to regain a balance by the use of some of the drugs available today. Occasionally certain foods trigger off an allergic reaction which causes, or contributes to, unbalanced behaviour.

Dr Rickard Mackarness in his book, *Not All In The Mind*, describes the situation of one woman who was so affected on eating a particular vegetable that she became mentally unbalanced and homicidal. Luckily for her and her family they discovered in time what was causing the problem. Some medical advisers were advocating a lobotomy, which might have left her harmless but brain-damaged.

Depression is hard to counter, especially when there is no sympathetic person available to talk things over with. For a lot of people who have to look outside their own circle or who are alone, that person may be found in the Samaritans. A voluntary organization, the Samaritans are on call twenty-four hours of the day. People from all social categories who are finding life and its obstacles difficult to handle, or who may just need someone they can talk to when they are feeling very low are clients of the Samaritans. Where anxieties may be serious and concern completely justified, no one can wave a magic wand and many situations are not always sorted out. But the opportunity to talk to someone who is willing to listen so often make people feel better and able to cope.

The clinically-depressed person needs some outside skilled help, initially to establish a correct diagnosis. There are many physical conditions of the body which can cause confusion in the mind. For instance, lung or kidney infections produce such symptoms which will disappear as the underlying cause is cured. Parkinson's Disease produces some dementia-like traits which lessen as the disease is brought under control. Brain tumours, strokes or concussion from head injuries may cause symptoms of confusion but these can sometimes be successfully treated.

Check Drug Doses

Sleeping tablets are a common cause of befuddlement since their effects last longer in an elderly person. A much lesser dose could be quite effective enough to give the required result. If unusual sleepiness is experienced during the day, then the doctor should be consulted.

When sleeping pills are taken in conjunction with some other medication, they can, together, produce confused symptoms. Quite often, some of the causes of mental deterioration lie with the medicines given to treat various conditions. Doses may be in excess of what we need, for when we are older we have less tolerance to drugs and this fact is not always recognized. Alcohol is also less well tolerated having a greater effect on us as we age. We need to be particularly careful with alcohol and drugs and as a general rule they should never be taken together.

Alzheimer's Disease

This is a comparatively rare condition which only occurs in a small percentage of people in their older years. It is one of the saddest diagnoses of all and is a type of dementia which is a progressive deterioration of the brain, affecting the ability to remember, to learn or to reason. Loss of short-term memory is the best-known symptom. My own mother-in-law was a most capable woman until well into her eighties. She was one day unable to find her way to the flat she had lived in for ten years; a year later she did not remember her much loved only son's name, nor could she recognize herself in the mirror. She would constantly exhort her image to 'come on out and have a chat'.

Alzheimer's can occur in much younger people and it is not unknown to strike men and women in their fifties. The causes of Alzheimer's are not fully understood, but it is known that they are linked with the loss of brain cells and not, as is often supposed, by hardening of the arteries, 'over-use' of the brain or stress. These conditions can have similar characteristics which can make a correct diagnosis more difficult.

Cause still Unknown

Several studies have suggested that aluminium may possibly be a contributory cause of Alzheimer's. Whilst there is much speculation no one can be precisely sure why this might be. It does seem sensible to take the precaution of using non-aluminium cooking utensils. There was some fuss about the use of aluminium in deodorants and this ingredient was removed by manufacturers in case of any danger.

There is hope that recent discoveries in research have

brought closer the day when there will be a cure for this tragic condition. Meanwhile, recognition of the problem will at least bring sympathetic counselling to sufferers and their families. It can be a great comfort to speak to others in similar circumstances, relatives of people with this disability and to learn how they are coping with all the attendant problems. Local groups have been formed in many districts where members meet and offer each other support and advice.

Diagnosing Cause of Confusion

Where a relative or friend has been recognized as having symptoms of a worrying nature, it is important to speak to the family doctor and get advice as to what might be causing the unusual signs.

Doctors have prepared tests to help decide whether confusion exists and often the simplest of questions may resolve whether someone needs further expert investigation or not. Sometimes even these basic questions are confusing to quite sensible but apprehensive individuals. We should certainly all know our own names and date of birth, but the current day or date, the name of the doctor, the local hospital or the prime minister might escape an older person who does not regularly read a newspaper or watch television. Panic or alarm before a nurse or doctor could well prevent someone from giving the right answers so that emotional stress could well be the correct diagnosis, rather than mental deterioration.

It is probably true that the most feared of all failings is that of mental incapacity. Impairment of the brain is regarded as the most pitiable of all afflictions; fear of such impairment is at the back of the minds of all of us, especially as we age.

Yet the fear and pessimism are often unfounded because there is so much that can be done. Sometimes, even seemingly hopeless conditions which have gone on for lengthy periods, can be treated and a great improvement. There has to be a reason for mental deterioration or senility and whatever fears or uncertainties one may have it is for the doctor alone to decide whether there is true mental illness.

Who has Gerontophobia

Society has been quick to label some members of the retired generations in an unflattering way as 'in their dotage', having 'lost their marbles' or simply as 'past it'. These unsympathetic terms are used by people with gerontophobia, those who are anti-old.

It is, in fact, a very small percentage of people of retirement age who become mentally unstable and less able to cope with the daily round of life. It is true that the brain shrinks with age and that by the time we reach ninety to ninety-five we will have lost a proportion of our brain cells. But the good news is that we all have more than we ever need or use, quite sufficient to maintain good memory recall and to continue to perform the necessary functions independently.

Memories alone are not ever unfailingly reliable, even in young people, but as we age we may come to depend upon our memories less. If it becomes more difficult to remember recent events, we should take to writing things down. The brain, like any other organ does lose flexibility and whilst there are drugs and substances which aid and enhance memory, some loss at the end seems inevitable, although for many it is minor.

A failing memory should never be expected or accepted, although there are certain causes of memory loss which we can do little about, for example, age-related illness which also brings about personality changes. But, too often it happens that we think old, when we should still think young.

There are many eighty-, ninety- and 100-year-old people who are bright, with good memory recall. One country doctor in Cambridge was proud of his patient who always enquired after his health, bustling around to give him a cup of tea. She fascinated everyone with her memories of bye-gone days, remaining fit and independent until shortly before her death at the age of 103.

We let ourselves down and lose out if we believe that

retirement has to be a time of failing senses. If we keep our brains involved, active and busy, eat well and exercise sensibly then we should stay mentally alert, proud of ourselves and a source of pride to our families and friends.

14 Drugs and the Relief of Pain

There is something wrong and you need help to be cured. The doctor has examined you and is considering a course of treatment, more than likely a prescription. But would you get better without it and are you prepared for possible side-effects which you may not have bargained for? How often will the doctor tell you to try the medicine but suggest that your diet needs correcting or that you need more exercise?

Almost thirty years ago, a close relative, Maurice, had a heart attack and was later diagnosed as having a high level of cholesterol. The consultant said that to reduce this a drug was to be prescribed which would have to be taken for the duration of his life. Appalled at this thought, Maurice asked whether there was an alternative. The doctor said that there was diet and exercise but as patients didn't like the inconvenience involved, drugs were better. But Maurice went on a strict, low-fat diet and walked every day for two hours. Within three months his cholesterol level was down to normal and he felt fit and well, as he does today. Some fifteen years later, that recommended drug was found to have such dangerous side-effects that it was withdrawn from the market.

Ten years ago, a close friend of mine, Marion, was in her mid-fifties when she felt extremely weak and ill, with painful joints. Tests revealed nothing but she was prescribed tablets for pain relief and was advised to reduce her work-load and to rest. Feeling worse she was sent to an allergist who found that there were certain foods to which she had an adverse reaction. Removing these from her diet she soon felt better and although to this day she is careful about what she eats, she feels well, energetic and works harder than she ever did.

Here, then, are two people who recovered their health and fitness naturally, without recourse to drugs. They have both now reached retirement age and are looking forward with pleasure to many years of post-retirement activity.

Nature is hardly given a chance to perform the cures she could effect if allowed to do so. The public is constantly updated on the value of drugs by the drug companies themselves through advertising and promotional leaflets and rarely does anyone get the chance to consider an alternative – the no-drug cure. Without doubt there are many excellent and efficacious drugs which have played their part in lengthening life and making it more comfortable, but there is a multitude of less than effective drugs which people are in the habit of taking because they hope or believe them to be doing good. I cannot help thinking of the many spirited seventy and eighty year olds I have met who told me that they felt old-fashioned about medicines and never took them.

Kay is a busy lecturer who was trained as a physiotherapist. She arrived at my office having travelled across London by bus and train on the day of the worst storm of the century and proceeded to regale us with advice on how we should sit, stand and walk, giving us illustrative leaflets as she did so. She then demonstrated the exercises she teaches and was amused at our reaction as she told us she was born in 1901. 'And' she said, 'I never take drugs.' On a rare occasion when visiting her doctor, 'to remind him of my existence in case I should become ill', but also to say that she sometimes gets a bit tired, she was incensed by his remark, 'What do you expect at your age?' 'Age', she replied, 'has nothing to do with it.'

Drugs almost always provide an element of hazard, sometimes subjecting patients to risks which outweigh the benefits. They are so often over-prescribed, needlessly recommended for mild and self-limiting conditions. What of the side-effects? Patients have responsibility for their own well-being and should know that drugs can have a powerful reaction, some of them undesirable, You should only take medicines if you and your doctor are convinced that you need them and cannot be cured any other way.

Drug Choice

The science of medicine has important primary aims. One is to promote and maintain good health, another to care for and treat those who are ill, relieving their pain and distress. Just a few decades ago, doctors had a mere handful of medicines or drugs to offer to their patients. Few of the names of drugs or what they did were known to the general public, except perhaps aspirin for the relief of pain, laudanum to encourage sleep and digitalis for treating some heart conditions. Today, there are literally thousands of remedies on the market, patients are familiar with many of them and often go to the doctor ready with a suggestion, sometimes even a demand for a cure for what ails them.

The drug industry plays an important part in all this, spending vast sums of money and employing the brightest of chemists in laboratory research. Occasionally there are valuable breakthroughs and an exciting development amazes the world, but in the last ten years – despite publicity and claims on the part of the drug industry for the fifty or so 'new' drugs produced each year – there have actually been only a few original and useful ones. There are new forms of existing drugs, some which claim to have fewer side-effects, others which claim to be more effective than those made by competitors but still more which are current versions just renamed.

Let the Doctor Advise

Doctors do want to please their patients, many of whom seem to like leaving the surgery with a prescription. Some patients complain to me about their doctors, who wisely refuse to hand out unessential prescriptions. I tell them how lucky they are to have such sensible medical advisers who are probably giving them more listening time, trying to find out what are the root causes for their ills, instead of providing pills.

Drugs may be prescribed for conditions affecting any part of the body but the doctor has to consider that what might assist in one ailment could well aggravate another, especially in older people. In addition, a drug or mixture of drugs might produce a slowing down or temporary loss of mental function and that can be frightening.

There are drugs which are specifically designed to have a calming, quietening effect but given too strong a dose a patient could be put into a state of confusion. Other medication might have a cumulative effect, which in the long term can cause conditions of a worrying nature. The family or carers of someone on medication should note any personality changes. There is not yet sufficient knowledge of geriatric pharmacotherapy and different medication or mixtures of drugs for older people should be dealt with cautiously. Smaller doses seem to be quite effective enough as we come to sixty and I find that a half aspirin will clear a headache where I once might have needed one or even two.

It should also be remembered that what will suit one person, in particular someone younger, will not necessarily suit another. The ageing brain can be extra sensitive, quicker at assimilating pharmaceutical compounds and one could more easily become addicted. If medicine is necessary it is a good rule to take the least and lowest amount and always with the doctor's and pharmacist's knowledge and approval. And even then take careful note of any reactions, don't trust your health blindly to anyone. It is you who knows your body best and must show responsibility.

Over-the-Counter Drugs

A danger exists for patients who diagnose and treat themselves when buying an over-the-counter drug which they have heard or read about. This medication might or might not be good for them but added to anything they are already taking could be dangerous. Unless the pharmacist or doctor knows of the full range of drugs prescribed, no alteration or addition should be made.

Understand the Instructions

When drugs have been prescribed by the doctor because he or she considers them right for a specific condition patients should be sure to take the drug in the way that has been advised. No one wants to take sleeping pills in the morning and feel sleepy all day or diuretics at a time which would cause them to rush out of bed in the night to pass water. Doctors may not give precise directions, they are busy people, but the patient should never leave the surgery without a clear, and if possible, a written instruction on how to take the recommended medicine. When it should be taken, how often, whether after meals or with plenty of liquid, whether it is unsafe to drink alcohol, whether one should drive, and so on. Every patient should be sure to find these things out and check with the dispensing pharmacist if they are not absolutely certain.

Many elderly patients have to take more than one kind of tablet and they should be taken in a certain sequence. It is hard to keep the order right, especially if, as often happens, a person does not know what a particular pill is for or what it does. I think it is helpful to know these things and to label bottles or pill boxes with whatever is most descriptive; for the heart, for the bowels, digestion, sleep, pain relief. Also note the time of day that they should be taken and make out a chart ticking off the pills as they are taken. As an alternative, line up the day's dose first thing in the morning in the correct order, ready to be taken through the day. Some drug packs are prepared with days written in. Ask surgery staff to help identify different medicines, for the doctor will appreciate the value of this exercise and it is easier for the patient.

Anyone who decides that they do not wish to take drugs which have been prescribed for them should always let their doctor know the reason why and should also return any unused drugs. The doctor needs to know if there has been an adverse reaction and to keep the records of the patient up-to-date. Some drugs cause an allergic reaction which can increase in effect each time they are taken, so it is important, sometimes vital, that they are never prescribed again for that particular patient.

Waste not Want not
A few years ago Brent Council in North West London decided to run a campaign to collect all unwanted drugs. In came pills by the thousand. Ken Livingstone, the Brent MP at the time, came with me to the Town Hall where we looked at the vast, transparent sacks of brightly coloured tablets, all to be thrown away. He shook his head at the waste and I thought of all we could do in the NHS if only we could reduce the unwarranted and escalating demand for drugs. The Department of Health has been working at the problem and new legislation is likely to produce a much more sensible attitude and, I believe, a more health promoting one.

Do not Store Drugs
There should never be an accumulation of drugs in any household. For one thing they deteriorate and for another, anyone temporarily confused could take them in damaging, possibly dangerous quantities or combinations. It is all too easy to go to bed at night, doze off and then awake, befuddled and wondering whether or not medication has been taken. This is when mistakes can occur.

Steroids

The use of steroids has become relatively common and they do a wonderful job medicinally, becoming an essential to the very life of many individuals. No doctor will lightly recommend them but, notwithstanding unwanted side-effects, it is still worthwhile for some seriously-ill people to take them.

Some Valuable Drugs

Narcotic analgesics serve many purposes and are not only used to induce sleep. Diuretics have been given to benefit those with kidney problems or to produce prompt weight loss.

Beta blockers slow the heartbeat and so can be used to have a steadying effect.

There are products designed to influence just about every organ in the body and while I am against the indiscriminate use of powerful drugs I share in the feeling of gratitude for those which improve the quality of life or even life itself. A recent example is the result of research to combat a deadly form of malaria which has been imported into this country and from which patients have died. This drug will undoubtedly save life.

Tranquillisers

It was once all too easy to offer a drug which quickly relieved anxiety and saved lengthy sessions of psychotherapy. It was not realized how addictive such drugs could be. Now patients have to kick their tranquilliser habit, either by self-discipline or through cooperative therapy clinics and meditation groups. There has been a high rate of addiction to tranquillisers and many men and women now in, or approaching, retirement must face the trauma of withdrawal.

Hormone Replacement Therapy

There is now a good deal of reputable scientific evidence which confirms that hormone replacement therapy (HRT) offers protection to women against osteoporosis and coronary heart disease following the menopause. HRT can also alleviate some of the more displeasing symptoms of the menopause and there are claims that it improves skin and hair condition too. Patients need to be carefully monitored when on HRT but if you think that you need it ask your doctor. It may do you a power of good.

Slimming Pills

Very few of us reach the age of retirement with the same body weight and 'vital statistics' as we had at the beginning of our working lives. We may be tempted to join exercise classes or weight-reducing clubs to lose a few pounds purely for cosmetic purposes. There is no reason why we should not. However, there is a temptation to speed up the weight loss rate by taking a course of slimming pills. Here there is a danger. There is a division of opinion in the medical profession about both the safety and efficacy of taking a drug as a suppressant to the appetite. Some of these drugs are similar to amphetamines and could become habit forming. The greatest danger lies in using any type of slimming pill when you may already be taking other medication. Certainly, continue to touch your toes and to watch your diet but before taking appetite suppressants or special diet foods, do ask your GP for approval.

Antibiotics

Always ask your doctor whatever it is you wish to know about the medicines you have been prescribed. There are misconceptions about commonly used drugs and it may be useful, for example, to clear some regarding antibiotics.

Many of us have good reason to be thankful to Sir Alexander Fleming and his team at St Mary's Hospital, London, discoverers of penicillin. It was hailed as a magic medicine which could overpower harmful germs and it was a means of saving many thousands of lives. It was the first introduction to antibiotics and was made from the kind of mould which we have all seen growing on foods. Substances were extracted from minute organisms and made up into medicines capable of destroying or stopping the growth of life-threatening germs.

This powerful instrument should have been reserved for use in serious cases of need. Instead, over the years it also became the means of a fast cure for a variety of mild illnesses. The use was justified where a doctor found patients had low resistance or conditions which predisposed them to dangerous developments. But needless over-use has caused a problem because bacteria have become resistant and stronger and more powerful antibiotics are needed all the time to combat them.

Each winter, as seasonal illnesses become prevalent,

sufferers arrive at their doctor's surgeries for antibiotics and feel aggrieved when these are denied to them. I have no doubt that some patients wear their doctors down and triumphantly carry away their prescriptions.

Do patients still not understand that antibiotics are useless to combat viruses which cause colds, flu' and sore throats? They are effective for non-viral chest infections, as well as for infections anywhere in the body, but the doctor has to identify the type of bacteria present and use the specific antibiotic which will destroy it.

There are many drug companies and between them they produce a wide variety of antibiotics, each designed to do particular jobs. Some antibiotics suit one person and not another, some control one kind of germ and not another. Progressively, bacteria have become more resistant so that eventually the antibiotic is ineffective, causing the patient to say, 'Doctor, this medicine doesn't work'. It remains for the doctor to advise which kind of antibiotic is best suited to the patient and for what purpose.

A secondary effect of taking antibiotic drugs is that too many bacteria are killed off and we may lose the beneficial little organisms which live in our bowels. Our stomachs then feel out of order and we could get other infections because alternative organisms have moved in which the antibiotic does not affect.

Some practitioners recommend that yoghourt should be taken at the same time as antibiotics since it replaces essential bacteria.

Chemical Reactions

One man's meat may be another man's poison and perhaps this is why certain people react to foods or chemicals so differently to others, sometimes becoming violently ill. Some scientists have made genetic individual differences their life study, endeavouring to show how we may each react in diverse ways to the foods, drinks and drugs we take.

In his book, *Biochemical Individuality*, Dr Roger Williams has shown that we are rapidly becoming the victims of our failure to recognize our own personal needs. It is up to each of us to be responsible for our own health as far as possible, to discover how we can be naturally healthy and to note what effects the food we eat and the drugs we take have upon us.

The Relief of Pain

Individuals are known to have different thresholds of pain and what one person will find tolerable another will find quite unbearable. Some will try heat, cold or massage to bring relief, while some can allow pain to wash over them, practising a form of self-hypnotherapy. Others must use medicinal help to reduce suffering which they find is unendurable. When all else fails, the doctor's advice is sought and analgesics are prescribed.

Analgesics are the drugs given to alleviate pain, although the doctor will always look for any underlying cause. An infection for example, can cause pain but analgesics will do nothing to cure that, although the body's natural defences, given time, might well take care of the infection. Often there is a chronic condition which is either slow to be cured or which can never be cured and which has bad crises of pain. Following certain operations there may be a brief period during which patients have the prospect of extreme pain, for which they will need help. For example, after an operation for haemorrhoids, patients may be given opium which is one of the most powerful of painkillers and is derived from the poppy. Morphine is another such derivative, as is codeine, also a well-known member of this group. The smallest of doses may be effective. All of these drugs induce sleep and may in addition have a constipating effect, requiring the corrective action of other drugs or preferably the consumption of extra fruit and high intake of liquids.

Aspirin, an extract of the willow tree and known for more than 200 years, is familiar to us all and is still one of the most useful drugs we have. But like all drugs, it must be used with caution because it can cause harm as well as good. It is a simple and effective pain reliever but may not suit everyone because of undesirable effects on the stomach or because it causes ringing in the ears. Paracetamol is an alternative to aspirin for the relief of pain and does not usually have adverse effects. Small, daily doses of aspirin have recently been recommended to prevent cardiac problems. All drugs should, of course, be taken sparingly and with caution and only on the advice of a doctor.

Natural Relief of Pain

Research has shown that a person's reactions can have a positive effect on pain. The degree of pain felt can depend not only upon physiological factors, the bodily causes, but also on psychological factors. How individuals cope with pain depends upon the environment they are in, a particular given situation, how they are occupied and also to quite a considerable extent, on their sense of humour.

People can distract themselves from pain or they can dwell on it, making it feel worse. Humour gives one something else to think about and laughing and smiling helps one to relax. Tension greatly increases pain while relaxing diminishes it, helping to undo tight muscles and allowing the body systems to work freely. Those in pain should try to relieve it by altering their attitude. A positive aspect, a reminder of the worthwhile things in life helps to make one glad to be alive and this alone reduces pain and the need for drugs. Recent research suggests that the act of laughing stimulates the brain to produce a hormone which enables us to want to fight on and also stimulates the production of endorphins, our own natural pain alleviators. The relaxation induced by laughter increases these secretions.

Depression usually follows an undesirable chain of events and lightening a mood with some fun or amusement can effectively break that chain. The whole situation can then be viewed more objectively, reducing the tension and leading to a more constructive attitude, enabling one to bear what has seemed to be almost intolerable. It is important to try to find diversion, perhaps by listening to some music or taking a look at the old comic movies, even though this seems the last thing one would want. Let Charlie Chaplin, Laurel and Hardy, Benny Hill or John Cleese perform a cure as they go through their classic routines. When one watches comedy TV shows or reads the transcripts of those programmes which caused amusement in the past, pain recedes. Inner reserves of strength are found and a light can be seen at the end of the tunnel.

No one can deny that there are times when doctors and patients alike are thankful to call on the blessed relief which drugs can provide. But we shouldn't take them unless we have to.

15 Exercise Means Fitness

Growing Younger

Is it possible to look and feel younger, to actually grow stronger and healthier, even after we have officially become senior citizens? A research study into the effects of changes of life-style for people in their sixties and seventies revealed that it is possible and is happening all the time. It takes a conscious effort but we can substantially increase our levels of fitness, make our hearts and lungs more efficient and strengthen our bones.

Start Early

Why do so many people wait until there has been a warning before they take health seriously and think of exercise? They act only after the stroke or heart attack, after rheumatism has developed, after muscles are stiffened and joints weak. Increasing physical activity confers many health benefits, one of which is a reduced risk of heart attack or stroke. But a word of caution, putting sudden strain on the heart can be dangerous.

It was for Tom, a man of sixty-one who led a sedentary life. He had a complete health check-up on a Friday and was declared fit. On the following Sunday he lifted his lawnmower from his garden shed and collapsed with a severe heart attack. He was unaccustomed to strenuous exercise and obviously was not in as good a state of health as had been supposed.

To keep ourselves in good shape we have to use our strength or we lose it. It is all too easy to get into bad habits, sitting and watching too much television, slouching deep into chairs as we relax or read the newspapers. Then we feel too weary to move and imagine that we need a rest before we go to bed. If this is the way we customarily behave then we must stir ourselves and our partners too, and start work on a programme designed to prevent premature ageing, sickness and debility and restore youthful vigour.

It cannot all be done overnight and we could do more harm than good if we rush into action in an effort to get fit fast. That would be counter-productive, causing injury, torn ligaments, stress fractures or needless stiffness. On the other hand we should not mollycoddle ourselves. Having had an operation or an illness does not mean that we have to live our lives at half-speed, unless we have been specifically warned to limit our activities. So many people who have had lung and heart transplants run in marathon races and men and women of seventy and eighty plus, even those who have had three-way heart by-pass surgery, are advised to increase their stamina and keep their hearts healthy by taking daily brisk walks.

The Royal College of Physicians and the British Cardiac Society are in no doubt at all about the benefit of exercise in preventing coronary heart disease, saying that physical activity should be encouraged at all ages for both men and women. Regular exercise to strengthen leg muscles could help older people to improve their walking speeds and to allow them to enjoy a more comfortable and independent life-style. Walking slowly is often just a habit.

The Doctor Needs to Know

If you have recently been unwell or put on medication, get advice about what activity you should attempt and for how long. You must be the judge of how you feel, but, if you have had any chronic or acute conditions then you must let the doctor advise what it is safe for you to do. It is your doctor, familiar with your record, who knows what physical stress you can take and is interested in the preventive aspects of positive health who will help you to devise the right programme of exercise. Therefore, do go to the surgery, get a check-up and if the doctor gives the go-ahead, you can proceed with confidence.

The Need for Physiotherapy

There are never enough physiotherapists and occupational therapists to meet the demand. They help to get us back in shape following accidents or operations, showing us how our joints and muscles must be constantly stretched and strengthened so that they work efficiently, allowing movement to be smooth and easy instead of stiff and awkward.

Therapists can tell us how we should bend or stretch, what equipment is available to help us in our recovery to fitness and how we can continue independent living. They can also advise us how to do things we thought we could no longer do, overcoming difficulties and suggesting alternative ways of doing them.

What Exercise is Best?

The most useful kind of exercise is that which will benefit the heart, other muscles and the circulation. To achieve this we must stir some of the sludge in our circulatory systems and that involves a continuous form of movement for an extended period. It is of no great benefit to perform a few minutes of bends and stretches twice a week and let it go at that.

Rowing is one of the best fitness sports for older people, according to Fritz Hagerman, physiologist and consultant to US Olympic rowing teams. He conducted a rowing study which included men and women over the age of sixty and virtually all showed improvement in cardiovascular function.

Walk to Health

We need to do something which moves our legs and arms for about half-an-hour at a time, twice a day, every day. Walking is a perfect example of an activity suitable for retired people, which can achieve this, something not too stressful but which can keep us going in a rhythmic way. It needs to be done at a fair pace to be really useful and five minutes is not enough although it may well be all that can be managed to start with. Exercise should never push a person beyond what is a comfortable limit of capacity.

A hundred yards may seem like a mile to the unaccustomed and under-exercised walker, but if the pulse rate is under control and breathing is easy, try a brisk walk for a quarter of an hour. Not in the cold, however, unless you are well used to it. Try the pulse rate at intervals and if it begins to race, stop and accept that a slower pace is required.

If you are unaccustomed to exercise or to any kind of brisk physical activity, you should start out with a warm up walk of just a few minutes, preferably in company. Try a little light conversation as you go and if you can talk while walking and without being out of breath or distressed in any way, then you should be alright. Follow this with a few simple exercises and if all is well, repeat the next day, extending the time spent on them.

If you go for a drive, stop for an occasional walk around. Don't fret if you cannot park your car close to your destination, be glad you are getting a chance of a walk and make it a bit longer each day. Don't use the car unless you have to.

With regular exercise the heart begins to work more efficiently, pumping blood around the body with less effort. The pulse rate will become increasingly stable so that the heart has more time to rest between each beat. Gradually, routines become more enjoyable and can be carried on for longer periods without incurring discomfort.

Reducing the Risks

Controlled activity is doubtless good for the heart. Inactivity is weakening and when this is combined with high blood pressure, smoking and a poor and fatty diet, the likelihood of heart attack or stroke is very much increased. Office workers or drivers, people who sit fairly still for a considerable portion of the day, suffer twice the number of heart attacks of those workers who have a good deal of activity or walking about to do. But anyone who has, or has had, a sedentary job and little exercise, may find it more difficult to break the habit of physical inactivity.

Brisk and daily exercise is one of the best meaures for all round health. It controls the build up of fat and it is common for energetic walkers to find that they can eat more without putting on weight. And because the circulation is so much better, people are more mentally alert with increased confidence and a greater interest in the world about them.

Fewer Aches and Pains

We all suffer from depressed vitality following colds. flu' or any illness or depression but once we are into a regime of exercise, health improves and the feeling of sluggishness reduces and disappears. We need 'tuning up' in order to be rid of the catalogue of headaches, flatulence, constant fatigue and aches which make us feel fed up with ourselves. Those who are subject to allergies often find that as the sense of well-being returns they can more easily tolerate the foods and substances which were upsetting them.

Exercise is Addictive

If it sounds boring to exercise that is only because you have not tried it. Once you become used to it, exercise is not only enjoyable, it is positively addictive. Prolonged activity releases a substance into the bloodstream which has the effect of putting us 'on a high'. We move effortlessly, feeling great. Some individuals say that exercise is not for them, it is not what they enjoy and so on. But exercise is not only beneficial and fun, it is essential to our well-being. Unless we keep our complex physical systems in order, they will deteriorate. No one can stay at maximum youthfulness and health unless they keep themselves in the peak of condition, as fit as they know how to be.

We can put our everyday routine tasks to good use by incorporating more movement into chores like making the beds, cleaning the car, hoovering carpets or sweeping the front paths. Take care not to overstretch but lean further and stretch higher, practise deep breathing, filling and emptying the lungs. Pull in tummy muscles, lift and rotate shoulders while washing up or preparing a meal. Get up on your toes and down again while ironing, folding clothes or doing any standing job. If you are sitting, move your ankles and toes, straighten fingers, they are always curled inwards and need stretching out. Try moving the parts which do not get much use. Gently turn your head from side to side, try leaning over to the left and then to the right. Do a little dance on the spot but don't be rough on yourself, do it all smoothly and slowly.

With a carefully worked out programme of exercise we become more agile, trim off excess fat, our muscles become firmer responding faster to the demands we make on them. Our skins improve, becoming clearer and brighter and we become more alert, reacting in a livelier and more youthful way, suffering far less from bouts of misery or depression.

The Right Way to Exercise

We all have different measures of ability. Obviously, someone accustomed to playing tennis or squash regularly or who goes on ten mile hikes is going to have no trouble with exercise. The routine that would knock out an office-bound company director would not inconvenience a postman.

There are wrong ways and right ways to exercise, for example, deep knee bends can damage cartilage behind the knee and cause lasting impairment. Any movements involving the joints should be done carefully and with no hard pulling. Always move neck and back slowly, without jerking. Exercising does not have to hurt to be effective. We should learn basic warm-up as well as cool-down routines to begin and end with so that nothing comes as a shock to the system or leaves us feeling stiff and sore. We assist in the elimination of waste products as we exercise and it is a good idea to finish any session with a five minute walk.

Wear comfortable, easy clothing and cover up after finishing a routine. We may work up a lather of perspiration and should take care not to sit about and get chilled. If we are out of condition we must be patient, building stamina slowly, finding sensible and suitable movements that will gradually lead to better physical and mental health and a wider range of activity. Never exercise if you are feeling weary or recovering from any illness, however minor. If you are feeling cold, warm up gently before subjecting your muscles to any sudden effort or strain.

Try simple bending and stretching exercises such as were learned at school. Do them whilst holding a nylon stocking or a scarf, stretched taut between the hands with arms extended, using it to help in the way we move. A skipping rope can provide easy-to-do exercise which uses all the muscles and improves co-ordination. If you can do it in the fresh air, all the better but go easy, as it can be strenuous. It is regarded by professional boxers as one of the most important routines in their training programme.

Massage is regarded as therapeutic and is used in some hospitals to benefit people with cardiac problems or hypertension. It is very pleasant to receive a massage but it is also pleasant to give one and I am not sure who benefits most. An arrangement between partners or friends to regularly massage each other could result in an improvement in tone for both. Use a pleasant oil and gentle friction, don't be hard or heavy-handed, particularly on the chest. If you need some tips on how it should be done, ask at your local leisure centre or health club if they can recommend a masseur to give you a sample treatment. It is best to use a firm table but you can manage quite well on a towel on the floor.

Golf is a pleasant social game and even if you do not enjoy whacking a ball the walking is good for you. Try playing billiards, it calls on back and neck muscles. Bowls provides relaxation, gentle exercise, indoor or outdoor and is ideal for the over-sixties.

Casual Exercises

Increase flexibility in the fingers by rolling a small ball in your hand. To increase leg power, lie on the floor and lift your outstretched legs, one at a time and slowly. Increase the leg lifts day by day until you are up to twenty. To strengthen back and stomach muscles try sitting on the floor with legs extended and inch across the room on your backside. To ease an aching back, lie flat on the floor on your back, draw your knees up to your chin and holding them with your arms, rock slowly from side to side; stretch legs out then draw them up again and repeat two or three times. To ease tension, lie down with the legs up the wall for a few minutes, then inch your body up the wall until you are resting on your shoulders.

Did you ever do 'a head over heels'? I did it for the first time at the behest of my little granddaughter. Even as a child I had always felt that this drill would break my neck but I survived and now do it regularly. But don't try it unless you are in very good shape and have a supple body.

Do you sit in a car for long periods? Try pressing the feet flat on the floor, one at a time whenever there is an opportunity and it is safe to do so. Press the palms of the hands together firmly, release and press again. Lift and drop the shoulders several times to relax them.

Perhaps you can combine pleasant social evenings and exercise. Ballroom dancing gets the circulation going and who knows, you may move on to learn something like tap dancing. You will then need little else to keep you fit.

How do you Feel?

Does walking and talking at the same time cause a coughing fit or breathlessness? Does running up stairs cause a feeling of faintness? Is there a sensation of total exhaustion and yet an inability to sleep? If the answer is yes, then you should go to see your doctor, ask if there is a special clinic for older people and don't be afraid to voice all your fears. You may need medical attention or a dietary change but it may simply be that your body is crying out for more activity to put you back into order. Remember that stamina must be built up slowly and there should be no sense of strain nor should you risk tearing muscles and ligaments with sudden movements. It may take a little time but have heart, don't lose confidence because you will increase your functional capacity, no matter what age you are.

Stop Smoking

It is harder to fill our lungs deeply when we are older even if we do not smoke. Help your lungs by giving up smoking before starting a new regime of exercise. Smokers' lungs are not in the best shape to undertake extra work and stopping smoking brings immediate advantages. In fact, many surgeons ask patients to cease smoking for at least a month before an operation.

No Late Exercise

Exercise can remove sleepiness so try to do workouts at least an hour or so before bedtime. A warm bath following a routine can take away some of the stiffness and prepare one better for sleep.

Keep-Fit Classes

Those who have not tried it often feel bashful at the very idea of performing routines in company. Most people are shy to begin with, but those who go to classes say that the last thing they would want to do is give them up. They have found the benefits too valuable, knowing that not moving around enough allows waste products to settle in the joints. This leads to stiffness in the mornings or after sitting for a while and an increase in those ominous creaks and squeaks as they bend, twist and turn.

Classes should provide a friendly atmosphere, giving advice and help to newcomers; it all depends on the teacher who needs to be qualified and competent. Once you join, don't worry about not keeping up or failing to do some of the exercises others can do. This is not a competition. Do what you are comfortable doing. Some people are naturally able to get into positions or perform routines which many of us would find quite impossible. We are not all built alike and it would be a dull world if we were.

Learn to Swim

We do not have to swim every morning to be fit, but it would be a good idea. In the water our muscles carry no weight and we can exercise almost effortlessly. Those who cannot swim should join a class. Men and women in their sixties, seventies and more, learn to swim, taking to it like the proverbial duck to water.

One grandfather of sixty-eight finally found the courage to ask his grandson's swimming instructor if he, too, could have some lessons. Donald had been too nervous of the water as a youngster to try swimming but he now does a stylish crawl and swims daily. His grandson is very pleased with him. The proudest record is held by a woman of ninety from an outer London suburb who swims regularly in her local pool. She came along in her wheelchair, was helped into the water and soon learned to enjoy the sensation of freedom. She relaxed and revelled in the mobility which the supporting water gave her and within only a month she had learned to swim a width!

Phyllis is a pensioner who, as a small child, fell into water out of her depth and nearly drowned. She thought that she would never get over the nightmares she had of fighting for her breath. Yet, she too, encouraged by her friends and the instructors, took to the water, soon learning to swim and to float on her back.

Convalescing

It used to be thought necessary to have days of bed rest after an operation. Then it was realized that muscles weaken quickly when they are not used and this can retard recovery. Following enforced inactivity, it is best to get out of bed and move about as soon as possible so that there is the least opportunity for loss of muscle tone.

Building Strength

When we lead busy and active lives, running up and down stairs, stretching and lifting correctly, bending properly to dig the garden, we are building up endurance and giving ourselves a supple body which will behave well and not let us down. In our house, we take a daily twenty minutes of exercise, starting off with a few minutes of deep breathing while standing by the open window. Each day we walk for at least half an hour and take a longer walk, perhaps five or six miles, twice a week.

TV and Cycling

If you are still thinking that you just could not manage to fit exercise into your life, try another approach. Do you spend more than an hour an evening watching television? Then get a static bicycle or a rowing machine, maybe both. Put them in front of the television set, push the furniture out of the way and never mind that your room looks in disarray. Something much more important is at stake because now you can achieve two objectives: watch your favourite programmes and get your slack muscles toned up. Start with just one minute the first evening and gradually increase. Watch that pulse rate, rest if you have to and once you build up, don't slip back and take days off unless of course you are not well or fatigued. If you find you do need a few days off then remember that you must start all over again, taking brief spells of exercise to begin with.

The Best Investment

By keeping ourselves in good shape, we will live longer, feel younger and stay healthier. The quality of life is vastly improved when we are in a healthy state. How often do we say,

'Health is everything, without it you have nothing'? What better investment could there be than one which will give such a return? In good and sparkling health, we look and feel better, we can perform better, finding enjoyment in all the things we want to do.

We could take courses of beauty treatment, go to expensive masseurs, find all kinds of therapy but when it comes down to it there is nothing to beat exercise. It is the key to good health. How nice it is to look in the mirror and see a straighter posture, a slimmer profile and a younger looking you.

16 The Best Food for You

The older generations were brought up on much more simple diets than we have today. They grew up on less tinned food, frozen foods were rare and most fresh food was unadulterated by the many additives now used. They were encouraged to eat dairy food and butter and cream and cheese were thought to do us good. The weekend joint, the 'roast beef of old England' combined with roast potatoes and Yorkshire pudding, all basted with fat, was a staple meal. Much of the fruit and vegetables people ate was grown locally. Today breakfast, lunch and dinner includes food from all around the world.

Grapefruit, lettuce and grapes from California, tropical papayas and mangoes from the Far East, avocados from Israel, bacon from Denmark, lamb, chicken, turkey and kiwi fruit from Australia and New Zealand and honey and salmon from Canada. Without the labels there is no knowing where anything has come from. The food buyers of the big stores travel far and wide to find what will please the shopper. We take it all as a matter of course, choosing from a more diverse range of food than was ever dreamed of in our youth.

Healthy Eating

Food is sprayed, radiated, tinned, frozen, until we are unsure what good may be left in it. We must do our best to eat as much fresh produce as possible and trust that the government will safeguard us against any harmful additives. We hear so many theories about why we should or should not eat one food or another that it can be quite confusing. The trouble is that nationally, we have some formidable diet-related problems. It makes far from satisfying reading to find that the British suffer a higher number of heart attacks and strokes when compared to most other Western countries and that the reason is likely to be found in our diet.

Is there some special advice we should be looking for? We have had to be fairly healthy in our eating habits to have reached retirement age and to be looking forward to enjoying a few decades ahead. It is said that as we grow older we eat less but that is not necessarily true. If we continue active lives and feel physically and mentally well we may eat as much as ever. We do not want to eat differently just because we are growing older.

We should enjoy our food but always in moderation, thinking about the good or the harm that the food is going to do us. We will not want to restrict ourselves but rather continue to enjoy the meals we are used to. Unless advised otherwise, we can continue our normal diets but stay within certain guidelines so that we remain healthy.

Being retired does mean that we will change our routines but should not limit the variety of food we have. Our needs should be satisfied from a wide range of food and drink. There is sufficient choice to allow us to omit foods we actively dislike and choose others which provide the essential nutrients. If our appetites are less than they were, it is all the more important that we choose the most nourishing of foods, buying what is the most fresh and appetising.

It is Worthwhile to Cook

It may seem to be too much trouble to cook for one or even two, but it is well worth the bother and nourishing and tempting meals can be produced with very little preparation. The first meal of the day is worth thought, although there are some who say that they cannot face food early in the morning. For staying power and getting the system going, little can beat a bowl of porridge, cooked or raw. Oats offer an additional bonus, they provide good health value, even a protection, some say, against heart problems. Add some stewed or fresh fruit such as a sliced banana for added nourishment. Half of the people in the doctor's surgery are there with constipation problems, many of which sensible diet and exercise would cure.

We can train ourselves to like the right food. If you adore cream cakes, but should not eat them then don't keep them in the house. If there are some left over after you have had guests, give them away. Likewise with biscuits or any other foods with 'hidden fats'. If someone has a high cholesterol level, buy the smallest amount of cheese and other dairy products.

If we are going to eat the food that is the best for us it has to be fresh and that means eating the food that is in season. Choose first from what is locally produced whether that means plenty of fresh root vegetables in winter like turnips, parsnips and onions (which can be chopped into salads or made into fresh soups), or tomatoes, marrows and lettuce in mid-summer.

You may be able to buy organically produced food which is free of sprays or irradiation. There is nothing mysterious about such food, it is what we ate when we were young. It won't look as though it deserves first prize in the local gardening competition but you will know that it is not adding to your store of harmful chemicals. Perfect looking vegetables and fruit are only achieved in quantity with the help of pesticides. We took some spray-free apples from a tree in the garden which were small and a little spotty but the taste was wonderful.

Some people hate to get the oven in a mess but casseroles of all kinds can be left to cook slowly and cleanly and served in the dish they were cooked in. Foil can be used to make a parcelled meal to include meat, potatoes, onions and mushrooms, tomatoes or other favoured vegetables. Whole oven-cooked onions, carrots or parsnips, spread with a little butter or margarine are naturally sweet and delicious and the foil wrapping leaves the oven perfectly clean. Try baking a stuffed apple or peeled pear in the same way. Remember, some nourishment can be lost in the cooking so don't overheat. The one thing we should all do is add an element of fresh and uncooked food such as vegetables and fruit to our daily menus.

Alternative Cooking Methods

Fish can be cooked in simple fashion between two dishes over a pan of hot water. Very little water or milk, plus some pepper or salt, is needed. If salt is forbidden, try a squeeze of lemon juice instead. Eaten with a boiled potato and a slice of wholemeal bread this provides an appetising meal. If someone is coming for dinner try baking a larger fish like bass or salmon trout, buttered and sprinkled with lemon juice and wrapped in foil.

Easy-to-prepare meals can be cooked in a pressure cooker as the compartments hold everything in one go and little of the nourishment is lost. Green vegetables retain their food value and colour if they are barely blanched or steamed for a minimum period.

Microwave ovens are so easy to use. A soup of fresh vegetables for two can be prepared in a few minutes; a jacket potato can be cooked in about three minutes and then split and served with melted cheese. Fresh vegetables take a short time and taste and look delicious. Fish in a covered dish with a little liquid will cook in only three or four minutes. At home, we have happily used a microwave oven for more than fifteen years. But we never use it for defrosting. Frozen food is better left out for some hours or overnight and we prefer to eat fresh food anyway. Roasted meat and poultry dishes, in our view, taste better when cooked in a conventional oven. The timing in microwave ovens varies, so you have to do a little experimenting to get it right. A few seconds becomes important. A cup of coffee or soup can be very hot in two minutes. Remember that cooking in a microwave oven is by a different method and twice the amount of food will take longer. It would not be practical to cook a dozen whole potatoes, better to use the regular oven. But slice two or three potatoes, alternate them in a dish with sliced onion, barely cover with water and dot with butter, a little salt and pepper and you have a delicious meal for two in about seven or eight minutes.

Packaged Food

Occasionally, take advantage of ready-prepared foods. They are fine for use once in a while as a meal, when you feel lazy or have little time but I would not recommend that anyone should have them as an undiluted diet. What with sprays, additives and irridation, I doubt whether that would be healthy. A wide variety of pre-packaged courses provides a selection for special occasions such as when you entertain, so that you only have to prepare the main course and can find a starter, ready made.

It is handy to have a stand-by store for those times when someone has flu' or the weather is bad and it is difficult to shop. Keep a small stock of canned or packet soups, meat, fish and fruit. Frozen foods can be kept for a limited time in the deep freeze but should be date-labelled so that they can be used in rotation and not kept too long.

Nourishing Snacks

The Earl of Sandwich started something when he began to eat food between slices of bread, a combination which afterwards took his name. Sandwiches can be served as a filler, lunchtime snack or as something quite special. A double or triple-decker toasted sandwich, filled with tasty meat, fish or cheese, garnished with salad and flavoured with mayonnaise can be a very satisfying snack. Accompanied by a bowl of soup and followed by some fresh fruit it makes a perfectly adequate meal.

Here is a family favourite for Sunday supper which the children learned to prepare at an early age. Now the grandchildren have taken on supper duties. Butter some brown bread sparingly on both sides as you make a sandwich of apple and cheese or onion and tuna, then grill it slightly crisp. Delicious. There are small electric machines which will seal your sandwich and toast it for you. Be adventurous, try different combinations for your sandwich, using up what you have in the fridge. Put some pickle or a little salad on the side.

The 'ploughman's lunch' of fresh French bread, thinly sliced cheese and pickles is a favourite stand-by. Invite me, and you would have to add a slice of Spanish onion.

Diets

There are literally dozens of diets to choose from and my only recommendation is to say that there is no magic formula for maintaining health or losing weight. To achieve this one must eat less than most of us normally do – and sensibly, everything in moderation. It doesn't do to keep weight going up and down and it would be advisable and healthier to settle for being a little overweight and stabilize at that. But don't keep on adding, even a pound a year is ten pounds in ten years.

In retirement we are probably going to spend more time at home and it can be tempting to 'nosh' when food is to hand. Make sure that snacks are healthy, include carrots, celery, bananas, apples, nuts and raisins. And not too much of those. Any food in excess will add weight.

We all have the occasional dinner out, when we eat too much of everything and probably put on some weight. Make up for it over the following few days by being careful to eat less, until your weight is back to average. It might take two weeks.

Food to Avoid

If there is a particular health problem we will be offered diet sheets by our medical advisers. We should all try to reduce our intake of hard fats such as lard, dripping, spreading and cooking fats and dairy products. Biscuits, cakes and pies, all those lovely delicacies which we have more than likely made at one time or other, contain hidden fats and these should be strictly limited. We can still enjoy them but only as a very occasional treat.

Limit the intake of eggs and offal as well as fish-roe and shellfish, which are all high in cholesterol. If we have heart or circulation problems we should simply cut out hard fats altogether and strictly ration others. We should use a thin oil such as sunflower seed oil, but sparingly. Using it twice or more, as is so often done in frying, renders it heavy and saturated. We should grill foods, avoid takeaway chips and fried foods because they are soaked in hard fat, use non-stick pans which brown with the least amount of fat and cut down on meat. Even if it is trimmed of visible fat it still consists of a considerable proportion of saturated fat.

Fish contains a thin oil which is considered more healthy and it can be baked or grilled but should not be fried in batter. Fish should be skinned if possible before cooking, it is healthier that way. Some fish, such as salmon and mackerel, have greater oil content and small quantities are very filling.

What we should eat more of are whole grain breads and cereals, oats, barley, brown rice, lentils and pasta, plus as much fresh fruit and vegetables as we wish. But if we are dieting then remember that fruit contains a good deal of sugar and we will not lose weight if we eat an excessive amount in addition to normal diet.

Hygiene in the Kitchen

Salmonella causes many cases of food poisoning each year and we should be particularly careful with food preparation in our own kitchens for that is where much of the trouble starts. Strict hygiene is vital. Eggs, fish and meat should be well-cooked in case they have been affected before they arrive in your home. Fruit and vegetables should be scrubbed or thinly peeled. Wipe all work surfaces clean before you start preparing a meal and keep food covered. Flies can deposit their eggs in barely visible places.

Do not Dehydrate

We come now to an important item of diet, one that is often neglected but which can cause quite a few health problems, especially as we age. Because our sense of thirst lessens as we grow older we tend to forget how much non-alcoholic liquid intake we need. At work we may have been offered many a cup of tea, a coffee or a cold drink. Retired and at home we can simply forget to drink from one end of the day to the other and a lack of fluids can cause us to feel quite ill. We could become confused and giddy. Each day we need about eight-to-ten cups of liquid and it is more interesting if we vary the drink. We might have two or three cups of herbal tea, plain or with milk or lemon, a glass of fruit juice, coffee, some soup, perhaps a cup of hot chocolate and just plain water, bottled if we prefer it. Just be sure you are drinking enough.

Limit Caffeine

Recent reports in the *British Medical Journal* state that a high caffeine intake helps to raise cholesterol levels. If heart problems have been diagnosed or are suspected then it is safer to leave coffee and tea out of the diet altogether. Caffeine-free tea as well as coffee is available if one misses these drinks, but where health is at stake it is surely better to play safe and choose one of the herbal drinks.

A well-known surgeon has said that to avoid bowel problems we should drink a glass of water last thing at night. So even if we have problems of night-time incontinence we should take that excellent advice. Remember that alcohol can be dehydrating and if we take a whisky, brandy, or wine as a night-cap we need to drink extra water to compensate.

About Vitamins and Minerals

A well-balanced, sensible diet should provide all the nutrients the body requires. If we shop carefully and eat home-prepared food we are probably getting the right amounts. If we are so unwise as to have a diet mainly composed of takeaway and junk foods, many edibles processed by dehydration, canning or freezing methods, we will run short of nutrients. Eating for convenience without considering the quality is asking for trouble.

The body requires a number of minerals such as calcium,

iron, potassium, zinc, iron and phosphorous, all in minute quantities. These are contained in foods like yeast, liver, wheat, garlic, honey and fresh fruits and vegetables. In other words if we have a normal varied diet we should get our fair share of these essential minerals.

In our later years we may have a reduced ability to absorb some of the vital nutrients and we could then need supplements. We may also be taking medicines which can reduce our ability to absorb vitamins; doctors will advise supplements when these are considered necessary.

An adequate supply of both vitamins and minerals are essential for optimum health. If we lack vitality, have unusual pains or skin conditions or feel nervy, we should see a member of the practice team at our surgery, perhaps the nurse, who will help us to find out why we feel low or ill and perhaps will recommend some needed supplement.

The elderly and those who smoke and drink alcohol are especially vulnerable and more likely to need supplements. But vitamins in excess can be harmful and should only be taken with professional advice.

Eating and drinking practices interest society a great deal. Switch on the television and so often there is a scene at the dining table or bar. We join friends to share a meal, compare our favourite restaurants and discuss the variety and quality of the food. If the contents of bookshops and libraries are anything to go by, we read cookery books at a great rate. Few magazines appear without articles on food, drink and diet and the dangers of this or that food or additive.

Food is important to us and rightly so. We want to feel as well as possible in these years of leisure and pleasure. Eating right will ensure that we feel right.

17 Are You the Right Weight?

Sophie Tucker was an international star, a great singer and during her long career she attracted large audiences on her appearances in nightclubs and theatres. A woman of ample proportions she had always hoped to be slim. We met in London at a dinner in her honour when she told me this, adding, 'The food is always too good, I guess I'll never make it'. She died in her seventies, never having achieved this particular ambition. It is not easy to slim.

It would never do if we all had to conform to a specific size or weight, but depending on build and height there is a range which gives the approximate right weight for each of us. For our health's sake we should not be much above or below this.

It has been said that inside every fat person is a thin one trying to get out. That saying is probably an accurate reflection of the truth and in the Western world one rarely hears of anyone who actually wants to be corpulent. As though to endorse it, a sign in a beauty-salon offered the message, 'YOU CAN BE THE SIZE YOU WANT TO BE'.

Is that true and if it is, why is being overweight a problem for people of all ages? For some it is no problem because there are people whose culture dictates that being large is attractive and a sign of prosperity.

Once excess weight has been gained and additional fat cells created, it is extremely difficult to deal with. The struggle to reach and stay a healthy and attractive size represents too great a trial for all but the most determined of us. Losing weight takes the most strong-minded commitment. It can be done but if by diet this must be adhered to for such a long time that it is all too easy to backslide and put on those lost pounds.

Kenneth went on a Weight Watcher's diet, became the 'Slimmer of the Year' and was proud of a photograph in which he stood in the single leg of the trousers he had worn as as fatty. And yet, within two years, he was once again a fat man, weighing over twenty stone. Now retired, he has since shed some of the excess pounds but remains well over the recommended weight for his height and build.

What does Overweight Mean?

If you are energetic and do not easily tire, if you feel fit and comfortable with your size, being plump may be no problem for you, but for optimum health it is better to stay within recommended limits and aim to be on the thin side. If you can pinch an inch of flesh between thumb and forefinger then you are overweight. That would mean that most of us could do with losing a pound or two.

It is now accepted that it is healthier not to go up and down in weight. Anyone who is overweight should either diet and maintain a lower level or stay at the same higher weight. Frequent gaining and then losing increases the level of fat running free in the arteries where it can clog and cause blockages in the bloodstream.

Studies confirm that it is remarkably difficult to reduce size and that comparatively few people succeed on a permanent basis. The reasons are complex, partly because when one becomes fat, additional cells are formed which are incredibly stubborn, resisting all ordinary efforts to purge the body of them. As weight is gained new cells are created to retain the extra fat and this process can condemn any but the most committed dieter to failure.

The most determined and sustained effort is required – not only to lose weight steadily until the desired target is reached but then to maintain it. A need for the comfort of food can be like a drug. It becomes necessary for the resolute dieter to become disinterested in eating for some months, to remember that once a healthier weight is achieved, the food will still be there.

Those people who reach the age of retirement and are on the plump side may not regard themselves as obese. Having come thus far a bit overweight, they may feel that little harm will come if they continue in their accustomed life-styles, eating whatever they fancy, no matter how ill-advised it may be to do so. They may feel that they are never going to be slim and no longer want to try.

A Bonus or Health Threat?

On the bonus side, it may be true that fewer wrinkles show when there is more fat under the skin. But it is really for the doctor to determine whether those extra pounds constitute a threat to health and future well-being. If we are to continue fit and active into our eighties, we need all the help that we can get. Take advantage of the health promotion checks offered in surgeries and act upon the advice which medical personnel may give. We want not only life, but quality life. So, if they say, 'Slim down' then that is what we should do. Would anyone willingly risk a heart attack or a stroke, the development of diabetes or the many other potential problems associated with overweight, as well as the years of helpless dependence which can follow? Surely not. It is unfortunate that there may always be some who cannot avoid these afflictions, but each of us should determine to do everything possible to reduce the risk.

Advice on Diet

There are so many diets offered; one will say eat tropical fruit, another recommends flavoured drinks with added vitamins, some are meatless, some veto dairy food. They will all work if the instructions are followed to the letter. We need to take in only a few hundred calories a day if we are to lose weight but it is hard to manage on that. Before embarking on any diet, however attractive the promotion for it may be, consult a doctor who is trained to understand your individual problem and who can give appropriate advice. A particular diet may be fine for some people and quite unsuitable for others. Many medically prescribed diets for weight loss ordinarily advocate a reduced intake of food. What is eaten should be unadulterated by preservatives or additives and be as fresh as possible: The diet should be varied for interest and contain a proportion of roughage and be supported by the consumption of plenty of water or unsweetened liquid.

Expending Energy

We need fuel for the energy we expend in daily activities and the amount depends upon how active we are. Ideally, we should all understand about the levels of food energy and nutrient intakes that our systems demand and make sure that we get these, no more, no less. It is important to recognize the risk to health if we fail to take sufficient nutrition.

We build up a store of energy and this is retained as fat in a layer under the skin, as well as around the heart, liver, spleen and so on. We burn up energy as we rest or as the body is exercised, but whenever we take in more food than we use in energy output, the store of fat builds up everywhere.

As a rule, overweight women are less at risk of ill-health than overweight men. Women retain fat lower down the body, around the hips and thighs while men store it around the waist and stomach. And the fat concealed beneath the skin in this area, in the abdominal cavity, can coat the organs with a heavy layer, reducing the ability to do their particular job. As blood journeys around the body, it deposits this fat in the form of potentially damaging cholesterol, to the heart, the liver, lungs, arteries and the linings of the abdomen. From a health point of view, what goes on inside the body of an obese person ought to tempt anyone overweight to make a dedicated effort to reduce.

The Right Diet

Diets should satisfy us in two ways. They should be palatable and they should be safe. GPs and their teams of nurses, dieticians and therapists are concerned with promoting health and can determine a right and safe weight for each individual. Only trained dieticians can assess the correct balance of nutrients, the right levels of protein, vitamins, salts, iron, minerals and trace elements which we each require. Your adviser will also monitor progress and change the proportion of food intake as necessary.

Generally, medical advice favours slow weight loss, as well as gradually increased exercise. During a diet, any change or disturbance in physical condition, any unusual or unexpected symptoms, must be reported. We are complex creatures and cannot afford to be deprived of the elements necessary for daily functioning. Slimmers do not only lose the undesired fat from their bodies but also other essential substances. The doctor or dietician can check whether this is happening and, if need be, revise the diet.

Once weight loss has been achieved the level reached has to be maintained and this means that eating habits must be changed permanently. A resolute personal commitment is required to lose weight and it is for each person to be self-motivated, to make that firm decision to practise restraint in eating behaviour and so keep weight to what it should be.

The motive for losing weight may be there but it can take an extra something to spark off the determination to achieve it. It may be the desire to look nice for an important occasion, a chance remark overheard or a grandchild's innocent comment. When Celia called for her six-year-old grandson at school he asked why she was fatter than anyone else. She decided she did not want such a title and shed several pounds.

It is fortunate for most of us that we naturally have balanced appetitites, not insatiable but able to satisfy hunger and take the food we need. We go through our lives eating to live but not living to eat. For the vast majority, being overweight clearly does not appear to be a desired option. I have never, personally, heard a person say, 'I like to be fat and I want to remain so'. And yet obesity is found among people of all ages and classes and with increasing frequency, often when there is an earnest desire to be slim. Judging by the numbers of weight-reducing diets which appear with such regularity in numbers of articles and books there must be a great number of people who read them and hope to find the one which will be effective for them.

Why Over-Eat?

Some people eat excessively because of habits acquired early in childhood. One father was so obsessed with the idea that his daughter would suffer from malnutrition that he awoke her at midnight to give her a meal and she grew to be a very fat girl. Many people will eat to compensate for shortcomings in their lives; they are unfortunates for whom eating is such an addiction that they are unable to resist any food available.

Less Exercise Possible

Add to overeating a decreasing amount of exercise (for it is doubtless harder to effectively exercise when overweight) and the result is obesity. And the obese have a difficult time. They are outside the 'norm', they do not have the same choice of clothes or footwear, they are hard on furniture and furnishings, and, most importantly, they are more prone to illness at every stage of life.

Fat and Happy

Some people accept philosophically that they love their food too much to diet. Maureen is happily married, the mother of two girls and a boy, all in their mid-teens. She is grossly overweight, approaching twenty stone and generally wears flowing garments to conceal the mounds of fat. A popular and intelligent woman in her early forties, she still has the self-confidence to appear on beaches wearing a bathing suit. We discussed her obesity and she admitted that whilst she would love to be slim she loved her food more. There have been occasions in her life when she wanted so much to be slimmer that she asked her understanding GP for help. He has twice arranged for her to have her jaw wired for a period of some weeks during which she could only drink liquids and remains under regular medical supervision. During both periods she lost considerable weight. However, in the following few months, she put it all on again.

Being pleasingly plump suits some people; many men and women say that they feel it gives them an added status in business to be of a more imposing size. Provided it is not causing health problems it is acceptable. But they have to be careful not to let more pounds creep on.

For the grossly overweight who finally do succeed in slimming there is another problem. One of the effects of great weight loss is a slackening of the skin and plastic surgery may be the only answer. Whatever slimming methods are used nothing can prevent the return of fat if people do not adhere to sensible diets and exercise.

Time for Self-Care

The development of a specific illness may mean that the overweight are urgently advised to reduce. Even then, knowing that their health and perhaps their lives are at stake, they have great difficulties. Achieving a healthy size produces the bonus of increased energy and a great feeling of well-being. During the retired years, when people have more time to look after themselves, they may achieve objectives they never managed earlier. It is certainly never too late.

When Jim and Barbara decided that they were going to lose thirty pounds each they had been overweight for many years. The pounds had slowly crept on during the first ten years of their married life and they had cheerfully acknowledged that they had 'middle-age spread', thinking it was quite natural. Occasionally they dieted but never succeeded in losing more than a few pounds which soon crept on again and, at sixty, they were each two stone above the weight they had been at thirty. On a routine visit to their doctor they had a check up which included a stern warning of the dangers of excessive weight. They went away with diet sheets feeling thoroughly chastised and promising to take some exercise too. Three months later, during which they had changed their pattern of eating, reducing all fats to a minimum and taken to walking at least a mile a day they were delighted to feel less out of breath and to have lost about eleven pounds each. A year later they were within ten pounds of their target weight and had become enthusiastic walkers, covering around fifteen miles each weekend. Their doctor told them they have greatly increased their chance of a healthy retirement. They said, 'We didn't know it but we must have felt ill because now we feel so well'.

Total Fasting

Total fasting would certainly lead to weight loss. Numbers of prisoners, both in this country and around the world, use this as a method of bringing their case-histories to the attention of the public. In the past, many famous suffragettes in pursuit of equality for women were courageous in abstaining from food and were force-fed when close to death. Total fasting has also been tried under close medical supervision for limited periods but it is considered to be unsafe and can be dangerous. There may be temporary or permanent damage of either a physical or mental nature or both.

Marion was an attractive girl whose excess weight worried her to the point where her doctor finally agreed to take her into a nursing home for a month of fasting. There was weight loss but she underwent a personality change, suffering severe psychiatric problems which have affected her whole life in a sad way. Too stringent fasting can also lead to loss of life, as was reported in the Department of Health (Report 31) prepared by the Committee on Medical Aspects of Food Policy, 1987. This can lead to a problem of a different nature, that of anorexia.

Anorexia Nervosa

This illness is an obsession with weight loss and many people believe that anorectics have the desire to be as slender as society's image of the model body. This is no more true than the other belief that they may wish to starve themselves to death. It is a very complex subject and difficult to define.

The anorexic man or woman has deep-rooted inner conflicts concerned with exerting control over their bodies. They always see themselves as much bigger than they truly are. One woman of my own age, who I know has been anorexic all her life, told me that it gives her satisfaction to say to her stomach, 'Don't worry, I can get you empty again and I will'. Anorectics fear putting on weight and need sensitive help and understanding and the realization on the part of family and counsellors that it is the anorexia which is in control of the person rather than the other way around. The anorexic feels trapped and can suffer great mental stress and feelings of desolation. They may resist all blandishments to eat or else they eat and vomit later yet somehow get sufficient nutrition to allow them to live near normal lives. They may come to terms with their problem and whilst in delicate health live well into retirement years.

18 Look Younger Longer

'Face up to the world', they say. It's a familiar phrase, making us brace ourselves, chin up, to take what is coming. By the time we are retired we have plenty of experience of meeting what the day has to offer and we know how important first impressions are. A glance in the mirror tells us how we appear, smiles look better than frowns, don't they? They reduce and lift the lines so no matter how hard we are concentrating we should try not to frown. Eyes are important since they mirror our thoughts, but vital to a youthful appearance is our skin and it is one of the first things noticed.

Can we do anything to improve its quality? We should give it as much help as we can, bearing in mind that as we age our glands secrete less collagen and valuable oils. The skin's topmost veneer which in youth renews itself about every three weeks takes a month of more later in life.

We don't have control over the kind of skin we will have – that is determined before we are born, at the time of conception – but we do have some control over how we treat it and how it will look when we are retired. If we take care to nourish it, both inside as well as out, staying healthy and taking sufficient rest, using moisturisers to correct exposure to the elements, then we are giving ourselves the best chance of having good skin throughout life.

Skin Composition

Skin is a tough and resilient substance, elastic and smooth in its normal condition. As we grow older it tends to change and toughen, the texture and colour alters and it creases, particularly when it has been allowed to dry out by exposure to the elements. It is composed of three layers and those of us with pale and delicate skins soon learn to avoid sunburn. The topmost layer with flat and rugged cells acts like an armour. The fine membranes which separate the layers above the deepest one, called the dermis, form part of the barrier which protects the skin tissues and the blood vessels beneath.

Never too Late

Facial skin is the biggest tell-tale of how old we are and though some people are naturally blessed with fine and unlined skins no matter what they do, most of us have to improve matters by taking simple precautions. It is never too late. Skin responds to careful treatment and so to a degree we can rejuvenate it. A cared for complexion should begin to show improvement within a few weeks. We tend to wash facial skin too energetically with harsh soaps, sit in the sun too long and we also expose our faces to blustery weather. Beauty experts tell us that if we use soap on our faces at all, it should be mild and unperfumed. We can determine our skin's needs and choose a soap to suit us, that is glycerine based for dry skin and medicated if it is oily. Over-washing removes natural oil and we should never cleanse the face more than twice a day.

The skin is a very effective barrier, naturally watertight as well as waterproof, holding moisture in yet preventing the absorption of dirt, germs and other harmful elements. Once the skin is grazed or scratched we cover it against infection and then, when a protective scab forms we are safeguarded until the skin is whole again.

Moisturisers

The specialized manufacture of products for skin care is an enormous business. Creams and lotions are carefully researched and formulated, usually expensively perfumed and packaged and cleverly advertised. Cosmetic companies vary in the claims they make for the moisturisers but, in truth, they all work pretty well on the surface skin. What has always been sought is something which would reach into and plump out those deeper layers. Twenty-five years ago there was a breakthrough and liposomes were produced, a form of carrier agent which because of its microscopic, molecular structure was able to successfully penetrate tissues and then deposit whatever it was carrying. However, these liposomes were not reliable enough and could have leaked their contents en route to their destination. Researchers have claimed that the latest results show that liposomes can now do an effective job. One company claims that their product goes right down to the bottom layer, the dermis. If there is an effective product of this kind available it could prolong the youthful look of skin considerably.

Skin cells virtually form a filter which allows the constant exchange of nutrition and waste products. In older skins the membranes harden, just as they do in arteries, forming a barrier which reduces the capacity of the cells to renew themselves and produce the all-important collagen and elastin fibres. It is these substances which keep our skin tissues plumped out and youthful. If the cosmetic companies can introduce these essential elements deep into our skins, then it may be possible not only to delay the ageing process in young complexions but also to improve matters for the older person, enabling a rejuvenating process which should result in a more youthful, firm skin.

Among the doctors who are concerned in this particular field of research is Christiaan Barnard, the same man around whom controversy raged when he pioneered heart transplants. He is determined to develop a treatment which will retard ageing. Working at the Schaefer Institute in Switzerland, Dr Barnard believes that he and his team will discover a method which will positively enable the skin to rejuvenate itself. If he succeeds we will certainly all hear about it. A youthful elixir or lotion has been sought for hundreds of years.

Meanwhile, we must continue to do the best we can using common-sense and the more prosaic products available. There is a wide variety on the market, some of which are perfume-free and non-allergic. They can all do a reasonably good job although no doubt some will suit certain skins better than others. It is a question of trial and error.

Some people claim that moisturisers can no more enter the layers of skin than socks can be absorbed by the feet, but massaging or patting emollient creams into the skin is soothing and pleasant and it is likely that the ingredients contain helpful elements. Gentle, cleansing lotions are easier on the skin than soap and water, which have a drying action.

When skin is unclean it holds dead cells on the surface and these give a greyish look, clogging pores and turning into red spots and blackheads. When the dead cells are removed, or exfoliated, the finer tissue beneath is revealed, producing a fresh and pleasing look.

Exfoliants

Exfoliants are materials which act upon the skin to remove the dead cells revealing the new layer beneath. Alternatively, a rough flannel will serve to loosen and remove this top layer. Some peel-off masks are produced to do this job but they have to be used with caution. The skin on the face is an extremely durable and protective covering but it needs careful treatment if it is to remain smooth and unlined, rather than tough and leathery. It may vary in its needs in different parts of the face, the part closest to the nose is often oily while other areas may be comparatively dry. Face packs are more gentle than exfoliants and are used as deep cleansers. Men remove the stale skin layer when they shave which leaves the skin looking fresh and some dermatologists say that this frequent routine helps to keep men's faces unlined.

The Sun can Damage

At retirement we often look for a place to live or holiday where we can enjoy warmth and bask in the sun. A certain amount of sunshine is essential for good health; we all benefit from some exposure and a tan makes us look well. However, too much sunshine can have the most damaging action on the skin layers, evaporating invaluable collagen which we need to plump out the skin.

Excessive sun tanning encourages skin cancers and at the Royal Marsden Hospital, London, doctors told me that after a hot summer they expect an increase of 10 per cent in skin cancers. Whilst these are the most easily curable forms of cancer, they can sometimes turn nasty and a more dangerous and life-threatening condition is created. Sun barrier creams should be used but even they cannot prevent the drying-out process. Since the effect of tanning is cumulative, the skin may not recover fully and every sunbath is paid for in a loss of moisture.

Skin Conditions

When the skin erupts with spots, pimples or a rash, we are signalled that either an infection or some illness is present, or that physical or mental stress has caused the skin condition. Irritating blotches can appear which may be caused by an allergic reaction to some food or chemical. We should try to trace the offending substances by eliminating foods we are especially fond of. Eggs, cheese, soft fruits and coffee are frequently found to be the culprits. Harsh soap powders are suspected of producing rashes, a form of dermatitis which usually disappears when the powders are no longer used. Even wearing clothes which have been washed in the offending powder and then rinsed, can still produce a reaction.

Eczema is a dry, itchy rash which often goes along with asthma, sometimes one condition being exchanged for the other as people grow older. Sufferers get to know what substances they should avoid in order to escape attacks. Eczema can appear on the face and neck but more often on the hands and wrists. It can also be triggered by stress.

Psoriasis appears without apparent reason but sufferers can usually recall an emotional upset or a particularly worrying period during the weeks or months beforehand. Attacks may be infrequent, but psoriasis is likely, in common with many skin rashes, to lie dormant, ready to erupt at any time. There is no permanent cure for psoriasis although much can be done to relieve sufferers.

Since stress may be a root cause of psoriasis and many other skin problems, doctors like to know all about their patients before attempting cures. More accurate diagnosis can be made if there is a holistic approach, a consideration of the person and of their problems, as a whole. A frank discussion with the GP may reveal difficulties of a psychological nature, with worries which can be allayed and result in better health.

Some of the complementary treatment centres which consider the patient holistically have been successful in improving skin conditions. Always seek the family doctor's advice before undertaking any kind of alternative health remedies.

Skin can Lack Vitamins

Deficiences in diet can affect the colour and condition of skin. Retired people, even as young as sixty, appear to be at high risk where there is a lack of vitamins. We do not absorb nutrients so efficiently as we grow older, tending to eat less of the right foods. We are more reluctant to prepare cooked meals, with a tendency to rely on pre-cooked, frozen or tinned dishes. The very elderly may eat less because they have ill-fitting dentures or are housebound, relying on haphazard shopping or on the WRVS service 'Meals on Wheels' which lose some of their nutritive value through being kept warm for too long.

Antibiotics and other drugs can interfere with the body's use of certain vitamins, with an adverse effect on our skin. We depend too much on drugs and tend to over-use them, relying too little on the self-healing properties of our systems. Antibiotics can prove over-efficient, killing off not only unwanted bacteria but also the bacteria which we need. Anyone on a long course of antibiotics will be likely to have vitamin supplementation recommended. Yoghourt can be beneficial, replacing the intestinal bacteria which are lost and so assisting in cleansing the systems and helping to clear the complexion.

Vitamins and Minerals

Vitamins are organic compounds essential to the body in tiny amounts. Apart from a few rare exceptions, we cannot ourselves produce these elements so we have to get them in our food or in supplements to our diets. No vitamin pills can possibly compensate for sensible and well-balanced menus, made with fresh and varied food. There is a standard, recommended daily intake for the most important of the vitamins and minerals which we require. Our needs must obviously vary according to sex and weight, degree of activity and state of health. A lack of vitamins or minerals in the diet will soon show in the skin, possibly as acne or as a dry or scaly condition. Sores at the corners of the mouth, or cracked lips may indicate a lack of vitamin C or of iron.

The skin on the legs thins with age and needs special care for if it breaks down it can prove difficult to heal. Pain may be felt just under the surface and this might be due to narrowing of arteries in the legs, a condition possibly alleviated by taking vitamin E. Vitamin deficiencies can add to the problem and your doctor or dietician will check the diet, recommending the element thought to be missing. There may be one or a mix of a variety of substances wanting, so that a combination of vitamins as well as preparations like evening primrose oil might be advised.

Vitamin and mineral supplements are invaluable but need to be used correctly, as prescribed. Overdosing can produce unpleasant symptoms and can even be dangerous. We have some twenty-five minerals within our systems, some of which we need in minute amounts. Examples are iron and calcium, which keep us from becoming anaemic or deficient in bone structure. The lack of iron soon becomes apparent, causing us to look pale and anaemic. It is surprising how quickly a deficiency of these factors affects us and shows in our skin, which may feel itchy or nervy. Eyes and hair, too, look dull and lacklustre, an early warning that something is wrong. A good balance is needed so that our incredibly complex systems can function.

Anyone switching to a vegetarian or vegan diet must be sure that they include all the nutrients they need, or make up for the deficiency by adding supplements. Similarly, those on a diet to lose weight may severely limit their intake of food, thereby also losing out on vitamins and minerals.

Pharmacists can spell out what vitamins or minerals will do for a person and will know what the correct intake should be. By all means ask their advice but symptoms which appear minor may mask conditions which only a doctor's knowledge and practised eye can correctly diagnose.

Home Remedies

An old Indian remedy was suggested for a patient who had a persistent leg ulcer, which was to lay fresh slices of papaya on the sore daily. Not very hygienic, I would have thought, but the ulcer responded well and was healed in a few weeks. I recently heard that a new pharmaceutical preparation contains an extract of this exotic fruit, so its properties must be widely appreciated.

My friend Pat, who is fifty-seven, was really fed up when her leg would not heal following an operation. Her daughter-in-law recommended an old family remedy, giving her an *aloe vera* plant, with the instruction that she 'take a leaf daily and gently rub the juice from it on the sore leg'. Within a few weeks healing had taken place.

The plant *aloe vera* is used in many preparations and is known for its healing qualities, but if you are planning to use medication other than that which has been recommended by your doctors, do let them know. If they say that there is no harm in trying, go ahead. But they may have reason to disapprove.

Cosmetic Treatment

No one wants a bland and smooth face at sixty or seventy – it would look odd and unnatural. We expect to look older as we age, although we hope that we will look somewhat younger than we are. The important thing is to look well. Nothing casts one down quite so much as to be continually told, 'You look really tired, you must be over-doing things', when all the time you feel as fit as the proverbial fiddle. There is a song, made famous by Stanley Holloway, which told of such a man who, despite feeling great, ended up feeling dreadful because everyone remarked how poorly he was looking.

In the ageing process, the natural elasticity of the skin reduces and it is most noticeable when the firm outline of the chin and jaw loosen and creases deepen at the corners of the mouth. Muscles around the edge of the face relax and the skin of the neck creases as it loses its underlay of collagen. In the windows of beauty salons you may see a sign offering collagen implants. This is material similar to that which we lose from under our skin and is taken from cows. Regular injections are needed since it is gradually broken down and absorbed into the system over months. It can be useful with deep wrinkles and also can help disguise some scars.

The removal of scar tissue or skin blemishes is probably the most common of all cosmetically desirable operations. When a mark is physically unattractive or causes comment it is not unnatural to want it to be removed. Some moles are attractive and regarded as beauty spots, others are hairy and displeasing to the person on whom they appear. We all have a few moles and probably think nothing of them.

Judging by the frequency with which advertisements appear offering 'Face-peel' this must be quite a common procedure. It is, as the name implies, a removal of skin by chemically burning off the top layer; in the new skin, lines and wrinkles should look fainter. With any of these procedures there is a greater sensitivity to sunlight afterwards and it is best to protect the skin from tanning.

The eyes may still be bright and unfaded well into later years but pouches and heavy eyelids can give that 'forever tired' look. Folds above the eyes can actually hang over the lids, making eyes look smaller, impeding sight and giving an aged appearance. If you are enjoying plenty of the right kind of food, fresh air and exercise and still feel that your looks do not do you justice, question whether cosmetic surgery could help. The short answer is, 'Yes, it could'. Cosmetic surgery is here to stay, faces can be re-formed, tummies tucked and thighs slimmed.

Face-lift procedures are now quite commonplace. People always ask how long they will last. The ageing process itself cannot be suspended and will continue, but there will be a more youthful look than there would have been without the operation. It would be most unusual for bags under the eyes to ever reappear to anything like the same extent, or for excess skin above the eyes to re-form.

The face-lift, technically known as rhytidoplasty, does not necessarily make one look younger than one's years, but it makes one look fit, healthy and fresh. Friends are likely to say, 'Have you been away?', or 'You look better than you have looked in a long while'.

Few patients are disenchanted with the results of cosmetic surgery. New noses usually please, higher cheekbones delight, flatter tummies thrill their owners. Anyone who is less than satisfied can always complain through the usual channels, but the most important precaution is to do your research and only put yourself in the hands of a well recommended cosmetic surgeon.

Once you make up your mind that you would like to have cosmetic surgery, there will be a number of questions which bother you and which you will want answered. Tell your own GP what you are proposing and ask if a cosmetic surgeon of good repute can be recommended. At the preliminary interview, find out about prices and duration of stay in hospital. Ask how long they think it will be before you can go out and about as there will be bruising and swelling which can take some time to disappear completely.

If you decide to go ahead the cosmetic surgeon will take a number of photographs and tell you what is recommended. Don't decide hastily, take time to consider. You might be able to meet a patient who has had similar surgery in recent months and from whom you can gain the confidence needed.

Depending on the extent of your own operation, you could be fortunate, facing the world in a few days, perhaps using some make-up over discolouration. It is best to be at one's slimmest and to wear one's hair longer rather than shorter, so that it can be arranged to cover the neck and ears until full recovery is effected.

Clinics specializing in cosmetic surgery say that they have as many enquiries from men as from women, which is not surprising. For men, with slightly heavier skin and bearded faces, there are different problems – for example, changes in hairline cannot be concealed by hair styles. Men must therefore ask exactly where scars will be and assure themselves that the surgery is going to achieve a worthwhile result.

Looking good gives you confidence and makes you feel good, but these treatments are not achieved without some discomfort and expectations should be realistic. Expect to look less tired and less strained which should make you feel well pleased with the result.

The common age for cosmetic surgery on the face seems to be between forty-five and sixty-five, and some people will elect to have a repeat operation some five years later. I know one woman in her late seventies who has just had a third. She was once beautiful and it matters very much to her how she looks. We all want to preserve youthful looks and while no one can turn the clock back or look twenty-five again there is no harm in taking advantage of modern medical technology. I am glad that I did.

Hair

Hair, the crowning glory, matters very much. However we are dressed, if hair doesn't look at its best the effect is spoiled. Hair and nail problems often go hand-in-hand with skin disorders and rectifying one may result in all-round improvement. Checking on vitamin and mineral intake may reveal shortages and when these are made up, hair, nail and skin health improves. Some swear by gelatine to strengthen nails, others say that cod liver oil capsules result in all-round improvement. It is all a question of trial and error.

One worry for older women is that hair appears in the wrong place, sprouting just where it is not wanted, on upper lip and chin. If it is not due to some glandular abnormality the only thing to do is to remove it. Electrolysis is effective but it must be done professionally, not by amateurs. Scarring could result. There are various creams or wax treatments which do a good job and one can keep growth under control. Shaving is not recommended because it also removes the soft down which should be left. Bleaching dark hair makes it less noticeable. If superfluous hair is a major problem obtain specialist advice.

We all lose hair from our heads daily throughout life, as many as a hundred or so hairs a day in our youth, but these are replaced quickly. Receding hair or balding is a different matter and is usually due to a genetic factor. Both men and women mind hair loss very much and can feel despondent about it but a bald head on a man is perfectly acceptable even if he is not as handsome as Yul Brynner. It is more of a problem for women in whom baldness would appear odd and they will be likely to wear a wig. Women find that their hair thins after the menopause when there is a reduction in oestrogen. Those on HRT tend to find that their skin is better and hair loss is less.

Little can be done about hair loss for either sex but we should use milder shampoos, dry gently under mild heat, comb and brush more carefully and try to do without perms which are drying and cause the hair to be brittle. Hair dyes and tints are also best avoided since they can cause more hair loss. Hairdressers can be very helpful, suggesting styles which minimize the problem. They can also advise whether any of the procedures such as hair-weaving and transplanting could be useful. Men are often advised to grow beards as a compensation for baldness.

If hair is really going fast and everyone is beginning to notice, don't fret. It is a less worrying problem today with the variety of wigs and hairpieces available which one can wear with confidence. Keep your sense of humour and make the most of what attributes you have.

Make-Up

Every decade brings a change of colour to our skins and we may need to alter our make-up accordingly. We want a light make-up on older skins, not something that will accentuate the lines. We need some colour but should try to achieve a natural look. Magazines are a good source of excellent articles and will often give a service advising on special problems about make-up. Sales people in stores, trained in beauty-care, can also advise about the most suitable products to use.

Blemishes can be covered with appropriate preparations and some of the make-up houses offer specialist advice. A patient with scars left from burns to the face and arms was given lessons at a Max Factor salon on how to conceal them and this increased her self-confidence greatly.

We should know what suits us in the way of make-up by the time we have reached retirement age but getting a fresh opinion can give us a new outlook and the chance to review the colours and types of preparation we are using. A new look is in keeping with retirement and a different way of life.

Reposed and serene, pleasant but not scowling, we can be secure in the knowledge that we are looking our best: not sweet sixteen, but sweet sixty, seventy, eighty, ninety – all the way to 120.

19 Young at Heart

Phrases like 'young at heart' convey the idea of someone grown older in years while remaining young in spirit. But to remain youthful we also need to stay young in mind and body. So why does it sound right to single out the heart and how do we stay, literally as well as figuratively, young at heart?

The Body's Pump

The heart is a solid muscle, as big as a fist. It pumps blood containing nutrients and oxygen all round the body, the beat of the heart ensuring not only a regular distribution of essential elements but also the regular cleansing of unwanted products.

To make all this possible we have an intricate network of veins and arteries which carry our blood supply to and from the heart. The smallest, the capillaries, have to be viewed under a microscope to be seen clearly, whilst the largest, which is connected directly to the heart and is known as the aorta, is as thick as a finger.

The reasons for damaged hearts are sometimes forgotten in the dramatic race to make us well again, either by drugs or by surgical intervention. How much of this treatment could be avoided if we understood our hearts better?

Major Risk Factors

There are three major risk factors which are out of our control: family history, our sex and age. Diet, smoking, drinking and stress are factors over which we do have control. If there is a familial predisposition to heart problems, others in the family have an increased risk and even the diets of the youngest members becomes important.

Until recently, men have been shown to have a greater risk

of heart disease than women, although this is changing as more women take to smoking and experience a more stressful role in work and life-style. The longevity of our parents is relevant since, according to statistics, our own expectation of life is the average age of our parents plus two years.

Heart Disease in the UK

Coronary heart disease is one of the nation's worst health problems, the biggest killer and approximately 30 per cent of all men and 25 per cent of all women fall victim to it. Our arteries should be of smooth, elastic and healthy material but as we age it is likely to become scarred tissue with ulcerated appearance and attachments of fatty globules. Scientific research indicates that much of the blame for cardiovascular disease lies with modern diet. We should not use any kind of fat or oil unless it is essential in the recipe. A low and polyunsaturated fat, high fibre diet with the added vitamins contained in fresh fruit, vegetables, bran and beans may well succeed in reducing cholesterol to safer levels.

Contributory factors to heart disease are diverse, but a great many are completely avoidable. A certain amount of cholesterol is vital in maintaining normal functioning for every part of the body. The two main kinds of fat in our diet are the saturated heavy fats which tend to raise the level of cholesterol in our blood and polyunsaturated fats which tend to lower it.

The plate which looks clean is evidence of a healthy meal, the one that looks greasy means that we have had too much heavy fat. Yet so many people love anything fried. When there was a campaign in Ireland to try to persuade husbands to eat less fat, the wife was pictured saying to her man that he would eat his socks if she would fry them!

About Angina

Angina is chest pain which varies in severity but is at best uncomfortable and at worst is described as an agonizing experience. It happens when the heart tries to force blood through clogged arteries, more especially at those times when additional oxygen is needed, as during cold weather, when taking exercise or when fear or excitement are felt.

Effects of Smoking

Whether it is cigarette, cigar or pipe smoking, the effects on the heart are bad and the introduction of nicotine can destroy the coating around our blood cells, causing clotting and arterial blockage. A constituent of cigarette smoke is a poisonous, lethal chemical. It may be a small part, only some 4 per cent, but it can reduce the amount of oxygen in the blood by up to 15 per cent. Nicotine is an addictive material, reaching the brain via smoked tobacco in about fifteen seconds and increasing the heart beat. Although the heart beats faster it gets less oxygen for the same effort. It also affects the smooth lining of the artery walls making them more liable to be clogged by the retention of fatty deposits. Each cigarette smoked releases nicotine into the bloodstream, remaining there for some eleven hours.

Everything in Moderation

If you enjoy a glass of wine with your meal or a nightcap of brandy it can do no harm unless there is a reason for you not to take alcohol. As we grow older, alcohol may have a more lasting effect on us and we should drink less of it. A regular excess of alcohol can damage the liver and put extra strain on the heart. Remember too, that alcohol has a dehydrating effect, reducing the level of body liquid and we should consume more soft drinks or water to compensate.

Crash diets do not do much in the long term, although we may lose a few pounds. It is our regular diet that is important, the way we eat, month in, month out. For our heart's sake we should try to keep weight low, limit our intake of salt and choose foods and drinks without added sugar. Don't overeat but do see that you get a good variation of fresh food, including some uncooked vegetables and fruit every day. A little of what you fancy does you good and, as my friend Gilbert Clark, a good GP if ever there was one, would say, 'Everything, in moderation'.

Hypertension

This is a term used for high blood pressure and is a condition which gives the heart an increased workload. If the arteries are already reduced in internal diameter, eroded and weakened, then heightened blood pressure increases the danger of a stroke or a heart attack. For damaged arteries and heart, even pleasurable excitement could be too much and if the heart beats fast when one is watching sport or engaged in sex, it could be wise to take some recommended preventive medication.

Effects of Stress

Stress can impose a burden on the blood vessels and the heart itself and is an important factor in blood pressure. A person who is often stressed, quick-tempered or excitable is liable to put the heart under strain. If there is already some damage then it may only need stress to tip the scales and cause serious problems. Steady, quiet breathing can be helpful at times of strain and should be practised.

If we are close to retirement age and business life is proving increasingly stressful and worrying, then it is worth considering retiring early. There are other things to be busy with which do not involve the risk of impaired health. The heart can become enlarged following a period of strain. If, in addition, there is high blood pressure, then a heart attack could be the outcome.

Signs and Symptoms

Symptoms such as swollen legs and ankles, adverse reaction to cold weather, shortage of breath during exercise and pain in the neck, arms or chest, should not be ignored. When we have early symptoms of something wrong and take sensible steps we can often put ourselves right without the need for drastic treatment. But if we ignore signs at an early stage we invite far more serious problems later. It must be for the doctor to decide whether the symptoms warrant a further investigation.

In any case, weight should be kept to a sensible minimum and a regime of supervised exercise gradually introduced and regularly practised. If need be, the useful drugs of today will be employed, but they must always be used with caution and a regard for their unwanted side-effects.

Medication and Treatment

A wide range of drugs is used to alleviate heart disease, the choice being dependent upon the condition to be treated. Sufferers from angina gain relief from glyceryl trinitrate pills which are placed under the tongue and dilate blood vessels, acting in a matter of seconds. A similar medication can be administered in spray form. There are drugs to reduce the level of cholesterol and others to reduce blood pressure.

Other prescribed drugs such as diuretics and beta-blockers are quite commonly in use to reduce hypertension although they can sometimes have significant side-effects. Among the more important of these are depression and a decrease in sexual function. Any noticeable difference should be reported to the doctor who may vary the dosage.

Hypertension can often be brought under control by a careful balance of food, exercise and medicines. There are many who do not like to take any kind of drugs, never even keeping aspirin in the house. When Isobel was forty-nine she had a heart attack and was found to have hypertension. Advised to go on medication she said that she wished to manage without. She and her husband both went on a strict diet which was low in fat, dairy food, salt and sugar. They went for daily strolls, increasing the speed and duration, week by week until they were doing a brisk walk of two miles a day. They were recommended to make certain additions to their diet, including herbs such as garlic, onion, ginger and freshly grown beansprouts.

At Isobel's next physical examination, the doctor found that her blood pressure was much improved. She had also reduced her weight by ten pounds and felt very well. That was fifteen years ago and the couple recently celebrated retirement with a long holiday, returning to the excitement of a first grandchild.

Pacemakers

Certain conditions call for the use of an artificial heart pacemaker. This might be recommended when the heart is not working properly, resulting in a slow heavy-feeling beat, together with a groggy sensation. The pacemaker helps to regulate the heart, taking over the natural controlling function. There are special precautions for those with pacemakers when travelling abroad.

Does Caffeine Damage?

A country family doctor was concerned to reduce a condition of hypertension in a diabetic patient who did not wish to use drugs with their potentially complex side-effects. The patient did not smoke, avoided all salt and took regular exercise. But when the doctor learned that the patient drank a dozen cups of coffee during the day, he advised him to not drink it at all for a two-week trial period. The result was that his patient's blood pressure became normal.

This experience caused the doctor to check up on the recent findings related to caffeine and its effect on the system. It was reported that caffeine has the ability to constrict blood vessels and he found that a single cup of coffee could elevate the pulse rate and raise blood pressure.

Heart Transplant

There are now many hundreds who have survived for years following heart transplant operations, enjoying life that they could otherwise never have had. Patients as young as a few days as well as the elderly survive very well. Artificial hearts have been made but considerable research is still needed before they can be regarded as acceptable replacements for the human heart.

Angioplasty

Angioplasty is now a fairly commonplace technique. Used in coronary artery conditions it enables doctors to get clear information about the state of the heart. A minute catheter, no bigger than the graphite in a lead pencil is threaded through a blood vessel in the arm (sometimes in the leg) and fed directly through to a coronary artery. By using contrasting colour agents a picture can be viewed on a screen. The picture allows the doctor to determine exact details about the blockage in the artery. Now, a second and even smaller catheter, carrying a minuscule balloon is inserted through the first and guided to the obstruction. The balloon is inflated and compresses the obstructive material so that the blood flows freely once again. The whole operation takes between one and two hours and the patient needs little time to recover and a mere few days in hospital. With new designs of catheters and non-toxic agents, it is expected that such operations will be done on an outpatient basis in the near future.

By-Pass

Blocked or unhealthy portions of coronary vessels can be removed and replaced with healthier sections from elsewhere in the body. This is a very successful operation, prolonging active life. But such operations are not cure-alls. They offer a respite and it is up to patients to adopt healthier ways of living if they want to extend their life-spans.

Edward, just over fifty, was rushed into hsopital with violent chest pains, the first sign for him of any serious health disorder. It was found he had severe blockages to three arteries, requiring urgent surgery. For years an habitual smoker, he was fond of a regular breakfast of eggs, bacon and fried bread followed by two or three cups of coffee with sugar and cream. Ten pounds overweight, he was a hard worker in a stressful occupation, running his own business and took little exercise. 'You', the surgeon told him, 'are a recipe for disaster. Whatever we do for you now will only be a temporary measure. Your life-style will soon either kill you or put you back in hospital and our work on you will be wasted.'

Edward was shocked. He certainly felt very ill. The chest pains had been frightening in their intensity and he had felt as though he had received a kick from a horse. The doctors had more grim news; they had discovered a blockage in an artery at the top of one leg which also needed an operation and they could not perform the heart by-pass at the same time. 'Your leg could be in some danger', they said, 'but we'll leave that for the moment.'

They were reluctant to operate unless Edward guaranteed a change of life-style, promising to cut out fats and dairy produce and eventually to walk three miles a day. Edward was a man who was determined not to die or to lose a leg. He had been given a second chance and he meant to take it and regain his health.

Six years later it is hard to believe the change in the man. He is addicted to his daily three-mile run and says that he could not face the breakfasts he once ate so heartily. Business goes on but he does not allow himself to become so stressed. He is slimmer and fitter than he has been in a score of years. Since that first tremendous stab of pain, he has never smoked another cigarette.

Be Sensible

I repeat, the sensible rule for a healthy heart is moderation in all things. We want to take every advantage of these bonus years, becoming a generation of independent, active and involved people. We want to be a credit to ourselves, to our families and to the community, and we can be. If we will just take care of our hearts, then our hearts will take care of us.

20   The Five Senses

Seeing

Not many can be like our friends, Anne Adams and Ken Butcher, who need neither glasses nor hearing aids. Anne is ninety years old and demonstrates her visual ability by reading small print with ease. At eighty-four, Ken's sight is so good that he can put minute details into his lovely paintings of country scenes and flowers, using tiny feathery brushes to obtain the right effect.

The impairment of perfect sight is regarded as being mainly due to the loss of flexibility in the eye muscles. If we could keep these muscles in better shape, practising regular exercises, then we might preserve our good sight longer, putting off the day when we need spectacles or a stronger prescription. A simple routine to try every day is to look hard to the left, to the right, then up and down. After two or three times, cup the palms of your hands over your eyes and rest them. Take two or three minutes to relax them, thinking, 'Soft, soft, softer'.

We require up to three times as much light to work or read by than when we were young and we should not struggle to read or work in poor light. Once we start to wear glasses we should return to our opticians at least every two years for a sight test, unless we suspect particular irregularities which need immediate investigation. If we do this we can expect to avoid problems, knowing that our eyes will remain as healthy as possible. Eye tests can reveal unsuspected ill-health which may have nothing to do with sight defects, such as circulatory problems and diabetes.

Cataract
The standard treatment for this disease, in which the crystalline lens of the eye becomes increasingly blurred and

opaque, used to be to wait until the obscurity had developed fully, or as it was termed, ripened. Now the wait is unnecessary. An operation is then performed to remove the clouded lens when a new lens may be inserted, or spectacles with strong lenses supplied.

Glaucoma
This is a serious condition which should be diagnosed and treated early if permanent damage is to be avoided. Fluids build up within the eyeball, often creating painful and potentially damaging pressure. This can happen without warning and is accompanied by sudden and persistent pain. Another symptom may be the vision of halos around lights. Glaucoma can also develop insidiously, slowly, over a long period and without the warning of pain. There is a gradual restriction of the field of vision until it is narrowed to 'tunnel vision'. This illness is detectable by opticians who employ sophisticated machines which help them to identify the condition at an early stage. Everyone in their late-thirties or over should make the time for regular check-ups, particularly if there is a family history of eye disease.

Glaucoma may be treatable by drugs alone although an operation may be necessary. There are an estimated half a million glaucoma sufferers in the UK, many of whom have not been diagnosed. These are likely to be among the older generation who neglect to go to the optician for regular checks. Where glaucoma has occurred in a family, other members have an increased risk of developing the condition and for this reason eye tests remain free to these families.

Eye Problems
Defective vision and even conditions like cataract and glaucoma could possibly be induced or advanced by emotional stress and strain. When people are away on holiday they frequently say that they see better and even manage to read without their glasses. This could be partly because they are in brighter, stronger light but could also be because they are feeling leisurely and relaxed.

With some viral infections such as flu' we get pain around our eyes, when aspirin and rest may be all that will be required for recovery. An occasional sensation of heat, dull ache, prickling and itching in the eye is quite common, but if these symptoms persist then it is better to obtain professional advice to determine the cause as soon as possible, hopefully avoiding serious illness.

Migraines, headaches and neuralgia can produce aches behind the eyes but these are temporary conditions which are self-limiting and pain soon disappears. Other eye pain producing conditions may be sinus related and if any of these symptoms, or others relevant to the eyes, persist for forty-eight hours, then the advice of the doctor or optician must be sought. Referral may be made to an ophthalmologist who can make a more detailed examination.

It is advisable to go to the optician's premises for eye tests where specialised equipment is installed. Local optical committees will probably know of an optician who is prepared to pay a domiciliary visit. Eye tests are available at a modest charge to anyone requesting them. They are free to those on limited incomes, as well as to families or individuals having certain eye conditions. People who are diagnosed as having eye problems and are required by their doctor to have eye tests will get these done through referral to a hospital without charge.

Ordinary Magnification
Magnification spectacles can be made for individuals at quite moderate prices or bought over the counter in some stores, but these only enlarge and do not correct faults. It is imperative to obtain a correct prescription and only a qualified optician can determine what is needed.

Bifocals
Where it is preferred to have one pair of glasses both for distance as well as for reading, the portion for reading can be made in a small section at the bottom of the lens. Graduated lenses can also be made so that they accommodate near,

middle and distance vision but these are costly, requiring a more sophisticated process in manufacture.

Choosing Spectacles
Choose glasses for comfort as well as style. Heavier lenses, such as are required for someone with poor sight, will need strong frames to support them and opticians will advise those which will be most satisfactory.

Repairs
Tighten the tiny screws in spectacle frames regularly to avoid losing the lenses and carry a kit containing a tiny screwdriver and spare screws, particularly when travelling abroad. Opticians the world over are always obliging about small repairs, finding matching screws and adjusting frames without charge, but not every High Street has an optician.

Complaints
Glasses which prove to be unsuitable for the purpose for which they were made should be returned to the optician so that they can be corrected. Complaints about NHS treatment by an optician should be addressed to the local Family Health Services Authority, who may determine whether there are grounds for taking the matter further. Complaints about treatment in hospital should go in the first instance to the department concerned, so that they are given a chance to investigate and explain. If this does not satisfactorily resolve the matter then an approach should be made to the local Community Health Council, with full details.

Contact Lenses
A popular development in recent times has been the production of contact lens within a moderate price range and which can be made to suit most spectacle wearers.

The idea is not a new one. Leonardo da Vinci, besides being a world-renowned painter, was a talented inventor and had produced designs for moulded contact lenses in the sixteenth century but lacked the modern materials and techniques which would have enabled them to be made. In 1887, the earliest versions of contact lenses appeared, but the greatest progress was made in this field in the 1950s, when small, plastic, corneal lenses were developed.

With the invention and development of suitable soft and hard plastics, the twentieth century saw the first experimental examples of modern contact lenses and during the last thirty years or so researchers and manufacturers have brought the latest versions within reach of the public.

Disposable lenses can now be obtained, designed to be worn on a daily basis for a week and then discarded. Also available are focal and bifocal lenses as well as those designed to block out ultraviolet light. Further interesting developments include a new diffractive lens. These are so made that the wearer can see both near and far. There may be a short period of a few weeks when a 3D effect is experienced but the eyes should then become adjusted to the new systems.

Spectacles are a necessary and indispensable aid to sight but they can irritate the nose and ears and can easily be lost, mislaid or broken. Once inserted, soft contact lenses can be forgotten for the day but they should be removed nightly, carefully cleansed and left in solution overnight. This is regarded as a somewhat fiddly procedure and some individuals cannot be bothered with it, but others have used the same set of lenses for years and would not go back to wearing specs for anything. The possibility of discarding spectacles in favour of contact lenses, soft or hard, is welcomed by those for whom the advantages outweigh the problems and the temptation to become unspectacled is great.

Daily Wear only for Contact Lenses
Ophthalmologists advise that there may be danger to the eye if lenses are not removed overnight as complex changes are caused when the eye suffers deprivation of oxygen. Irritation from substances which get underneath the lens could lead to corneal infections and ulcers which are a serious threat to sight. The eye has the ability to recover from minor abrasions if left open to the air but not if covered and damage can go

unnoticed until it becomes severe with permanent effect. Lens users who keep them in for days are far more susceptible to damage and it is well worth the trouble to remove lenses daily.

Holidaying in a lake-side camp in Vermont in the USA two years ago, we were intrigued by the unusual eye colouring of some members of staff. We assumed that a rare genetic factor must be present in the local community until we discovered that tinted contact lenses were in fashion. Anyone can now have stunning blue, violet, green or brown eyes.

Hearing

Whether or not we reach retirement with perfect hearing may depend upon a number of factors, including the genetic one which may dispose us to a weakness. Some illnesses have an adverse effect upon the hearing, as might the pitch of noise we have been subjected to in our daily lives. Noise levels in places of work or amusement are often so high that they cause hearing loss, as do loud and sudden noises severe enough to shock the system.

For hearing to be normal there has to be perfect functioning of the outer, middle and inner compartments of the ear. If something prevents vibration and transmission of sound then a hearing problem results and is known as conductive hearing loss. It may be possible to alleviate or to cure this condition. Should there be damage beyond the middle ear and along the pathway known as the inner ear, sensori-neural deafness is caused, which is a much more difficult condition to deal with.

When there is trouble in hearing all that is being said in normal conversation, we should investigate the cause. It could be just an excess of wax which is a natural secretion in the ear and which lubricates, waterproofs and protects the inner parts. It can be gently removed from the outer ear but needs a doctor's attention if it is blocking the interior portion. We should heed the words of the audiologist who said that people should put nothing in their ears but their elbows.

Other causes of deafness require specialized knowledge, possibly referral to a consultant audiologist to diagnose what is wrong and to advise the treatment necessary. If a hearing aid is recommended be sure that you completely understand how to use and care for the appliance. NHS aids are bigger than commercial ones and are worn on the body. Some hearing aids are quite tiny, fitting behind or in the ear. Others can be incorporated into the earpieces of spectacles.

Check carefully before responding to newspaper advertisements, some of which make extravagant claims for their hearing aid appliances and which may be comparatively highly priced. Once bought, a hearing aid should be used constantly and with patience for it takes time to become accustomed to new levels of sound and the benefits may not immediately be realised.

Speech therapists will offer useful practical advice to those with hearing problems. They recommend that anyone who has deteriorating hearing should learn to lip-read and there are local clubs which offer plenty of opportunity for practise as well as the chance to learn about other people's experiences.

Tinnitus
Nothing can be more aggravating than tinnitus, a constant noise in the head. If this has been investigated by the doctor and there is nothing apparent causing it, the only thing remaining is to get on with life and ignore the noise. After a time, it merges into the background and can be forgotten. Playing a music tape which will mask or blanket the tinnitus gives temporary respite.

Tasting and Smelling

A healthy fresh-feeling mouth is a prerequisite to feeling well and looking one's best. Nothing is worse or more off-putting than approaching someone whose breath is bad or sour-smelling. We need the assistance of our dentist and hygienist if we are to achieve optimum dental health and we can help by being scrupulous about cleaning teeth after every meal, whether they are our own or dentures.

We keep our teeth far longer than our parents did and it is

not unusual to find people well into their seventies and eighties who still have their own teeth. Professional attention is needed if we are to keep our teeth as long as we live and regular visits to the dentist should be a high priority. Dentists can give treatment almost painlessly with the equipment at their disposal today, saving teeth where they would once have had to take them out. Getting teeth capped is expensive but a high priority for many who will do anything to save a tooth.

A small proportion of dental care is paid by the NHS to everyone using the national service and it is free to those on a low income. Ask your dentist if NHS care is provided and how much of the charge you will have to pay. Quite a few will only do private work and you should ask for an estimate for whatever work is to be done. If you have a problem getting a dentist or choosing one, ask at the Community Health Council or Family Health Services Authority if they can help. They have lists of dentists and may be able to recommend one near to where you live. Your GP or practice nurse may also be able to advise you.

Most dentists have hygienists who will clean your teeth professionally for a modest charge and having this done twice a year will help to keep your mouth pleasant. Cleaning your teeth after every meal will ensure that you are always nice to know. 'Using a mouthwash regularly is a must for me', said one seventy-eight year old. 'I mean to be a fragrant old lday.'

Dentures may need refitting after a few years because our gums and mouths may change shape. Nothing is more unsightly or discomforting than to watch someone with ill-fitting dentures, nor can the person concerned find them pleasant to eat with.

If you have had dental treatment which you regard as unsatisfactory, take advice about how to complain. You may be able to get work re-done.

We want to feel and look as good as it is possible to do when we smile so it is worth making our mouths a priority. Spend whatever is needed and count the cost as money truly well-spent. With our mouths in good order we can enjoy our food better although our taste-buds become less sensitive. We may not have such sensitive noses, noticing cooking odours and perfumes less. Still, the sense of smell remains a useful sense until a great age, some people in their eighties and nineties finding little difference in their enjoyment of the smell of food cooking or of their favourite perfume.

Touching

Hands should be treated as well as I ask you to treat your feet. They respond to massage with some fine oil, rubbing and moving the joints until they feel more supple and the skin feels smooth. Treat them to a rub with Vaseline if they feel rough, wash and dry them, file the nails and gently push down the cuticles. Your hands can be used to massage your body, touching, feeling and easing the tension. Press your fingertips to your head and if there are tender spots, rub them with a circular movement. Give your neck a few minutes massage with your fingers, gently going over the spinal knobs. Now sit back and smile, hold it and cover your face with your hands, feeling relaxed, breathing quietly, eyes closed. Touching, smelling, tasting, hearing, seeing, all the senses complementing each other. Nice, isn't it?

21 Dancing Feet

Feet deserve Respect

There are few people, either men or women, particularly among those in the upper age brackets, who have the kind of feet which they can display in sandals without any feeling of embarrassment. Why should this be? We are all so dependent upon our feet to carry us about and yet few people give them the kind of care and attention which they merit and which would ensure trouble-free mobility.

Foot problems affect a considerable proportion of our population and are to be found most frequently in elderly people. Some 75 per cent of the older generation have trouble with their feet causing all kinds of difficulties, limiting mobility and in some cases causing their owners to become housebound.

Before retirement, we may already have these problems, in which case we should be taking extra care not to aggravate conditions. Whilst tasks like ironing or hobbies like carpentry are more usually done while standing, it is easier on the feet as well as the back to do them whilst seated. Sitting or standing, it is better to wear well-fitting shoes because slippers do not support the feet properly. They cause you to shuffle along, whereas the well-shod foot makes correct movements, heel first, then toe. It is better for morale too, if you are properly dressed, right down to shoes, even if you are not going out.

Circulatory problems occur more frequently as we age and anyone who notices that their feet are often cold or become swollen should always visit their GP to obtain an opinion. Don't think that it is not worth going because nothing much can be done. That is far from true today and it is important that the condition be correctly diagnosed. Exercises and bathing may be helpful and elastic stockings can provide comforting support, where a doctor recommends them as part of the right treatment.

Making Feet Last

Feet do show signs of age and this is not to be wondered at considering the job they are required to do. The fact that we are going to live longer and more actively means that our feet may have to last another two or three decades and they deserve all the care they can get.

Most older people have some evidence of osteoarthritis in the bones of their feet although this may be without any symptoms or cause no problem. Let the chiropodist advise as to whether any treatment, medical or otherwise is needed.

Apart from arthritis, the majority of causes of painful feet are associated with weak muscles, relaxed ligaments and deformities. Fortunately, most of these respond to treatment if they are attended to promptly. But if they are neglected they can cause serious disabilities.

Pain in the sole of the foot should be diagnosed by a doctor since the reason for such a symptom is not readily determined. In older people who do not take much exercise or are in the habit of walking slowly, there may be circulatory problems manifested by cold feet. But it is essential to consult a doctor of this is persistent since there may be a serious underlying problem.

Gouty Attack

Anyone with gout who has experienced the burning pain of a suffering big toe is unlikely to forget it and will do anything to avoid a recurrence. No joint is exempt from gout but it is the big toe which is commonly affected, often swelling, becoming hot and exquisitely tender. First attacks usually occur after middle age but they do subside quite quickly leaving only a painful memory. The doctor should be made aware of the condition and will often recommend a change in diet in addition to some medication, both to reduce pain and hopefully to prevent any recurrence.

Diabetes and Feet

Great care must be taken by anyone suffering with diabetes. Once this diagnosis is made strict recommendations are always given to patients concerning foot-care. They will be told of the dangers of infection and that they should pay regular and frequent visits to a chiropodist. Even trimming one's own toenails can be hazardous and should be done with the greatest of care; anything more, such as treating corns, definitely needs professional attention.

Well-Fitting Shoes

Nothing ages the face as much as the strain of walking or standing on aching feet so choose shoes with care and regard for the long-term effect they will have. Appearance is important of course but there is such a range of styles and fittings nowadays that it should always be possible to satisfy both vanity and the need for comfort. It is not a question of cost. Shoes do not necessarily have to be expensive to fit well, be elegant and stylish, easy to wear and of good value.

The choice of footwear depends upon the kind of occasion they are needed for. Most women, young and old, love to wear high-heeled shoes but to stand about all day in them cannot be sensible no matter how the wearers may protest that they are perfectly comfortable. Men of all ages too, can be guilty of sacrificing comfort for a fashionable look. Toes get crowded into narrow shoe-caps, curled over and liable to suffer from corns, calluses, bunions and other such unsightly problems.

Once these common foot ailments occur, they do not easily disappear and they make finding comfortable shoes more difficult. An examination of some worn shoes will probably reveal the cause of the owner's problems, the wear showing where the contact points are. Pressure can cause nail deformity, fungus infection and sores, apart from those problems already mentioned. And when these conditions arise, they take up a lot of the time of doctors, chiropodists and nurses to deal with, to say nothing of the distress for the patient. It is scarcely credible, but one man said that he had suffered discomfort until his forties when he realised that he had always bought shoes a size too small.

Take a critical look at your own shoes. Are they worn down and are the linings undamaged? Are the heels in need of repair? When I asked these questions of a group of pensioners, we uncovered some shoes which were causing their owners to walk in quite a distorted fashion. Backstrain follows inevitably. And we all agreed that well-cared for shoes made one feel smart. Don't ever make do with old and tired footwear.

Common Conditions

Bunions are a particular problem for many who have worn too-tight shoes and if they become painful, surgical treatment may be recommended. More simple treatment may be just to wear broad and comfortable shoes, a bed-cradle at night to lift the weight of bedding and perhaps a corrective cast for night wear. Exercises are useful but if all this fails and pain persists then an operation may be advisable. Complete recovery time can be as much as three months.

Many of the over-the-counter cures for corns and calluses are quite drastic and contain powerful chemicals. Self-treatment is not advised and it is safer to see a chiropodist. Twice-yearly visits are a wise investment for anyone of adult age, but I would say essential for those of us who are retired and most people say that their feet feel so much better after professional care that it is well worthwhile.

Avoiding Problems

Good foot sense means good shoe sense and both men and women, even at retirement age, are guilty of breaking the rules, especially when it comes to kow-towing to high fashion. Pointed shoes, slim-fits, too-narrow court shoes, high-heels, non-supportive sandals, all of these and other kinds of unsuitable footwear seem to tempt buyers into making serious mistakes. Many of us have experience of making the wrong purchases and we know only too well that we will suffer for our vanity when feet end up deformed, causing pain and reducing mobility. The self-inflicted troubles resulting from ill-fitting shoes can be agonizing, resulting in a need for corrective, possibly surgical intervention.

It is not just the shoes which are at fault. Even tightly tucked-in bedclothing can limit movement. Socks, stockings and tights must fit comfortably and should be discarded before they are misshapen or shrunk by washing because they could cause the toes to be drawn into unnatural positions. Try taking off shoes, socks or stockings on arrival at home and enjoy the freedom of walking in bare feet for a short while. Flex the toes and give them a little exercise. Bathe feet in tepid water, not too hot, for this would remove the natural oils from the skin. Dry gently and thoroughly and massage a little oil or Vaseline around the toes and over the hardened sole and heel. Wipe off the surplus and then slip into comfortable but supportive sandals or shoes.

When to Buy Shoes

Buy shoes later in the day since feet do tend to swell when they have been carrying several stone of weight around for some time. The fit should be easy and comfortable and there should be no pressure on bony protuberances. The soles and uppers should preferably be of leather since this is a material which breathes and allows for movement. There is a certain amount of give in natural materials but if they are too snug a fit on purchase it does not do to take them home and try stretching them. We should value comfort more as we grow older and do not want to have cause to regret our purchases.

Results of Bad Posture

Bad posture is another outcome of poorly-fitting shoes because this disturbs the muscle balance in the foot and leads to weakness. This is a cause of a great deal of the chronic backache from which so many people suffer. The foot is, in a way, like a spring and bears the full weight of the body. Left to themselves and in a natural state, feet will perform faultlessly and indefinitely, as they do in animals. But we like our feet to be protected and encased in leather or synthetic materials, too often in such a way that we end up misshaping and deforming them.

What does a Chiropodist do

State Registered Chiropodists are specialists who are trained to provide a comprehensive foot-care service. They will treat for the immediate relief of pain in the feet and lower limbs. They will advise on the general way to care for feet and may be competent to carry out certain surgery techniques. They can also prescribe, supply and fit necessary appliances.

The letters MChS mean that the chiropodist is a Member of the Society of Chiropodists and has undergone an approved course of training for State Registration. FChS indicates those members of the Society who are Fellows and who have passed the higher Fellowship examination.

Every older person should get to know a local chiropodist who can recognize those aspects of disease which first manifest themselves in the lower extremities. They may treat patients privately or on the NHS. As professionals they are much underrated since they do provide an invaluable service and yet many people only go to them as a last resort. Since they can prevent or reduce a great deal of pain and suffering they can improve looks, probably as much as a visit to a beauty salon.

Book appointments with chiropodists early for they are in great demand and there may be a waiting list for patients who are referred to hospital or to the health clinic.

Students are being trained as foot-care assistants to practise under the supervision of qualified chiropodists and this will reduce the time patients have to wait.

The scant respect shown by the majority of people to their precious feet is costly in terms of health, comfort, time and money. The worst of it is that foot problems may become acute just at the time when their owners want to be mobile, when they are looking forward to the excitement of retirement with time to enjoy themselves and to get around.

Talking of getting around reminds me to remind you to walk, not at an ambling pace but briskly, stretching your feet and ankles, feeling the muscles in your calves and thighs pulling. Take a stick with you, it's handy as you stride along and can offer some support as you go uphill and help your balance as you go down. This is a walk for health so don't stand about chatting to the friends you meet. Take them with you or arrange to meet them later. Twenty minutes of rapid movement, swinging your arms and you will have moved some of the sludge around and your feet should feel like dancing.

Undressed Feet

A look around the beaches will disclose some ghastly looking feet. What a pity, when they could be pretty and natural looking. They are a big help in making the enjoyment of life possible, no matter how we choose to spend our time. So, in preparing for retirement, be sure that feet get a fair measure of respect.

22 Keeping the Works in Order

Can it Be?

Incontinence at any age is seen as the last straw, something that surely cannot be happening. When it occurs in the comparatively youthful individual of fifty and sixty, it feels almost insulting and is something people will struggle with for ages before acknowledging what is wrong, even to their doctor. But no one should feel embarrassed to admit to what is, after all, a very common condition. All manner of subjects are discussed today, but the one of bladder weakness is still taboo, which is a pity. And yet, since as many as 60 per cent of women do have the condition, it should surely be talked about quite openly. This may happen in the future because many magazines, for example, nowadays contain articles which freely examine the various aspects of this problem and there are also a number of medical seminars where such issues are discussed.

The good news is that in a full third of cases a cure for incontinence is possible; where it is not, much can be done to alleviate the condition.

An Encouraging Trial

A woman doctor found that with only minimal training and no specialized resources, she successfully treated those of her women patients who were suffering from incontinence. When reporting her findings, she said that the majority of patients showed improvement and some had achieved a complete cure. This success rate was reached within three months of the commencement of treatment.

Anyone experiencing a leakage of urine, however slight, at

times of moderate physical stress, such as when they laugh, cough, sneeze, reach to a shelf or change position quickly, are probably suffering from a weakness of the muscles supporting the bladder. When these symptoms occur, treatment should be sought at once. Neglect will allow muscles to weaken further.

Women are more often affected than men for the reason that during childbirth they strain the base of the pelvis which supports the bladder, womb and bowel. Women with prolapsed wombs can find that they suffer urinary leaks, especially when they exert themselves, placing muscles under stress as when they carry parcels, laugh or cough.

Men and women are equally reluctant to raise the matter with their GP, resisting this step for as long as possible. This means that there are often years of distress before help is finally sought. In many areas Continence Advisers, who are trained and experienced nurses and who have a no-nonsense, sympathetic and matter-of-fact approach, have been appointed.

Approaching retirement years, men and women find that incontinence becomes increasingly serious, intruding into and spoiling life. What a shame that this is allowed to happen when there is more often than not an easy remedy. Symptoms may indicate different causes and advice will depend on many factors. It is important to isolate any serious condition and also to overcome the sense of stigma which attaches to the whole matter.

Incontinence is associated with age and weakness but feeling old is a negative state of mind and we should think positively. Why do we fail to take the problem of incontinence to the doctor early? Is there shame in admitting that we cannot control a function? We would find it easier to accept that we could have such a condition if we realised that such problems can be beaten or at least made manageable.

Refusing to accept that there is a problem can mean much needless misery. Some people actually become housebound, unable to go out for fear of having an accident which they would find too mortifying to cope with. Unburdening one's mind to the doctor can reduce the stress which makes things worse.

The Old Days

Visiting homes for the elderly was often unpleasant because of the smell of urine which permeated the building. The residents were often scolded for getting out of bed at night to pass water. An elderly bladder is not as resilient as it once was, so not unnaturally it was easy to become incontinent. It is not only the elderly though who are disturbed for this reason and anyone who feels the need to go to the toilet, should of course go at any time they want to. Facilities in any case are easier to reach in modern homes, hand rails can be provided for those who need them and this kind of provision means that incontinence can be averted.

Find the Reason

There is a belief that with increasing age a weak bladder is as natural as the need for spectacles but there must be other reasons for weakness. Improvement often follows a change in diet and the elimination of some food and drink which has been irritating to the bladder. Tap water contains many chemicals, one or other of which may cause irritation. A switch to boiled tap water or bottled spring water may prove helpful.

At fifty-six, Laura had tolerated a weak bladder for twelve years during which the condition had become progressively worse. Every couple of hours or so she had an urgent need to pass water and it became a nightmare if she was driving and was caught in a traffic jam or attending the theatre or any kind of function. Acutely embarrassed, she felt unable to tell her husband or anyone else in all those years and was considering early retirement from her job. But reading an article on allergies and water changed her life back to normal. She stopped drinking tap water and the improvement after a week was, she said, like a miracle. She also stopped eating the highly-seasoned meals and any irritant foods such as pickles which she had been fond of. She now practises simple, daily exercises which are helpful and the incontinence has not recurred.

The Restrictions

Incontinence imposes restrictions which vary merely from the need to reduce fluids to having to wear protective pads. There may also be a reduced ability to carry or lift shopping or articles of any weight. It may become quite impractical to travel by public transport and social gatherings become times of anxiety instead of pleasure. Sufferers feel unattractive to their friends and mortified about any suspicion of a smell.

Sexual relationships are often ruled out as people assume that they must be undesirable. This causes hurt misunderstanding when partners, unaware of the problem, do not realise why they are rejected.

Occasional urinary incontinence, a minor dribble, can happen to almost anyone. Regular bouts should not occur in the normal course of events and anyone having frequent problems should lose no time in getting round to the doctor. A slight chance exists that there is an underlying, more serious reason for the weakness so there is all the more urgency to seek attention quickly. Doctors and ancillary staff are sensitive, understanding and ready with helpful counselling and medication. The regular practice of a few simple exercises may be all that is needed.

What can Cause Incontinence

An increasing number of men are found to be suffering from urological disorders, many of which can be corrected, especially if they are seen early on. Older men quite commonly suffer from incontinence, either from a weakening of the bladder and surrounding muscles or from an enlargement of the prostate gland. Sometimes it is because they fail to empty the bladder completely, causing irritation which prompts an urge to go often.

A recent study claimed that about three-quarters of all men over the age of fifty have some problem with the prostate gland. It is recognized by a weakening of the urinary stream, incomplete voiding and a dribbling incontinence. There may, however, be few symptoms and the sufferer may be reluctant to go to the doctor with what could appear to be a minor problem. Symptoms related to incontinence must be checked out by the doctor before minor problems become major ones.

The operation for a prostate gland condition is considered to be a simple one and recovery is usually trouble-free. It may be even more simple in the future if a revolutionary new treatment proves as promising as it now appears to be. This method involves placing a tiny microwave generator so that it can specifically treat the prostate gland. Patients report fewer adverse symptoms than in the more accepted form of treatment and the urinary flow is significantly improved. Israeli researchers at the Beilinson Medical Centre, Petah Tikva, have reported a high success rate in patients with benign enlargements of the prostate.

Infections

An over-active bladder may be a temporary condition brought about by an infection, by some medicine, by constipation or even the mental stress of an emotional upset.

Cystitis is a very common problem for women of all ages. There is a burning sensation on passing water and a feeling of tenderness in the area. Frequent bathing is a must and a course of antibiotics will often cure this condition. During a bout of cystitis, it is better to wear cotton undergarments rather than nylon and skirts rather than tight trousers in order that there should be a better circulation of air.

The Pelvic Bowl

The pelvis is a ring of bones in the lower half of our bodies. It is made up of our hips and lower back. Within this circle, we have the bladder and bowel and, in women, the womb.

The bottom of this bowl-like arrangement is the pelvic floor which has a range of muscles positioned in such a way that it acts as a support. Cup your hands together and you have an idea of the size and thickness of these muscles. The tubes from each of the organs, the bladder, womb and bowels pass through the bands of muscles to reach outside the body. A common reason for the leakage of urine is the inability to adequately control those muscles.

Ordinarily, the muscles squeeze the tubes strongly so that there is no leakage of material. Women have an additional problem because during childbirth, the pelvic muscles must stretch to accommodate the baby's head and long-term weakness may be caused. If you can picture this you are in a better position to understand and combat the weakness. At the time of menopause, as the hormone levels change and women's muscles become thinner, any weakness will become magnified and leakages may occur.

Preventative Measures

We can learn to do exercises which will strengthen the muscles and bring them back to normal and we can ensure that we do not put on weight. When women reach the time of the menopause it might help matters for them to take Hormone Replacement Therapy which has been found to be valuable to many. There were fears in the past about ill-effects from this treatment, but it is now thought that the benefits far outweigh the disadvantages.

Expert Advice

Here is a sample exercise recommended by a consultant to a group of practice nurses, for them to teach to patients.

Sit on a chair, knees apart, arms loosely by your side and lean forward in a relaxed position. Imagine that you need to get to the toilet in a hurry but you are delayed in getting there. Now tighten up both front and back passages, pulling up and in, hard. If there is a feeling of tightening in these areas, then you have found the right muscles. You may find that you are clenching everything, fists, feet, hands, mouth, and pulling hard on the stomach. But this is not the result you want. Concentrate on the right area and relax everything else. Do not get disheartened or discouraged, giving up and saying that you can't manage to do it. You can. We all can. For some it will mean practising for weeks at odd minutes of the day, but you will succeed in the end.

Once you have the muscles identified and can work them at will, hold for a count of four seconds and then slowly, gently release. Repeat at least three times. Do it every hour, on the hour whenever possible. And do it at least ten times a day, standing if you cannot sit. That means your muscles are going to be exercised in the right direction about forty times a day and with this level of correction they will soon be doing their job again. Incontinence will be coming under control and you will experience a real improvement within the next few months.

In a short time, you will be able to do these exercises without anyone being aware that you are doing them. Sitting in the car, in a bus, at a meeting or just standing in a queue. Meanwhile, as long as the condition continues, women should try to wear easily removable clothing so that there is no delay once they get themselves to the loo. Men too, may find that Velcro fastenings are easier to deal with than zips which may catch just at the wrong moment. Practise control before you start to empty, holding on to get those muscles stronger and accustomed to the idea that they can do their job. Give yourself time and once you do start to pass urine be sure that the bladder is properly emptied so that there are no residual drops left to cause irritation.

Maintain Liquid Intake

Don't reduce the amount of liquid you take during the day but regulate it and limit drinking strong tea and coffee. We need a good deal of liquid to keep our insides healthy. Even a moderate level of dehydration is possible when people cut down their liquid intake and it can have the most unpleasant consequences. Don't drink when you know you have to go out. Limit what you have after tea-time, especially alcohol or fruit with a high liquid content such as water melon, which can make you pass water more often.

If you are on special tablets, say water tablets, determine the best time to take them to suit your activities and try not to let anything disturb your night's rest. Your own doctor may have other ideas and you should follow the advice you are given, since this will take into account factors that are relevant to you.

Share the Problem

Don't continue to conceal the problem if you are not getting better. Don't be nervous, help is readily to hand and even if a repair job were to be found necessary, it is a minor thing these days and over in no time.

Medical Check-Ups

Your own doctor will check your urine and may want to refer you to the hospital for a specialist opinion. If the problem turns out to be a simple case of incontinence, arrangements will be made for you to have individual advice and training and you will be supplied with pants and pads if these are thought necessary. There may be a special service for the collection of disposable items in your area.

Therapists may suggest electrical treatment for those whose muscles cannot easily get going again. There are cases when an electrical current may be employed which stimulates the muscle fibre. Once the muscle comes alive, the brain accepts that something can be done and the pelvic muscles can be trained in the ways described previously. There is no danger or pain involved in such treatment.

Remember, incontinence does have some specific cause and is not a natural outcome of normal, healthy living, nor is it an inevitable part of growing older. Never accept that you have to live with it, get it sorted out. We want to have a problem-free old age without worries or cares of a physical nature and should exercise all of our muscles. It is our responsibility to keep them strong and healthy to go on doing their job for life. For independent advice and further information write to the Incontinence Adviser at the Disabled Living Foundation. (See Useful Addresses.)

Constipation

Age is no reason at all for being constipated. Improper diets, insufficient exercise or the lack of personal self-care that comes with depression can cause this condition at any age. It is better and more usual to clear the bowel daily and although some will go twice a day there are others for whom it is quite normal to go three or four times a week. What is important is regularity and that week in week out you maintain the same pattern. Be patient and be sure that you give yourself time, never rushing away before you have allowed the necessary minutes it takes. Laxatives provide a temporary answer but using them regularly only makes the problem worse. A dish of all-bran with some stewed figs or prunes should be help enough for the occasional bout of constipation, which no one should worry about unduly.

Incontinence of faeces is quite another matter. It needs urgent attention and is caused when hard material impacts in the bowel and only liquid faecal material can trickle through. It may be supposed that one has diarrhoea but that is an unmistakably different condition. If there has been no satisfying bowel movement and this leakage occurs, you need your doctor.

The design of our toilets is partly the fault of our problems. We find them easier to sit on and to rise from but physiologically we would be better off if we crouched. Raising the feet on blocks can assist people who find they have difficulty in passing stools.

Haemorrhoids

One outcome of constipation is piles and that can be so agonizing that sufferers put off going to the toilet, so things get worse. 'Anyone who strains while on the toilet', said a medical lecturer, 'is foolish. The effort of straining can damage other organs in the body.' He advocated a change of diet, saying that we need more bran and roughage to keep our digestive systems active, we need to drink more water and take more exercise. He also thought it a good idea to gently pat and massage the stomach and lower back, to help stimulate and activate the bowel. I thought he offered a recipe of sound and sensible advice.

You are being given a message if you suffer haemorrhoids and ignoring it can take you a stage further to more trouble, for example to a split in the back passage and this would require surgery. An operation in this area can be painful, far better to avoid it in the first place, adopt a healthier life-style and do all you can to ensure regularity.

When we retire, we want to have as comfortable a life as possible, with few of the problems outlined in this chapter. We certainly don't want to spend a lot of our time having to cope with these conditions. Keeping in order is the best way to forget all about it.

23 Relaxation and Sleep

Relax and Let Yourself Go

By the time our second daughter, Andrea, was born in 1952, I was enthusiastically into practising relaxation. When the first one, Alexis, had come along a year earlier, I had yelled for help during her birth, not understanding how my failure to relax was keeping muscles tight that should have been loose. A nurse in the recovery ward explained briefly to me what I should have learned, what books I should read and how easy I could make the birth of my next child. I didn't realise then how valuable her advice was to be during my life. Four months later I had mastered the technique of complete relaxation, lying on the floor feeling weightless, mind emptied of thought. A quarter of an hour of this and I would rise as refreshed as though I had just got up from a good night's sleep. I couldn't wait for my next child in order to try it out during the pregnancy and childbirth itself.

The nurse had explained to me that if my abdominal muscles were tight the baby could not get out easily but if I relaxed there would be no problem. Clench your fist and place it against your shoulder, arm muscles tight. Ask someone to try to open your arm while you are holding it clamped. It is not easy, but when the arm muscles are loosened, the arm falls down naturally. That gives you a rough idea of what is happening during childbirth.

There I was in hospital, the midwife telling me to place a mask over my mouth and breathe in the gas and air mixture, while I insisted, 'No, I am perfectly alright'. At last and in irritation she asked, 'Now mother, do you want to feel this baby arrive?' 'Of course I do,' I told her and watched in wonder as our second child's head was presented, one more hard push and she was on the bed. It was all so easy. So it was with our son, David, four years later. I heard my husband telling the maternity staff that the birth was imminent while they assured him that there were still several hours to go. Half-an-hour later he was amused at the frantic hustle as the action speeded up and in no time at all he held our son.

The benefit of learning this relaxation technique greatly increased my capacity for work. From then on I needed far less sleep and was able to take refreshing naps of a few minutes whenever I felt tired, consciously undoing all the tightness, saying, 'Let go, let go.' The extra time I gained was invaluable. While the world sleeps you can get on with jobs that would be endlessly interrupted during the day. If I added up the extra time I have usefully spent awake instead of asleep it would come to years.

Relaxation is of help during periods of pain because if you fight pain you grow more tense, whilst relaxing and letting it wash over you, reduces it. When we hold muscles clenched in any part of our bodies, head, neck, chest, we are reducing the blood supply which can cause discomfort. If you have the opportunity to learn how to relax, take it, it will bring bonuses you will benefit from and enjoy. You will probably never again need sleeping pills.

Did You Sleep Well Last Night

It's a polite question but if you are asked and wish to stay popular don't give chapter and verse about how you woke after two hours and had to get up and then couldn't sleep and so on and so on. You might send your listener to sleep.

As young and busy parents coping with a growing family we may have merited at least seven or eight hours a night. In middle age, we manage on less sleep and as retirees, four or five hours can be quite sufficient. Our habits change and whilst we can enjoy an afternoon rest, our requirement for sleep at night is reduced. Doing little during the day, exercising neither our minds nor our bodies we cannot expect to sleep much at night.

Sleep Patterns

If we understand the pattern of our sleep we can capitalize on that knowledge, extend our time awake and use it to advantage. The usual tendency at night is to fall into an initial light sleep of about twenty minutes, followed by a deeper sleep lasting some fifteen minutes. Next comes that deep, totally 'out-for-the-count' slumber which continues for about an hour. During the last quarter of an hour of this period, although the body is profoundly asleep, the brain is active. The person asleep is subconsciously aware of these changing depths, surfacing to the edge of wakefulness at the end of each period and then subsiding into the next stage. This whole pattern then repeats itself.

Our personal sleep habits may be disturbed by unusual events. We may have stayed up late for a party or have had to care for someone sick during the night. A long journey by air often causes jet-lag and time-changes certainly affect most travellers. As a matter of routine, we are ready for sleep at about the same time every night. However, if we have to go out for some reason, the tiredness may disappear, then we may say, 'I'm wide awake now, yet I was so sleepy before'. But our normal sleep pattern will have been disturbed. If sleep is regularly disrupted, as it is for doctors when they go out on night-calls, an average once or twice a week, a new sleep pattern may replace the old one.

There are dramatic exceptions to sleeping habits. One man who denied that he ever slept at all was subjected to scientific tests which showed that in fact he did not fall into what is regarded as the usual pattern of sleep. He rested but never fell into deep sleep; nevertheless he appeared to be in good health, mentally alert and well-adjusted. There are few such exceptions in this world as was confirmed by Pierre Flauchaire, of the Ecole Centrale in Paris who has made an extensive study on the brain's activity. His findings showed that there is a defined sleeping cycle for us all, man or beast. The single exception he noted was the shark, said to live its entire life-span without sleep, forever wakeful.

As we age, the tendency is to awaken more frequently. At seventy plus, we might expect to wake up four or five times a night for short periods, so that only about four-fifths of the time in bed is actually spent asleep.

Fatigue and Accidents

The wisdom of our years will tell us never to ignore feelings of fatigue, especially when driving. If it is evident that sleepiness is overcoming us, it is safer to find a side road and take a ten minute nap. Anyone who drives on over-tired can risk temporary memory loss and even a form of momentary dementia. The need for sleep can overtake any one, during any activity, coming so suddenly that the mind refuses to work normally. It is better to stop whatever task one is engaged in and take the rest which the system is demanding. Studying or reading can be non-productive if the brain is weary and begging for a short respite.

Lack of Sleep

What are the main worries about sleep or lack of it? One concern is waking often, another the inability to get to sleep easily. If there is a change in habit and a new pattern of breathing, sleeping and waking occurs, consider whether there is a reason, perhaps a catarrhal problem or some other physical condition. A post-nasal drip into the throat and on to the chest can be irritating and cause coughing which brings one awake. One way to determine if the lack of sleep is serious is to consider what the days are like. If your days are enjoyable, if you get along well with people and achieve all that you want to, then there can be no major problems. But if you feel irritable and out of sorts, try eating your evening meal earlier, take a walk instead of sitting reading or watching TV and see if you don't sleep better.

Help may be needed to determine reasons for changes in sleep patterns. Has there been a recent shock, a newly prescribed medicine, a change in life-style? If self-help does not work and there is no improvement then see your GP.

What does your partner think of your sleep habits? Do they find that you sometimes awake with a choking sound, coughing to clear your throat, then falling asleep again, unaware by morning that anything untoward has happened? Do they feel that you are tired despite an apparently good night's sleep? If you both find this worrying, it could be checked out, possibly by an all-night study called a polysomnogram. If sleep is regularly disturbed, then this may be the reason for weariness or fatigue during the daytime. You need to be warm at night but also to have some fresh air and try not to go to bed to read or to watch television. Go to bed to sleep.

Night-time restlessness may be due to a condition known as nocturnal myoclonus, with jerking movements of the legs and arms. If this disturbs you or your partner, advice should be sought because it can be successfully treated.

Narcolepsy is a rare problem which can run in families and more commonly affects younger people. Sufferers fall asleep suddenly, without warning. It might be any time, any place, driving, at a meeting or during a romantic interlude. Help for this condition is provided by stimulant medication and by spacing naps throughout the daytime waking hours to counteract the sleepiness.

Apnoea

Apnoea is a condition in which breathing is shallow or momentarily ceases during sleep. There are various reasons why it happens and two are important. The neurons of the central nervous system which signal impulses to the respiratory muscles temporarily fail to function, as happens with polio victims. Or, there may be a failure to get air through the pharynx at the back of the throat and so into the lungs. As many as 25 per cent of those above the age of sixty-five may have this condition to some degree. If it should develop, then a stiff drink at bedtime is not the answer and might be harmful.

An American professor of psychiatry, Dr Hartmann, has studied sleep patterns for twenty-five years. He tells of one patient, a lawyer, who developed bouts of apnoea, incorrectly attributing it to premature ageing and therefore thinking it incurable. In fact, the doctor was able to prescribe medication which successfully overcame the problem. It may not always be so easy to cure but if you believe this is your problem, let the doctor know about it.

Feeling Low and Depressed

Do not feel dejected because you are feeling more sleepy than you used to and assume that nothing can be done about it. In most cases it can be so much improved by altering life-style, increasing the range of interests, taking regular exercise that people feel better than they have felt in years. Daytime sleepiness should not be confused with Alzheimer's Disease, although it is a symptom of that disease.

Depression is a partner to lack of sleep and if you notice that you or someone close to you is exhibiting symptoms of depression and fatigue but still cannot sleep, then outside advice may be indicated. Anyone could need help who shows an unaccustomed lack of interest in what is going on around them, in their personal appearance and with unexplained loss of weight or decreasing pride and care within the home. No one should dismiss these signals or take sleeping pills as a long-term palliative. Patients often benefit more from a talk with a member of the surgery team than they do from a prescription. At times drugs are necessary and we can be thankful for them; however, sleeping pills when taken over long periods can cause daytime drowsiness, be habit forming and withdrawal can mean misery.

Sedatives and Stimulants

As we grow older, drugs, and in particular sedatives, may have more effect on us and those which were once effective for only a few hours may continue to produce a calming effect into the next day. Let the doctor or pharmacist know about all the medicines you are taking, including anything bought over the counter since the collective effect could be harmful.

Caffeine

If falling asleep is difficult then limit coffee, tea or any other stimulating, caffineated drink to the mornings only. A wake-up cup of coffee is a good idea but several cups throughout the day can produce jittery nerves and a hyped-up person. I love a cup of fresh coffee but after a second cup I feel distinctly unwell and so I limit myself to one a day. The effects of caffeine can last for many hours so be moderate and you won't go far wrong.

For most of us alcohol induces drowsiness but it can cause you to wake up after only two or three hours of sleep. Never take alcohol and medicine together. The unpredictable interaction of these is well documented and the effects are potentially harmful, particularly for the older person.

Natural Sleep

Regular habits are best since the body likes to work to a recognizable routine. Rising, bathing, eating, taking exercise, going to bed, all should be done to a regular programme. Ideally, we should find the bedtime that suits us best. Try going to sleep at the same hour each day, in a quiet room at a comfortable temperature, perhaps taking a light snack and a warm, milky drink. Mothers used to favour this for their children and it was not such a bad idea. It is now known that milk contains tryptophan, producing a chemical called serotonin which takes about twenty minutes to induce sleep. A warm bath is comforting, increasing the blood flow and helping one to relax so that sleep comes more readily. We need fresh air but ensure that open windows do not jeopardize your security. Warm the bed by all means but I would never recommend getting in a bed with an electric blanket left switched on. What is unhelpful is to change routine or to go to bed just after a heavy meal.

Sexual intercourse at bedtime is a fine exercise, decreasing tension and distancing anxieties. Masturbation produces a similar reaction and if it offers comfort and satisfies a need there should certainly be no guilt attached.

The Daytime Doze

There is nothing wrong in taking a refreshing doze but constant daytime sleepiness may be due to a lack of oxygen which can produce extreme tiredness. What is then essential is a brisk walk in the fresh air or at least some deep breathing by an open window. Check that rooms are not over-heated and are well ventilated, obviously we cannot be at our best breathing stale air.

Long spells of daytime dozing may occur in the extremely elderly but should not be habitual to anyone in their sixties, seventies or eighties. Some of my ninety-year-old friends are quite outraged at being termed very elderly, it is all a question of attitude. They are energetic and youthful and if they felt sleepy during the day would be wondering what was wrong. We can form bad habits, winding ourselves right down by doing less and less and this leads to lassitude. To counteract such drowsiness try to introduce a little more activity into the day.

Natural Movements in Sleep

During sleep, movement is reduced and breathing slows but we still move about constantly, shifting position and turning over. Under closed eyelids our eyes move and occasionally breathing is irregular. At intervals there is rapid eye movement, the body systems increase in activity and it is at this time that dreams occur which are sufficiently dramatic to be memorable. We may call out, speak as though awake or even sleep walk. This is when men of any age may experience an erection and women may find that there is an increased warmth in the vagina. Dr Charles Fisher and his colleagues at Mount Sinai Hospital in New York City observed a number of men in their nineties who, despite their age, had average patterns of erection when asleep.

We are often busy as we sleep, our minds coping with the problems we are occupied with during the day. It may help to offer them to our subconscious selves to sort out for us. When we awake at the end of a cycle, we must be ready to record any ideas. So, keep pencil and paper handy and notes can be taken down straight away. Some people awake to find their midnight scribblings are of no use at all but many of us find them valuable.

Tired or Bored

The need for sleep is expressed quite clearly and is usually difficult to conceal. Frequent yawning, a loss of concentration, boredom with conversation, these herald a powerful urge to drop off to sleep. A few deep breaths of fresh air or some tensing and release of muscles may help us to stay awake. But if such impulses occur at night and we go straight to bed, we may get a better night's sleep. If we allow ourselves to fall asleep in a chair, we may have that deep sleep then and should not expect to sleep so well once we do go to bed.

Getting more Done

People in all walks of life feel that they have too much to accomplish to spend a large slice of the twenty-four hour day lost in sleep. They work until late and rise early, accomplishing a great deal at night with no telephone calls, no doorbells, nor any meals to prepare. During a normal life-span our sleeping time could be decreased so as to provide as much as an additional five or six years of alert and wide-awake time. More time to spend reading, writing, going places, on hobbies or with friends.

Distracting Noises

We should try to do something about noises which prevent us from sleeping. There are heavy sleepers who nothing can disturb, others sleep lightly and are awakened by the least sound. Airplanes, traffic, noisy neighbours or birdsong, they can all be aggravating when we are trying to sleep. But the noise which some people find more maddening than any other would appear to be that of a snoring partner. No one deliberately snores but what can be done about this very common practice and why does it happen? There are many ideas offered to help cure this problem and your doctor may have the right answer. One recent innovation has been designed by scientists in Chicago and consists of a device which is a tube placed between the lips and which holds the tongue forward. The designers claim that it is a certain cure for snoring.

It would be a boon to many a marriage. But I like best the comment of one woman whose husband snored. 'When I hear it I know where he is and that he is enjoying a good sleep and it sends me off to sleep too.'

24 The Key to Good Health

A Partnership

The key to good health lies in our taking an equal part in our health care. Health is such a precious commodity that it is a wonder we do not all treat it with more respect, doing all we can to preserve it. But the fact is that most people do what they want to do regardless of whether it is good for their health or not. Inviting life-threatening illnesses doesn't seem to bother those who persist in unwise life-styles. Even when serious illness hits, as soon as we are well many of us slip back into the habits we are fond of, ill-advised though these may be. We're only human after all and no one has an infallible recipe for health. Basic common-sense is as much as I would ask of anyone. That, and a reminder that being old does not equate with being ill.

Over the age of retirement or not, are you really as fit as you would like to be? Are you keen to learn how you might improve your health, anxious to eat food that will do you good and ready to work hard exercising your way to a more active life? Even at seventy-five and more, those who have followed advice about how to be healthier have improved their state of fitness.

An aim of good government is to raise the standard of health for everyone but a substantial part of that responsibility must lie with individuals themselves. We of retirement age will recall when the Beveridge Report was published in our youth, during the 1940s and the emotion with which we received the news that we were to have a comprehensive health service, free to all. It was thought at that time that the provision of such a service would result in a population having a standard of fitness so high that the use of the service would lessen. It did not take long to realise that this would not happen. Demands grew and self-dependency reduced. Even when it was scientifically confirmed that poor habits damage health, the public failed to respond in the estimated numbers, expecting that however they chose to live and whatever happened, the health service would take care of them. Now however, that tendency has begun to reverse, there is a growing emphasis on healthy life-styles with the expectation and hope that this will produce less demand on health services.

Expectations of better health care for the disadvantaged among the population, including the very elderly, will continue to rise; they have many problems and are owed special support. But the idea that the community in general should continue to be so dependent on medical attention, so demanding of a treatment to cure any and every ailment, cannot be right.

No one anticipated that demand would rise at such a rate and that with research constantly producing expensive new procedures and drugs, those demands would continue to spiral. Transplantation of hearts, lungs and livers is becoming commonplace and if there were more donors the numbers would be even higher. That is wonderful, but it also means a big bill for drugs and nursing care.

We may know what the charge is to bring out an electrician, a washing machine engineer or a plumber but there are few people, even in the health service itself, who know precisely about health costs. What does it cost to call a doctor out, to have a hip operation or to provide essential life-long drugs? Measuring these services in terms of money is far from easy but it has to be done. We do want a health service which offers comprehensive care but it all has to come out of a given budget and even in the richest of countries, some control has to be exercised. Patients must have necessary treatment and medication but too often they will visit their doctors ready to demand a prescription or a referral which the doctor, for good clinical reasons, is reluctant to provide.

You and your Doctor

Most people sign on with a general practitioner who is nearest to where they live, often without investigating the services offered or that particular GP's qualifications. Everyone should exercise more care in their choice and find out something about the doctor to whom they will entrust their future health care. Surgeries now have leaflets which give detailed information about the doctors, their teams of health workers and the various clinics they offer, including hours of opening. If there is a choice of surgeries in your area, make enquiries so that you choose the one best suited to your requirements. If you have been registered with a doctor for many years and have a good relationship then there is every reason to stay put. Find out if there is a Patient Association at the surgery which helps in offering ideas for improvement and even raises money to improve surgery facilities. You have a part to play in making your surgery one of the best. Don't just sit back and grumble about the premises or the service you get, take a positive role.

If you have not visited the surgery for some time, staff will be interested to see you and check you over to ensure that you are in good health. It is better for your doctor to see you when you are well so that he can appreciate the difference if you should happen to fall ill.

I could sympathize with Megan, a bustling cheerful woman always ready to help out anyone, who at sixty-six and over the course of a few months contracted a mystery illness. She hated 'Giving in' and going to her doctor who she had not seen in years. Thinking it was 'some bug or virus' she tried resting and getting to bed earlier but she felt no better. Her friends were worried and persuaded her to go to the doctor who, in her view, thought that she was exaggerating the illness and told her that she had been overdoing things and that at her age she should be taking things easy. 'I'm not old,' she said. 'Why should my energy suddenly disappear all in a few months?' The doctor did finally, and Megan thought sceptically, make arrangements for further tests. It turned out that she had hypo-thyroidism, a disease with the kind of symptoms which make it difficult to diagnose with certainty. The loss of energy, tiredness and feeling of cold which Megan had experienced could have been attributed to a number of diseases. With correct medication she began to feel much better and although she suffered lapses and had to take things a bit easier she was determined to be well and this positive attitude helped in her recovery. When Megan finally felt better and showed something of her previous healthy sparkle the doctor was quite astonished at the improvement. Had he known her previously he would have recognised how ill she had been at the outset.

Frank is another patient who had not visited his doctor in twenty years since he turned sixty and thought it was best to 'steer clear of them'. During an accident he received a blow to the ribs and despite the hot baths and liniment rubs the pain became so severe that he reluctantly visited his woman doctor and came away full of respect and gratitude. 'She was great. Gave me a thorough MOT and said I was OK except that through this knock I had shock shingles, whatever that is. Gave me some painkillers and a few weeks later I was right as rain.' Frank wondered whether he should buy her a bunch of flowers. Why ever not; such gestures help to make a doctor feel appreciated and they are as human as anyone, perhaps more so.

In going through their list of patients, one surgery found a couple aged over seventy-five who they had never seen since their registration several years previously. Ernest and Margery were surprised to receive a telephone call from the practice nurse asking if she could call and see them. They were suspicious but she promised to write to them and explain that she wanted to be assured that they were fit and well and finally they agreed that she could call. It was found that Margery bore stoically with a painful hip and arrangements were made for her to attend some physiotherapy sessions which gave her much relief. Surgeries too, must play their full part in the health care of their patients.

Establishing a good GP/patient relationship is one important step towards health and in this partnership each has a role to play. Doctors are well trained, knowledgeable and keep up-to-date with post-graduate education. Their surgeries should be modern, bright and inviting and they should offer clinics which encourage the promotion of health. Patients, for their part should be reasonable in their demands. For example, your doctor cannot be expected to come to the telephone at a moment's notice but you should ask when it is convenient for you to call back so that you can talk together. Write down your symptoms and requests so that you don't take over long in thinking about them when you have the doctor's attention. Go to the surgery for a consultation unless you are really too ill to come out. If your own doctor is not available, it is quite reasonable that you should see a partner or assistant in the practice. They are fully qualified. In case you have to be examined, wear clothes that are easy to get in and out of and never demand prescriptions or referrals to hospital. State your reasons for your requests reasonably and let your doctor advise you. Remember, your doctor can require the Family Health Services Authority to remove your name from the practice list if they believe the relationship has broken down or they consider you to be unsuited to their practice. They do not have to state reasons. If, however, you are dissatisfied with your treatment you may go to another doctor and ask if they will take you on. If you are unable to get acceptance then the Family Health Services Authority is empowered to require a doctor to take you on for a minimum period. In my experience this usually turns into a long-term and satisfactory association.

You and your Dentist

It is equally important for you to choose your dentist with care. Some will work solely within the NHS, some will only do private treatment and others may give you a choice of either. Whichever you opt for, find a dentist who is progressive, well thought of and whose surgery looks bright and hygienic. Establish whether you are going to receive National Health Service for which you will have part of the treatment without charge or private care for which you will pay the entire bill. You should always make it clear in advance that you want an estimate of the cost and make a note of what it is at the time. You are in no position to argue when your mouth is open and the dental care is begun. Don't stint on your dental care, your personal appearance matters very much. Make regular use of the hygienist who can remove plaque and stains and help you to keep your teeth looking nice. People retain their teeth far longer these days. Should they require attention but cannot be filled they can usually be capped and while this is an expensive treatment many will prefer it to having dentures. Getting the best possible care for your teeth can be a good reason for dipping into savings. Those on low incomes will get dental care free on the health service.

Use the Pharmacist

Your pharmacist is an under-used source of expertise, well-versed in health-care and aware of the action and interaction of drugs. Take advantage of this when you next visit your local pharmacy. The pharmacist may be able to arrange for you to talk quietly and privately about any problem you have with medication rather than discussing it more publicly over the counter.

Going into Hospital

Admission to hospital is usually preceded by an explanation of all that will happen. Once in the ward, an examination is standard no matter what the reason for entering. Obviously, the hospital staff need a good deal of information about you so be prepared to answer their questions. You may be taken off drugs if doctors have to assess your reactions or if they want you to try something different so you should let hospital staff have all your medicines as soon as you go in. If you have never been an in-patient before, the routine may seem strict but there is a lot of work to get through. As much as everyone wants their hospital to seem like a pleasant hotel, there are limits and there must be strict regulations and discipline. Seriously-ill people are being cared for and staff time is very precious. Patients must be woken at early hours for ablutions, meals, medication and treatment and by the time doctors arrive for ward visits all must be shipshape and orderly. If you have had an operation you will be got up as soon as possible, not only because vacant beds are always in demand but because this is best for you and could help prevent other medical problems. Co-operate with your hospital staff, take your physiotherapist's advice and you will be out and about in the least possible time.

The standard of service is generally very high throughout the NHS and complaints are comparatively few. But the public today is better informed and more likely to question the actions and decisions of professionals, which they would once have accepted without question. It is not unusual to come across complaints about rudeness or arrogance but these are held not to be a breach of contractual duty. It must be remembered that there are limits to the kind of complaints which health authorities can hear and when anyone suffers injury, damage or loss through medical negligence the law must be studied in order to decide whether there has been a breach of the duty of care owed by the medical staff involved. Patients often feel aggrieved by the guarded responses they receive as a result of their complaints but the medical profession is cautious and alert to the possibility of litigation. The patient often only wants to have an explanation about why something occurred and this would be likely to satisfy them. However, once complaints have been officially lodged, a proportion of cases will come before a court, some rightly but some needlessly. Annually, a number of cases of complaint result in considerable damages being awarded. Professions have their own strict rulings about the behaviour of their members who can be struck off lists and denied the right to practise if found guilty.

The Future of the NHS

Modern technology makes possible treatment and cures undreamt of a few decades ago. Operations which were too dangerous to contemplate are becoming matters of routine because so much information is available and in such a wealth of detail. Even in brain surgery, neurosurgeons know exactly where they must probe to produce the results they want to achieve. Tiny tumours can be recognized at a very early stage and removed to effect a cure when a few years ago the death of the patient would have been highly likely.

New and simpler operations supersede difficult procedures with less danger to patients and even cancer is no longer regarded with anything like the fear that it used to be. Many cancers can be cured whilst numerous others can be treated and held in remission for years. As one example, scientists at the Imperial Cancer Research laboratories have recently used computer graphics to help them in their pursuit of cures for cancer and their research leads them to believe that they could prevent the uncontrolled growth of breast cancer cells. They would do this by exploiting the new knowledge they have gained about amino acids and which would, in effect, instruct the cells to cease their growth.

Much remains to be discovered about osteoporosis but new knowledge and preventative steps will reduce the prevalence of this condition. People will become aware of how much they can do to escape it, thus avoiding much misery and illness and consequently very considerable expense to the NHS. Osteoporosis happens as the result of the loss of calcium and protein from our bones faster than these can be replaced. Bones then become fragile, brittle and weak and in this state they break easily. Patients already suffering from the condition are now told how they can halt further deterioration and hopefully even restore bone loss. Women are much more commonly affected than men because of the hormonal changes after the menopause or following hysterectomy.

Whatever discoveries lie ahead they will mean that more resources must be poured into the NHS to finance them. And however much goes in, more will be wanted. One resource which is under-exploited is our own determination to be healthy. We should use it more often, especially in our older years, as a magical key to good health.

Our health service has endured for more than forty years, the envy of the world. It is something to be proud of and it will continue as a model instrument in providing health care to the community. Despite the efficiency of the NHS and for many reasons, the view has grown that there is room for private health care to run in parallel. Many people who can afford it, and in particular those of us who are retired, may well decide that they prefer to make an additional contribution and so widen their choice of care and treatment.

25 Private Health Care

Who Needs It?

Although at present some four-fifths of our population still rely upon the NHS to look after them when they fall ill, an increasing number of people, many of them retired, elect to 'go private' for at least part of their health care. Because many worry about the lack of choice they may have if they need care in hospital, they take out some form of health insurance as a precaution and a safeguard.

Private or NHS Doctors?

The national primary health care service is a very popular one and few patients find fault with their NHS general practitioners, their GPs. They like the principle whereby they can have a walk-in service or obtain an appointment within a day or two for consultations and have easy open access to surgery teams for treatment and advice when they need it. It is a well liked and efficiently run comprehensive service operated by caring doctors. These are independent contractors working single-handedly or with partners and supported by well-trained staff.

For people who prefer a private service there is an alternative. There are a number of doctors who elect to be in private practice, working on their own account or in partnership; there are other doctors who work for private health companies.

Patients who go to private doctors are charged for consultations and prescriptions must be paid for separately. Patients who register with a private health company either pay for consultation and treatment when they go to see their doctor or get a home visit, or else they can contract to pay an annual rate which includes the cost of their consultations. They then pay additionally for extras such as home visits, pathology, X-rays and, of course, medication. Private companies will also offer a range of services to people not registered with them, the fee charged being dependent upon the check-up or treatment required.

The Hospital Savings Association

The HSA will accept enrolment from anyone under the age of sixty-six who is in good health at the time of joining. This non-profit making organization (see Useful Addresses) offers limited cash payments whenever hospital or nursing home care is needed, either in this country or in Europe. It can also make payment towards such items as optical tests and spectacles or contact lenses, dental treatment and dentures or private physiotherapy bills.

Take some Cover

Insurance companies offer widely differing ranges of health cover to those approaching retirement age, with particular regard to the needs of this group. Insurers will stipulate health standards for those who wish to take out policies. If you decide to take out private insurance you should go to an independent agent who can advise impartially about which type of policy is the most suitable. The best cover will allow you a choice of consultants and hospitals and may be linked with life insurance, having a surrender value should it be necessary or desirable to cancel the policy. Special cover overseas to specified countries is provided by some policies and may include transfer costs to the hospital nearest to where the patient is staying. If need be, and dependent upon the terms of the policy, insurance companies allow repatriation costs to the UK under medical supervision. This can be a very comforting thought when you are ill or injured if local facilities are inadequate. Hospitals and nursing homes abroad may not have the kind of equipment or standards of medical care which we tend to take for granted in this country.

Some policies will give you cover for any illness for which you need treatment once you have paid the first premium. Some will not cover existing illnesses immediately but may give cover after a qualifying period of perhaps two years. Others will allow protection for almost anything after a qualifying period of only a few months. There are certain exceptions where the cost of care can become extremely high and you should contact your insurance company when consultants recommend treatment, in order to be sure that you have cover for this particular procedure. The amount and type of cover you can get in any one year may be limited so do read the small print before you decide to sign a contract. The extent of cover is strictly related to the cost so check it out, understand exactly what protection you are paying for.

Prompt Treatment

The NHS is at its best for those needing accident or emergency services but for the treatment which is not of an immediate and urgent nature there are often waiting lists. It is the idea of having to wait for an operation which prompts some people to take out insurance so that they are more or less guaranteed immediate treatment. Often, private ambulance cover is available too, which many would regard as worthwhile. For all sorts of reasons, instead of NHS hospitals, people might prefer the seclusion and solitude which some private hospitals can provide. You might find *en suite* bathrooms, as well as the more hotel-like services and luxury touches of carpeted rooms, soft lighting and designer decoration. Visiting hours are usually much less rigid and meals can be offered to visitors. Efforts are being made to raise the standards of food in hospitals everywhere but private establishments have to provide the kind of amenities which will attract custom and they generally manage more exotic menus and wider choice. Good food can certainly raise morale and patients react favourably to interesting and well-presented meals.

There are few people who could afford such standards of opulence and this kind of personal care and treatment out of their income or even capital. Costs escalate rapidly and charges can amount to considerable sums within a relatively short period of time. No matter how secure people may feel, if they do have to dip into their pockets to pay for health care, savings can melt away like the snow in spring and financial security disappears.

While the medical care in some private hospitals may be very good, matching the standards found in NHS hospitals, it may not be so good in others. You should be assured that you will get medical treatment of a high standard before you agree to become an in-patient.

Hospital consultants may choose to work wherever they wish and frequently have contracts with NHS hospitals as well as private ones. Patients on waiting lists for operations and who have private health insurance may be advised to go to a private hospital where they can see the consultant of their choice and receive necessary treatment earlier. Other medical staff are usually NHS trained and with post-graduate experience in that service, before electing to go into the private sector.

Look for High Standards

Private hospitals are profit-motivated businesses. They are generally equipped with the most up-to-date facilities, able for example, to take complex X-rays and with operating theatres designed to cope with advanced surgery of all kinds. Many have hi-tech diagnostic facilities equal to those found in the best of NHS hospitals, including CAT scanners and pathology laboratories. Their staff are highly qualified and regularly take post-graduate education to ensure that they remain in touch with the latest of methods. Be sure that the private hospital or nursing home that you are going to is highly recommended, well-equipped and with expert staff.

Most private hospitals also offer health screening for both men and women, using a wide range of tests designed to detect disease in the earliest stages. Admission to a private hospital is usually through the patient's own GP who will refer to a specialist when hospital care or treatment is thought to be necessary.

What to take with you

Those who have never been in-patients in any hospital can find it a daunting experience to have to look forward to, whether going privately or not. Take the minimum of things with you, there is generally very little space in a hospital room or locker and friends or relatives may be asked to take your clothing and unnecessary articles home with them. Bring your own soap, towels, face-flannels if you prefer, although these will be provided. You will need a dressing gown and slippers to wear when up and about. Both men and women should spoil themselves with favourite toiletries to take in to hospital. Pleasantly perfumed soap, fragrant talcum powder and body lotions make you feel good as well as taking away that antiseptic smell which is necessarily common to most hospitals. Take a book or two in with you, preferably paperbacks – a hardback can be heavy to hold when you are feeling fragile and lying down in bed. Be sure that you make the most of the luxury of being taken care of, it doesn't last long.

Is Choice Desirable

The idea of choice between NHS or private treatment for those who can afford it may still be opposed by some people but the ideological arguments are lessening. People have the right to spend their discretionary income or their capital as they please. I could wish that NHS health care and conditions in hospital would overall not only be very good but of such a high level that no one would be interested in private health care. That is unlikely ever to be, given that luxury hotel standards, in conjunction with the best of medical attention, are considered important and desired by so many. Nevertheless, we can continue to feel justifiably proud and confident in our NHS which, in all its branches, offers an enviable standard of medical care.

Many of today's retirement groups are affluent, wanting freedom of choice when they need medical attention and well able to afford it. The retired sector is encouraged to buy the protection which its members feel suits their needs and they can now get tax relief on health-related insurance premiums. This is another reason why the private health-care industry is growing so rapidly, preparing to cope with the expected increase in demand.

We don't have a choice about being ill but if we can choose where to be ill, why should we not do so? What is your preference? My choice is the NHS. I can relax in a big ward, undisturbed by surrounding activity. Much as I may love my friends and relatives, I like the idea of limited visiting so that I can be undistracted for a period of time, particularly if I am feeling unsociable. And when I feel better, I personally like meeting the other patients on a ward, hearing about their interesting lives and families. And, I like being allowed, when up and about, to remember my nursing training and help in the ward duties.

26 Complementary Treatment

Complementary health care is a term which reasonably describes what we call 'natural' or 'alternative' treatments. These are diverse and outside the mainstream of conventional health care, but most utilize the self-healing powers of the body. These treatments have always had their ardent followers and are increasingly popular, research indicating that as many as 14 per cent of the population have consulted complementary practitioners. That is a lot of people, approaching 8 million.

There are over 100 complementary healthcentres ranged across the country, in each of which a number of alternative therapists have combined to offer clients a choice of treatment. Apart from these centres, there are many practitioners who work single-handed or in partnership. In all, it is estimated that there may be as many as 60,000 alternative health therapists operating in the country. A variety of skills are offered and some of them are briefly described here. Libraries have books about each of these therapies should you wish to learn more about them.

There is a degree of mystique surrounding many of the treatments which are available and which promise better health. Some aim to improve or cure individual conditions, others offer techniques which promise a whole new way of life. The British Medical Association is rightly reserved in its views and cannot sanction any discipline which is not scientifically proven. Orthodox medical doctors go through many years of study, have a great deal of experience before they qualify and enjoy well-deserved high regard. The medical profession must remain concerned that any treatment should offer bona fide help and that the public are not being misled by charlatans. Therapies need to be validated if they are ever to be fully accepted by the mainstream of the profession.

There will be more protection for the British patient when the European Community directives are enforced. These will call for at least three years full-time training for all 'medical practitioners', conventional or otherwise.

There is an increasing acceptance of certain treatments: acupuncture, chiropractic and osteopathy are among those which a proportion of doctors do approve of and for which some private medical insurance will allow cover. Either these doctors learn and use these special skills themselves or they send their patients to trusted practitioners.

Many of our ills are self-limiting and it follows that some treatments will be credited with a cure which would have happened anyway. However, I have known many cases where individuals do seem to have been helped by alternative treatment and I do, therefore, always keep an open mind about any claims. It is perhaps understandable that on occasions, when people find that ordinary medicine fails to cure them, they turn to other forms of help. They may hear from family, friends or neighbours of some cure or improvement that was obtained. Others do not wish to take medicines and look for a more natural way to better health.

Remember always that any one who feels ill or suffers with high blood pressure, a heart condition or other serious ailment should seek approval from their doctor before undertaking alternative treatment.

Acupuncture

Two thousand years ago acupuncture was practised in China where today it is still often used as the sole anaesthetic so that the risks and post-operative effects associated with general anaesthetics are avoided.

Acupuncture is now a recognized treatment in this country for the relief of pain and it is claimed that certain conditions can be relieved, possibly cured. It offers, too, preventive treatment since it is said to build up energy levels. Once relief is obtained, it can last for varying periods and if symptoms do return then further treatment promises a good response.

Acupuncture involves the insertion of sterile, stainless steel needles into the skin at strategic places known as trigger points and some practitioners obtain an enhanced response by the use of an attached electric stimulator. A recent innovation has been the use of soft laser beams. It may take anything between four to ten treatments to obtain alleviation of pain. If this has not been achieved by the end of the fourth treatment this method of treatment is unlikely to succeed.

Alexander principles

This method of teaching a philosophy about living a new way, using our bodies differently, reflects in better health and looks. Teachers show how to change the habitual pattern of movement and bearing, demonstrating how their methods can relieve many problems such as muscular tension, arthritis and backache as well as mental stress. It is also useful in rehabilitation following injuries through accident.

Allergies

Allergies can mimic most physical illnesses, causing problems as serious as any they imitate. They can also trigger off emotional disorders. Allergic reactions to substances can cause just about any symptom, too much like the real thing for comfort. These lead at times to incorrect diagnosis and treatment.

A number of ills are caused by an inability to cope with certain chemicals, foods and additives. We may react with arthritic-like symptoms, an ordinary headache or a splitting migraine, stomach ache or an irritable bowel. The notion that an intolerance to food or any other substance can cause illness is not a new one. We probably all know of someone who will say that they cannot abide a certain food because it brings them out in spots or makes them feel ill. Some react badly to chemical odours, traffic fumes or to cigarette smoke.

An allergy can be taken to mean an altered or abnormal reaction by the body, either externally or internally, following exposure to some food or chemical. Dr Richard MacKarness in his book, *Not All In The Mind* was able to show how he cured a number of patients with severe mental disorders by identifying and removing offending substances from their environment or diet. Many say that their own illness has been found to be rooted in some hitherto unsuspected allergic reaction to a particular element. Once this was removed, the condition improved.

Dr Jean Monro has had success with a number of cases involving allergic problems and her clinic in Hemel Hempstead receives patients from all over the country. Dr Monro says that with many more new chemical compounds around, it is scarcely surprising that people must absorb some of them and will suffer in so doing.

A great deal more is now known about the ill-effects of food additives and some chemical elements. Many people are addicted to the very substances which cause them to feel ill, for example, tobacco and alcohol or perhaps tea, coffee or fruit juice. Patients can be tested by a doctor or trained staff member at an allergy clinic to determine this.

Allergies are not always easy to discover. One simple test suggested is to abstain from a suspect food or element for a few days. Before exposure to or eating the substance, take the pulse rate. Then, either take or sniff the substance or place some under the tongue. The pulse rate should be measured again after ten minutes and once more after half-an-hour. An increased pulse rate may indicate that there has been an adverse reaction. Do give voice to suspicions about allergies to your own GP to whom any recurring symptoms should be referred.

Aromatherapy

Aromatic oils, we are told, each have their particular uses. Practitioners will select from as many as forty or fifty to use separately or in groups to produce improvements or cures.

They are applied with deep and prolonged massage lasting up to two hours at a time. It is a pleasant treatment, both soothing and relaxing. At Charing Cross Hospital, massage has been used with some success to reduce tension in suitable cases, some of them elderly patients with heart conditions.

Cancer Treatment Centres

Many cancers are successfully treated, especially if they are diagnosed early and it is important to be able to recognize symptoms and get a doctor's advice. The importance of simple and fresh food and a healthy life-style is stressed by cancer treatment centres where cures for some cancers have been claimed.

Chiropractors

The British Chiropractors Association defines chiropractic as 'concerned with the diagnosis and treatment of mechanical disorders of joints, particularly spinal joints and their effects on the nervous system'. It is based on the belief that many medical problems stem from the spine and can be treated with massage and manipulation. If one is to judge by the full waiting rooms of, and the praise accorded to, the practitioners of chiropractic, the treatment must have resulted in a successful outcome for many.

Faith Healing

Faith healing must be distinguished from spiritual or psychic healing. The first is really assisting a person to marshal their willpower and energy to use their self-healing capacity. The second needs no action or faith on the part of a patient, it involves the transference of some kind of energy which can be felt as heat from the healer. The ability to perform psychic healing is looked upon as a gift, some discovering it in themselves by accident, others developing it from a deep desire to help others. Healing may be claimed to be done through an entity previously of this world. The nature of this therapy is mysterious, but during healing, Kirlian photographs have been taken which reveal flares invisible to the eye. This type of electrophotography, when properly done, records a bio-energetic aura. Healers claim that some disorders give off radiations which are perceivable to a sensitive healer.

Absent healing is carried out through prayer and is not limited to human beings. It has been shown to be successful with animals in scientifically conducted experiments. An analysis of brainwave patterns shows that healers and clairvoyants show similarities of patterns while they are practising their abilities.

Graphology

Medical graphologists claim that handwriting can not only reveal character but can say a lot about the writer's health. The theory is that different parts of the body correspond with the way letters are formed in handwriting and irregularities will indicate ailments or disorders. It is claimed that these can be identified by the trained graphologist.

One practitioner is Maureen Ward who has a weekly radio phone-in programme and regularly confounds listeners with her apt diagnoses from samples of writing. She explained that illness is often diagnosed by this method even before any symptoms have been felt. Treatment is offered by means of written exercises.

Herbal Medicine

Plants are used as the base for many of the drugs manufactured today and herbal remedies come from the same source, but the latter are said to produce less reactive responses and are considered to be more 'natural'. They are also said to purify body systems in a way that no other therapy is able to do. Practitioners have to acquire a knowledge of herbs and their different powers. Many plants such as aloe vera, garlic and valerian are familiar to households for their qualities of healing of wounds, fighting bacteria and for sedative effect. Among many favourites, ginseng, royal jelly and honey are held to be exceptional and effective in sustaining health and retarding age.

Homoeopathy

Homoeopathic doctors are medically qualified in addition to being trained in this branch of medicine. Homoeopathic treatment has developed from the idea that cures can be effected by administering tiny, diluted doses of substances.

Hypnotism

The trained hypnotist hopes to induce complete relaxation in the patient and so reach the subconscious. In this way the mind can be persuaded to reject ills and take positive steps to gain health. Hypnotism is also used to help reduce pain and to cure addictive habits, such as smoking, excessive eating and drinking alcohol.

Ionisers

These portable machines manufacture and release into the air electrically-charged particles known as negative ions which freshen the air, allowing easier breathing and are recommended for people who have chest problems and hay fever. They are said to relieve tension and reduce stress levels.

Iridology

Iridologists claim that marks and colour changes in eyes can assist in diagnosing certain conditions, present or potential. An early practitioner, a physician, was accused of being a quack and his defence was an accurate analysis of his accuser's medical history. While this form of alternative treatment has not yet had full scientific trials there are doctors who believe that it could be a useful adjunct to orthodox diagnosis.

Naturopathy

Students of this method of life-style eschew all forms of medicines, drugs or invasive treatment such as surgery. People are recommended to eat fresh, additive-free food and not to smoke or drink alcohol. Moderate exercise, swimming and walking are advised and exposing the body to sun and air is all part of the recommended way of life. Naturopaths are concerned with treatment of the whole body and not with separate ills. They need to know about basic mineral and metal content and could for example use hair analysis to determine levels of these substances. If levels are toxic they will prescribe a method of purification.

Osteopathy

The function of the osteopath is to treat pain by manipulating joints. In the hands of an experienced practitioner many people find relief from spinal disorder and strain. Osteopathy is also said to reduce tension headaches which so frequently originate from the neck. Manipulation is no longer considered an unorthodox treatment but since it is easy to aggravate actively inflamed joints, care should be taken to find a reliable and recommended practitioner.

Reflexology

This method of diagnosing and treating illness is based on the assumption that there are pathways in the toes and feet which connect to corresponding parts of the body. There are pressure points along these pathways where massage and pressure can be applied in order, it is said, to produce improvement in health.

Transcendental Meditation

This is a study, sometimes known as 'TM', based upon ancient teaching and is promoted as a powerful means of improving health. One has to feel relaxed with eyes closed and a clear mind, then whilst breathing quietly, repeat a single word which has happy connotations. Repeat the performance during the day. No one could teach TM in a brief paragraph, it takes several hours of tuition and a great deal of practise. Meditators are said to be less prone to illness, are able to think clearly and be capable of sustaining greater workloads. If TM can do all this, it is not surprising to learn that it is also said to slow ageing.

Yoga

This popular form of relaxation and exercise is practised by thousands of people all over the country. Attending regular sessions improves health and breathing control and helps to ease stiffness. Students are assessed individually so that they are not offered exercises which are beyond them. This is a favourite means of therapy for retired people.

Summary

These are some of the more popular complementary therapies which are practised and I know there are many more. Mostly they are painless and some should even be quite enjoyable. But before you commit yourself to a course of treatment, please consult your GP for an opinion as to whether it will help you.

27　The Carers

Few of us want to think about that daunting time in the future when we may no longer be independent but will need support in one form or another. No one wishes to be in such a situation but since more people are living on to a greater age some of us will undoubtedly need help, someone who will help us to care for ourselves. We will need a carer.

Greater Expectations

People who are debilitated by illness or disability no longer accept limitations as they once did but now have greater expectations. They want to continue to get out and about and provided they receive the right sort of help this is possible for many. Staying indoors because of a weakness is likely to increase the failing, so it is worth maintaining mobility for as long as possible.

Historically, people who needed some kind of assistance in caring for themselves either received help from volunteers, professionals, or entered some kind of institution. The philosophy today is that, following disablement or illness, an impaired person should not be shut away, but belongs out in a caring society with entitlement to remain in the community in a familiar environment, among people they know. Whilst this was often managed in the past by care provided at home, it was frequently given at great personal sacrifice by spouses, family members, friends or neighbours.

Family Carers

There is a considerable difference between paid helpers, whether related or not, and unpaid ones. The relationship between partners or families provides a long existing tie that can be damaged by the wearying duties and burden of full-time caring. People say that the last thing they would want is for their frailties to impose restrictions of any kind on their loved ones, or cause them to alter their life-styles.

Traditionally, the duty of carer with its expectation of self-sacrifice was a role that a member of the family, usually a daughter, was expected to undertake, often foregoing marriage and any personal life. It happened to sons too, and the unselfish devotion of such children to their parents, although commendable, was often at great personal cost.

The extended family group is becoming more rare, often splintering into smaller units. Higher divorce rates and the opportunity to move elsewhere in the country or abroad, breaks up the family network and because women are more often out at work in full-time occupation they are less willing or able to take on the responsibilities of caring for a dependent, elderly person. Even so, most community care is still family care, with personal attention given by a family member. The Association of Carers has estimated that there are more people caring for elderly or disabled relatives than there are bringing up children of under sixteen. The association also estimates that 60 per cent of carers are women, many of whom are themselves over sixty.

When a family member slips into the role of a designated carer there are many pressures and problems and much will depend upon the relationship that has endured up until the time the dependency began. In an attempt to relieve the pressure on people while keeping their dependent relatives in their own homes for as long as possible, a new type of carer has come into being.

Paid Attendants

This new category of attendant, trained in care and able to go about with the disabled person, is a welcome innovation. It offers the kind of assistance which either allows a person to be completely independent of voluntary or family help, or gives what is most valuable, a period of respite to the permanent carer.

Both attendant and attended need some education in how to behave so that the delicate balance of relationship can be maintained. Attendants are not servants and should not be ordered about. But they are there to do a job and don't want a thank you or please every two minutes. It is best to work out what is acceptable to each and then to keep to those guidelines. No one would want to stay with a crabby or petulant person who showed no gratitude. Neither would an individual with a job to do want to work for anyone who felt too embarrassed or too indebted for services rendered, to give any instructions at all.

Someone unused to a household would have to be told about how it is run and attendants might well have suggestions of their own, which in their experience had proved to be beneficial. These must be listened to with courtesy and should perhaps be accepted for trial.

Any relationship which involves private and personal care is a tricky one. People are thrust together for long periods, often having to share intimate duties in body care. A sense of humour on both sides helps.

When Sophie, sixty-four and arthritic was stuck in her bath, all her own efforts and those of her attendant failed to budge her. They had to get her daughter over to help and Sophie said ruefully, 'It was a bit embarrassing but we all laughed so hard that it passed off as a funny episode'.

At present, the status of paid attendants is not sufficiently high. Yet attendants can enable people with disabilities to lead active and comparatively independent lives for many years and such care does make it possible for people to stay in their homes when they would otherwise have to move into sheltered or nursing home accommodation. And most people infinitely prefer to stay at home.

Temporary and Permanent Dependency

Health care in a partnership role may be temporary, reversing as when one of a couple has flu' one week while the other gets it the next week. They each take care of the other as needed.

Sporadic care is quite different from the day-to-day care needed when a person loses the ability to see to their own daily personal needs. When permanent deterioration has resulted, the caring alters radically, is very demanding and makes a difference to the family, especially to a spouse. Nursing may be required, and additional help may be needed in respect of toiletting and feeding. This is very demanding and carers themselves are often quite elderly people whose spouses or older relatives look to them for support.

Many carers, both men and women, nurse their dependents with tenderness and skill, willingly permitting the disruption to their own lives. They accept the lack of recognition, pay or respite relief but the strain inevitably shows in time. It is imperative that there should be adequate support services so that carers do not sacrifice themselves altogether or drive themselves prematurely into similar dependence.

Devoted Partners

In many marriages there is such devotion that when a partner needs care it is given without question, lovingly and unselfishly. Neither partner would dream of leaving the other or allow anyone else to provide the necessary attention. But each should recognize that carers bear a burden for which respite is essential if the help is to be maintained at the necessary level. A break of a short space each day should be insisted upon, perhaps a walk or a visit to the shops. There may be some outside interest which both partners can share and take pleasure in and this can be enormously helpful.

A couple had been married for fifty-one years when the wife, Eleanor, had a stroke which totally incapacitated her physically. She had been a capable housewife and found her dependency distressing. Eleanor's joy had been to tend the plants and flowers in their garden which passers-by stopped to admire. Her husband Tony was determined to keep the garden as his wife liked it. He employed a home-help assistant who provided him with respite from the care of his wife and freed him to work outdoors. Eleanor remained keenly interested in her plants and this helped her rehabilitation although she never recovered sufficiently to work actively again. Still, for the next six years, until Eleanor died, the couple were able to stay together in their own home, enjoying each other's companionship.

Getting Help

Often it is up to families or partners to assess the services offered in their area and to obtain the best available. Ideally, there should be a choice and whether it is a private or a local authority service the range and type of care chosen must be matched to requirement. Expectations may not match up to reality and relatives often demand care which is quite unrealistic, sometimes when they themselves are providing no input.

Doctors have a heavy responsibility and it is helpful when a member of the patient's family is willing to co-operate. Frequently, a competent relative can carry out procedures when instructed by the doctor but if the situation demands the services of a qualified nurse then the doctor will arrange for one to call.

Physiotherapists and occupational therapists may also be brought in to help in rehabilitation. They can visit the home, suggesting new and easier ways of doing things, providing advice on the best way to cope with ordinary problems of bathing, toiletting, feeding and mobility. Their assessments may result in a recommendation for the provision of equipment which can restore a measure of independence and confidence. Items such as stair rails, bath grab rails, outdoor ramps, walking frames, etc., are immensely useful and most can be supplied or loaned on demand from the council.

There are numbers of helpful gadgets which are available and which should be given a fair trial. Too often, useful small aids are dismissed without having been given a long enough term of use. It is all too common to find expensive appliances, even deaf aids, lying around unused and perhaps needing only to be serviced properly to be useful.

District nurses can visit regularly if need be and assist with various procedures at home, providing invaluable support for carers. They share with them the more personal problems involved in full care.

There are Neighbourhood Task Forces in some areas which can offer help to people in straitened circumstances and who need maintenance or gardening work done. Social services departments and health authorities offer a variety of helpful facilities such as an incontinence laundry service. They may provide a bathing attendant who will regularly visit to help people to bathe. The quality and type of provision varies between areas across the country. Anyone in need of advice should enquire at their local Citizen's Advice Bureau, the doctor's surgery or Duty Social Worker, as to what is available locally.

In every social service area there will be found a duty officer who can be contacted at times of real emergency, whether this is during the day or at night. Important telephone numbers, those of the doctor or emergency service, hospital and close relatives should be carefully noted so that in times of urgent need they are readily to hand.

If the person cared for still lives alone then home help may be provided to visit and to share the burden. The WRVS provide Meals on Wheels, which is a real help, providing regular support for a housebound person as well as reassurance for a carer who knows that a visit and a hot meal are arriving daily.

There may be a laundry service in the district which can take care of another duty, that of keeping clothing, towels and linen clean. Heavily-soiled clothing or bedding will need special treatment and for this there is often provision made by the local council.

Need for Counselling

The care of a dependent relative may be readily undertaken, but for some it is a burden from the beginning, never more than an interim and compromise situation and fraught with resentment. Ideally, the love that is strong in a marriage or between family members should continue and be strengthened by sympathy and concern when someone becomes ill, but sadly that does not always happen. Carers should be able to discuss their situation with someone, perhaps surgery staff, if they are to be responsible on a long-term basis. Personal dilemmas on both sides can be expected when one person has the care of another.

Filial Duty

Sarah cared for her mother, Ella, who was an alert but bedridden ninety-two year old, very demanding of attention. Theirs had always been a good relationship and mother and daughter had loved and respected each other. Sarah's husband Bill, had agreed that his mother-in-law, having suffered a stroke, should come to live with them. The old lady, who had just celebrated her ninetieth birthday and until then had been fiercely independent, now grew increasingly fractious, missing her own home and hating her dependency. Sarah became resentful of the time consumed by the caring role and by the restrictions placed upon her and her husband.

They were unable to carry out their plans for enjoying their retirement and saw the years slipping away. Although they had two married daughters who were willing to help on occasion, each of them had young families and Sarah and Bill were adamant that the responsibility for the old lady was theirs alone.

It was when Sarah became ill and had to go into hospital that the social services were called in and took over the responsibility for her mother. This event proved a blessing in disguise because thereafter frequent respite was provided so that Sarah and Bill were able to take some of their planned holidays and begin to enjoy their retirement. Ella too, enjoyed the change and the break from unremitting care by her daughter.

Respite Care

Both carers and cared for need breaks from each other and such arrangements can be made, allowing for accommodation in local homes for the elderly dependent person. Beds are generally reserved for short-stay emergency respite needs and this stay can occasionally be extended. There are districts which will take people in for two weeks at regular intervals, perhaps every two or three months. Alternative arrangements may be made with sympathetic families who will, for modest payment, take an elderly person in for brief periods. Some social services are able to reserve funding to offer people seaside or country holidays.

Day centres offer a range of activities which interest and stimulate elderly and disabled people, occupying them for several hours during the day. During this time carers may enjoy some freedom to pursue their own lives and can resume their caring duties refreshed by the break.

Home-Care Treatment

Home-based diagnosis and treatment follows lay beliefs about the workings of the body and mind. Home-care treatment can be simple and effective, often without resort to medication other than something as simple as aspirin. Common-sense prevails and for some conditions a cure will depend on keeping warm, resting and eating some special food, often administered as a form of medicine. The chicken soup of Jewish people, regarded as 'natural penicillin', the spicy, hot food of West Indians believed to be the cure for 'rich blood' or a good thick Irish stew, a great pick-me up. For some illnesses, fasting is traditionally regarded by many cultures as beneficial and old sayings are quoted 'Starve a cold and stave a fever'. Among Hindus, fasting is regarded as curative and, in addition to a recommendation to fast when unwell, there are many days when only foods considered pure and natural such as nuts, fresh fruits and vegetables are eaten.

Whatever is done, home care often works a treat. After all,

being dependent and needing care for minor ills probably only means wanting a little attention and comfort. At times we do need to call the doctor but most illness is self-limiting and recovery will take place no matter what anyone does or does not do.

Mobility

One of the worst aspects of losing independence is to lose mobility. In some areas of the country, there has been an effort to overcome this problem by setting up Taxicard schemes. These allow people with disabilities which prevent them from using buses to travel at greatly reduced fares. Disabilities of a temporary nature however, do not count.

The Depressed Patient

People who are in the position of having to be cared for frequently suffer from depression. This can have an equally depressing effect upon the carers who become despondent about the effectiveness of their work. This extra strain becomes a problem and counselling is needed. The social network tends to decrease when people are gloomy and it is the cheerful patient and household which gets most visitors.

Adequate Support for Carers

Carers, both paid and unpaid, are owed a debt of some magnitude by families, the community and the government. Those who become attendants should receive proper training and be paid an adequate wage, under contract and be provided with pleasant and reasonable working conditions. Their status and that of dependent people everywhere would then be raised and the absolute necessity for dignity in the lives of us all would be recognized. Support services must be adequate to help carers in their often onerous task and to enable doctors and nurses to guarantee the best of possible care for their older patients and the highest attainable quality of life.

Anyone in need of care should be able to remain a part of the community, fully participating in everyday life. Much depends upon what can be afforded and central government is hard put to make sufficient provision since demands spiral upwards continually and there are other priorities. It is up to retirees to help national charities, both with time and money so that they are strengthened and can help those of us who unfortunately are not able to maintain independence to the end.

28 A Place of Your Own

Make yourself Comfortable

There is nothing quite like the feeling of being at home with a familiar roof over your head and your personal things all around you. We may wish to remain in accustomed surroundings, continuing our lives after retirement at the address we have made our own. It's nice to be in a district that is familiar, where you get many a friendly 'Hello', where people care about you and everyone knows your name. But there are other options open to us. Do you hanker to go back to where you grew up? Were you ever attracted to a place you visited and where you would like to spend the future? Plans should be firmed up well in advance of actual retirement so that you know in plenty of time what you are going to do.

Moving to a Familiar Place

It is hard work moving, preparing the new place and giving up the old. For Joan and Peter, just retiring, it was especially hectic as they had also decided to move Joan's mother in with them. At ninety she reluctantly conceded that she should no longer live alone so they had her home and contents to deal with too. They all moved some sixty miles into the countryside to a village they had spent many happy times in and knew well. But it was a priority that the new place should be big enough to accommodate their daughters, Sally and Elizabeth, who with their husbands and children were to be frequent weekend visitors. These four generations who like each other very much will often be together now.

Going Abroad

There are valid reasons for choosing to live abroad; good weather is tempting and in many countries the cost of living is less than it is back home. For example, accommodation is still relatively cheap in Southern Europe when compared with equivalent property in the UK and of course there are tax advantages to be enjoyed if one is prepared to emigrate. But never take this step without detailed investigation as to what is involved. You certainly ought to take a lengthy vacation in any place you propose to make your future home.

Not many would be as adventurous as a couple I knew approaching eighty who astonished their children by moving from the chilly north of England to South Africa, the favourable rate of exchange permitting them to sell their modest home and buy a bungalow complete with attractive garden and swimming pool. They love the warm climate and have made enough friends in the area to make life very pleasant.

Emigrants might decide on a place not quite so far afield perhaps to the island of Mallorca, the Spanish mainland or Portugal.

Setting up with a new partner can be one reason for emigration as it was for Gwen. She was fifty, long divorced, en route for a holiday in Lisbon and reading a new book by one of her favourite authors. Next to her sat Richard, widowed, a few years older than she was and who was returning to his home in Portugal. They were attracted to each other and began to chat but it was a while before he revealed to her that he was an author and that she was reading his latest book. They saw a great deal of each other during her month's holiday, fell in love and she needed little persuasion to return and marry him. They have so far had eleven happy years together and she too has become a writer.

Returning Home

After many years abroad there is the temptation to return to one's place of birth to live after retirement. It is not easy to uproot and Mildred at seventy is finding this a problem. She has established herself in her own successful business and comfortable house in Spain. But it is lonely and she is torn between the desire to return to England or to remain in the country she has grown to love. Financially it could be a problem for she still needs her income and even though she is beset by ill-health and is unable to move easily because of arthritis, she runs her export agency from her bed. It takes courage and spirit to carry on but she never allows herself to be downhearted and presents the picture of a woman of beauty and style. You cannot think of her as old.

Reasons not to Move

Most of those people anticipating retirement or already retired live in their own homes, independently and in accommodation which they own or rent. A big house where the children grew up is an asset in many ways until you calculate the cost and difficulty of upkeep. A smaller place would almost certainly be easier to manage and less expensive to run and some additional capital is likely to be generated, to be invested for income, spent on extra holidays or a long wanted luxury.

But moving is a big step and you must be sure that you really want to. John and Pearl decided when they reached sixty that they should give up the lovely home they had designed and built twenty-five years earlier and move to a more manageable apartment. Natural hosts, they enjoy nothing more than receiving visitors. Their friends, children and grandchildren congregate in what is regarded as 'the family home' and during the summer their swimming pool is the scene of much fun and laughter. The plans to move produced a chorus of dismay and to the relief of everyone, including the couple themselves, they are staying put.

Reasons to Move

If stairs are a problem because of ill-health, single floor accommodation could be the answer but a stair lift can be installed in a house and would almost certainly be less expensive than moving. I visited one home with an outdoor flight of steep steps where the occupant, although in her eighties and with a hip problem, made nothing of them. 'I wouldn't give up my home because of those,' she said. 'It's hard work sometimes getting up and down them but what else would I do for exercise?' And she smiled.

Big gardens can be a liability and finding someone to help is always going to be a problem although friends without gardens might be found to share the work. Such an arrangement has worked well for Martha who is in her seventies and generous with her lovely garden but the friends who enjoy it also give time to looking after it. Group activities like these provide an interest that can be depended upon to improve the quality of life. Community contact is a vital link, enabling people to remain part of their familiar world, living in the way they want to for longer than would otherwise be the case.

Choice of Accommodation

Ownership of housing by way of the purchase of council accommodation has been encouraged and this can widen the choice that people have since after a period of time they can sell at a good profit and then buy elsewhere. However, the modern popular, purpose built units are frequently higher priced than larger accommodation. Management fees in such units must be taken into consideration, since they tend to rise, often steeply. It is far preferable that they be managed by a consortium of the owners so that there is a measure of control and the profit element is eliminated.

Housing Associations

Housing corporations and associations are normally non-profit making and operate in districts of the greatest housing need. These areas contain high numbers of elderly people, often found living in housing which has received little maintenance over many years. They may be in homes in which their families lived and grew up. Better use can be made of such existing larger houses either by providing them for younger families to occupy or by dividing them into smaller and easily run units suitable for independent older people. Conversion costs, however, are high. One association specialising in this particular area is Abbeyfield which buys houses suitable for conversion into perhaps eight or nine units of bed-sitters where the retired occupants run the house, sharing duties rather like a large family. (See Useful Addresses.)

Housing trusts and corporations work closely with local authorities, complementing and supporting local needs and policies. They remain independent entities and usually choose for occupation of their housing people from a wider range than are to be found on the waiting lists of local authorities. They always have long waiting lists of would-be tenants since they are generally able to offer moderately priced, good quality accommodation. They may specify the kind of tenants they are prepared to consider. These may be of a religious persuasion which matches that of the providers of the funding which originally set the trust up. The preferred tenant may be of a specified profession, calling or trade.

Tenants of privately rented but unsuitable homes may be advised to apply for housing association accommodation and it is always worthwhile going on to a waiting list. One never knows how quickly a vacancy may come up so applicants should never feel discouraged. It may be hard to contemplate leaving behind beloved gardens and rooms with precious memories, but if these homes are difficult to heat and need extensive repair then it could be better to move.

Buying or Renting

The home owners' choice is greater since they can sell and either purchase a more suitable property or rent one using income from the invested proceeds. Some housing associations do allow for a 70 per cent ownership by the tenant, with 30 per cent remaining in the possession of the association. They remain as a management body, responsible for communal facilities, for all repairs and upkeep. In some cases they will provide for a twenty-four hour or daily service by caretaker or warden. Some will provide a residential porter or warden service, others an emergency telephone service available daily for twenty-four hours.

Housing in the 1980s

A great deal of the private housing built from the mid-1980s on has been one bedroom accommodation meant for occupation by elderly people. These are small and centrally heated apartments, often planned close to shops and all amenities. But they are in high demand and the prices for them have risen dramatically. So much so that almost as soon as new ones are built they seem to undergo a significant increase in price. Maintenance costs may be built into the contract of purchase or offered as a separate contract and need to be considered carefully. Do they include care of gardens and common parts such as landings, lift maintenance, window cleaning and external decorations? Is there a residential porter service offered on the premises or a non-residential one present for limited periods only, during the day? Is there a telephone service available at times of need? One should try to ensure that the charges for any of these amenities are reasonable and fair.

Provided such units of accommodation are thoughtfully placed within a mixed housing community of varied types and as part of a general residential area, close to shops and services, then they will successfully fulfil a need. It is very important that we who are older should remain part of a natural mix of all ages, both young and old and do not become distanced as an elderly, segregated group. We are not fixed by our ages into rigid patterns, some of us will always remain youthful, continuing to enjoy and to serve the community and to be a natural and respected part of it. We need to see children and young adults as well as our contemporaries and they need to see us.

Family Units

I am all for the extended family exchanging and sharing visits occasionally, depending upon each other for support at times of need in a natural way. But it is important to recognize the value of privacy for the small family unit. The jokes about in-laws are founded on fact and can mean a great deal of misery when a dominating parent of either sex attempts to run the family against the wishes of the younger people. The unit of parents and their children should be allowed privacy wherever it is possible and desired.

In a large and wealthy household it may still be possible to tuck lonely elders into a big home of many bedrooms and assorted living rooms with substantial kitchen quarters. But in the more usual smaller homes of two, three and four bedroom houses, grandparents and close elderly relatives may not always be welcome. The general consensus of opinion is that they should be somewhere reasonably close but in an independent household. The most contentment comes when it is possible to live in harmony with relatives who love and sustain their older members of the family. But in practice this happens infrequently. One third of people above the age of sixty-five live alone, either from choice or because they have lost their partners of long standing or because their families want privacy and have no wish to give it up to care for a relative.

Moving to an Hotel

Some people, whether couples or single, may prefer to relinquish the responsibility of running their own home. Depending upon funds they could look around for a suitable boarding house or hotel. It is usually the custom for permanent hotel guests to get preferential rates which can make this a tempting alternative. If there is a recommendation from a friend or if the accommodation and food have already been tried and tested then the move can be made with some assurance. If you consider this option, check that you can take personal items and that the room itself offers bed-sitting facilities. It's nice to be able to invite someone up for a cup of tea without having to perch on the bed and it is a real boon to have a private bathroom and toilet. If these prove too expensive then at least there should be toilet provision close by. Think about arrangements for personal laundry, whether there are facilities for making a hot drink and whether heating is adequate. Overheated rooms are not healthy and we should remember that as we grow older and feel the cold more we should wear extra clothing.

No one wants to spend their years of retirement inhibited by overly restrictive house rules. Prospective hotel guests should determine whether and when visitors are welcome and if they may be invited for teas or lunches and also whether there is a strict ruling about lights out in lounges at specified times. Most guest houses have communal television sets and allow at least one late night. But it is reasonable to expect that noise after hours should be kept to a minimum for the sake of the majority of guests who may go to bed earlier.

The decision to move into a guest house as a permanent resident should not be taken lightly. There are all kinds of small and apparently inconsequential matters which may be of importance and these should all be thought about. All extra charges should be specified and no one can assume that there will be free anything. Consider matters such as the cost of the room if it is vacated during holidays and whether possessions can be stored elsewhere if the room is going to be let to another occupant during absence.

Final Moves

At some stage it may be necessary to recognize the practicalities and consider a move to sheltered housing, perhaps to a residential home or somewhere which offers nursing care. It is important to have as few changes as possible because moving at this time of life can become a traumatic event. The use of all available resources must be considered as there is a steep rise in cost as the need for more care becomes inevitable.

Going into residential care is sometimes a preferred option, particularly for those who realise that their independence is becoming limited. Responsibilities are fewer and one feels less of a burden and liability to relatives, neighbours and friends. But leaving home is a sad business for most older people and if adequate supportive care can be provided at home then residential care is always a last resort.

Choosing a Nursing Home

Should you need to find a reliable nursing home the first step is to get a list of registered places from your local authority. Visit those homes you think might be suitable, arranging your call at a meal-time and ask to look at bedrooms and bathrooms. Ask too, about the numbers of staff on duty during day and night and if possible meet some of them. A trial stay is best since it should reveal whether you could be happy and comfortable there.

Home Safety and Security

While we are still working and have maximum earning capacity we should make our homes as convenient, as safe and secure as possible. Take a look at your accommodation with an eye for comfort, quality and convenience. We are more liable to have accidents in the home as we grow older and many of these occur on the stairs and in the bathroom and kitchen, so let us go over a few basic rules and see whether any have been neglected.

Never leave food cooking in the kitchen just for that minute when you might be distracted and forget to return. We have all had the odd burned saucepan to tut over, it happens so easily. Any electric kettles or irons or indeed any electrical appliance with cables which have weak spots should be checked and if faulty must be repaired or renewed.

The bath itself should have hand-grips fixed at an appropriate height to aid getting in and out and a non-slip mat in the bath makes you feel more secure and comfortable.

Shower stalls could be safer if it is difficult to use the bath and, again, hand-grips should be fixed to the wall, with soap trays within easy reach.

Flooring should be non-slip wherever possible and remember that uncarpeted floors, tiles or lino are slippery when wet. Always use a non-slip polish. Check if there are any worn patches of carpet or lino which could cause an accident and ensure that all the rugs have non-slip backing and lie perfectly flat.

If you have not managed to give up smoking be sure never to smoke where or when you may doze off, endangering yourself and others. Bedding and upholstered chairs, as well as clothing burn easily unless they are made of fire-resistant material.

Double glazing provides security as well as reducing heat loss and it is worth having it fitted if you can. Single panels of glass in rear or front doors should be shatterproof. But in case of fire be sure that you can get out; it is quite difficult to smash through double glazing. You may still like doing your own decorating but be safety conscious. My stepfather was never so happy as when he painted the outside of the house and the last time he did it he was over eighty but he was very careful to see to it that his ladders were sound and securely positioned.

Be Security Conscious

The increase in attacks on people who are alone, whether out or at home means that we must all be security conscious. Many incidents take place where they are least expected and it is only sensible for everyone, men and women, to be alert and aware of potential danger. Check locks on outside doors and fit door chains. If possible, have a peep hole fitted which you can see through without being seen. Do not admit unexpected callers. Ask them to write for an appointment and only admit those you know to be bona fide. Be very suspicious.

If you have reliable friends living nearby leave a set of keys with them. It is such a relief to know that you can get in easily if you happen to lock yourself out or even lose your own set of keys. Don't secrete keys out of doors, someone may watch you put them there. Look around outside and see to it that the approaches to the house are safe, easy to navigate and well-lit and have repairs done if they are needed. Once inside, lock your doors and check that your telephone is in order.

For people on their own, some comfort and feeling of security may be gained from using an alarm service. An example is the innovative idea of the Constant Careline which has been set up to provide a national twenty-four hour emergency service and which can be installed wherever there is a telephone. It offers peace of mind for older people and their families and comprises a small remote unit kept on the person and an infrared-activated two-way telephone unit. An alarm can be activated by a touch on the remote unit or telephone, when a signal is sent down the phone line to the monitoring centre. Personal details are then flashed on to a screen, including name and address of the caller, their families, neighbours and local emergency services. A loudspeaker built into the telephone allows the Careline helper to speak to the caller without the receiver being lifted. Additional features include a timed pressure mat which is activated if no one treads on it for twelve hours, a room temperature monitor which warns of dropping temperature, bathroom alarm cords and smoke and burglar alarms. These features allow for automatic communication with Careline so that rescue action will be taken.

People should collaborate to look after each other's property. The Neighbourhood Watch Scheme is a real deterrent to crime and, if there is not one locally, your police station can advise you how to start one.

Neighbours and friends who can rely on each other for mutual help and comfort not only make it possible that independent living will continue for longer but make life richer and more rewarding.

29 Money Matters

Walking along a suburban high street one afternoon I was stopped by a woman who I guessed to be in her mid-sixties. She said, 'Forgive me, but I have to talk to someone about my problems and there isn't anyone'. In the next few minutes I was appalled to find that she was entrusting me, a perfect stranger, with all her personal financial details. From my experience in advice bureaux I know that there are many older people who need professional advice about money and do not know where to get it. You, of course would go to an advice bureau or a bank, wouldn't you? But in any event you would never ask a stranger for you could be unlucky and run the risk of being taken advantage of by someone unscrupulous.

Let's face it, the most knowledgeable of us are hardly financial wizards, we tend to muddle through life hardly knowing how our bank accounts stand and with only the vaguest of plans or goals for the future. Which of us makes proper financial provision for sickness or an emergency, let alone for retirement? But if we are going to make our senior years the best of all we will need the most income we can get. That means we ought to have done some careful and well-advised planning at an early stage of life.

Are you completely familiar with your own financial affairs? Do they still match present needs or do they require updating? With retirement imminent, we will want answers to many questions but the final result we are seeking is for our living standards to continue to be as comfortable as possible. Inflation is likely to remain with us and we must do the best we can to secure our income by developing a detailed plan of action and that requires some expertise. The question of future income is far too important to be left to casually acquired information and one needs the expert advice of experienced and reliable professionals. Care taken at the stage when plans are made for the future can make all the difference between easy comfort and a penny-pinching existence.

However, we can do little about unstable national or international finances. No country can be an island, each nation is interdependent with all the others; political instabilities in a distant zone affect money values across the world. This means that however secure we may feel in our financial arrangements we simply cannot be completely proofed against reductions in value of money. We ought to be optimistic in our outlook but also realistic, protecting our money as best we can.

Looking Ahead

One of the first things you need to know is just what your financial situation is. Set down on paper exactly what your assets are. These will include real estate, that is freehold or leasehold property and any realisable possessions. Then try to make a practical estimate of future financial prospects.

Evaluating possessions is an interesting exercise since owners may have little conception of how their values might have increased. The home is the first thing to consider and if it is owned outright it is a considerable asset. What is its present day price? It will have almost certainly appreciated quite a bit since it was purchased and is likely to be your most valuable possession. What other precious goods are there which you probably undervalue? Do you have an old Persian rug, some fine porcelain, silver cutlery, a Victorian escritoire? These are realisable assets which you will perhaps wish to keep or you may decide to sell and capitalize on their value.

House Owners

For most of us the biggest purchase we will ever have made is our own home. Few of us recognize that we have in this large item a wealth resource which we can keep for life whilst at the same time enjoying income from it. There are options for the older person who lives in a house which is too large; to sell, re-model and let or sell part, or capitalize on part or whole in exchange for an annuity.

Annuities

A husband or wife who own their home have a resource which could increase their income while permitting them to remain where they are during their own lifetimes. This is particularly useful for those couples who do not have children or anyone else to whom they wish to leave their unencumbered property.

A number of insurance companies offer annuity schemes which provide income until the death of the second partner. This allows the occupants to continue to live in their home and receive an annuity income, normally paid monthly. Various types of schemes are available from most of the reputable insurance companies and building societies. Since schemes may be tailored to suit your own particular circumstances, you must take financial and legal advice and consider all the options. Some of the income from annuities may be tax free since it will be regarded as a return on capital. Your decision must be based on accurate knowledge and complete understanding.

Pensions

Many companies today have excellent pension schemes which offer some alternatives to employees according to their personal status and family commitments. It is quite usual for a spouse, more often the man, to take steps to ensure that his wife will not find herself in reduced circumstances if she should be widowed. A typical pension might provide for a lump sum for her should he die before retirement, plus a proportion of the monthly pension to which he would have been entitled.

Most people now enjoy longer periods of retirement and on balance, most of us agree that it is well worthwhile making the effort to save that extra bit of money when we are in employment in order to secure additional income when we are older. Everyone must make their own judgement but the happy-go-lucky character who spends to the hilt and talks of a short life and a happy one may live to regret it. Life is a bit like an obstacle race; people fall at every hurdle, but more of us are going on. And the golden years hold more possibility of the good life than ever before.

Company pensions will offer the chance for a spouse to receive part of the pension in the event that the employee dies after retiring. If this is thought to be insufficient, then any spare money might well be employed in buying some additional life insurance or an annuity. Virtually everyone who has worked whether for themselves on a self-employed basis or for an employer, will have paid National Insurance contributions. This will entitle them to receive state retirement pension.

State Retirement Pension

Some weeks before the pension age is reached (sixty for a woman and sixty-five for a man) a form will arrive from the local DSS office. If it does not, it should be requested. No one should disregard this form, even if they do not intend to retire for some time. Once the form is completed and received at the DSS office, the right to a pension is established and there will be no delay when it becomes due. All individuals must apply independently, whether married or not. Women may be favourably affected by recent legislation and should look at the special leaflets relative to their circumstances.

Anyone who is at home and unavailable for work because they are caring for someone, could quite possibly qualify for a pension. There is some protective legislation for people in these circumstances but much depends upon individual situations and advice must be sought from the DSS or the local CAB. Do enquire if you think that you belong to this category.

A Source of Advice

A bank is a reliable source of financial advice and you do need a friendly one. It is best if there is a member of staff you can get to know and talk to when you need assistance. Their time is valuable and you must be reasonable in your use of such a facility. Choose a bank which is conveniently located; you may want to consult in a hurry and it is easier if your advisers are situated close to where you live. Banks have investment departments to which you can be referred if you have large sums to invest but think over any proposals with care and be sure that you understand the issues. Some people will more easily make decisions about the big sums than they will about buying a pair of shoes. You have a lot of questions to ask and you should get answers you fully understand.

Building Societies

You can invest part of your savings in one of the better known building societies which over the years will guarantee a modest but secure return of interest on your money. They have recently extended their facilities to equate with those operated by the major high street banks, providing current accounts, cheque books, cash dispensing points and so forth.

The Stock Market

If you know all about stock markets and understand the risks involved, you can if you wish happily splash out on buying shares. If you are inexperienced, remember to spend only what you can afford to lose.

Should a particular commodity appeal to you, that is as good a reason as any to buy shares in the company manufacturing that product. And if you like the way a major store is doing business you might wish to back your judgement and buy their shares.

Many public companies operate an incentive scheme by offering perks to attract people to buy their shares. These may take the form of special discounts on the products they make or sell or be concessions on the services they provide. For example, on some cross-Channel ferries, a shareholding above a certain amount would entitle the holder to a considerable discount on the normal fare. Tour operators may offer shareholders special deals on holidays provided they hold a certain minimum number of shares.

The usual way of buying and selling shares is either through a stockbroker or your bank. A fee is charged for this service and this adds to the cost of the shares.

Unit Trusts

Unit trusts are a way to invest money, using the experience of professional management who will invest in a spread of companies whose future success they believe is assured. Choose unit trusts which have a good record of achievement and which hold what you consider to be safe portfolios. You should regard your holding as a long-term investment as it is unlikely to turn a quick profit but could steadily increase in value over the years. But money can be lost in the investment market, so be very wary.

National Saving Certificates

These offer a secure home for your money giving a relatively high tax-free return on your investment. Look out for the Retirement Issues which are index linked and attract an additional rate of interest if held for five years or more. The interest does not attract tax and the increase in value is free of Capital Gains tax.

Other Investments

Your advisers may use terms you are quite unfamiliar with, such as 'gilts' which is merely a popular term for government stocks or gilt-edged securities. Capital bonds give a guaranteed rate of return over a full five years, good for non-tax payers who keep the gross interest. Savings certificates give tax-free return over the five-year period, so offering a good deal to the tax-payer. It may all seem bewildering, but tell your adviser what you want: high income, security, an occasional flutter on the stock exchange, the choice is yours. With a reliable adviser you should get just what you want.

Income Support

Anyone, young or old who is in need is entitled to a basic income even if they have never paid National Insurance contributions. Income Support is a means-tested cash benefit and is paid by the DSS. Those who qualify will have the sum added to their national retirement pension and usually will find it is paid from the same order in their pension book. Anyone who has not enough money to pay for basic needs, food, clothing, heating and lighting etc., should enquire about their eligibility for assistance.

Because Income Support is a means-tested benefit there is a cut-off point and no one can apply for help if they have capital above a certain amount. There are certain types of income which are regarded as necessary resources and which are tax free. For example, allowances which are paid to those with disabilities or who need attendance for personal needs, or certain resettlement and housing benefits. It is possible for claims for all these kinds of benefit to be made and interviews conducted at home if people cannot travel. Information must be provided as requested and any subsequent changes in circumstances should always be relayed to the relevant social security office.

When to Save

People who have been careful with their money during their lifetime may well say that they are penalised at the end. Those who are spendthrift get their incomes made up. But it is surely far better to know the feeling of security which comes from having money set aside for a rainy day. If that money goes down below the ceiling amount, extra benefits will be provided. No one is expected to use up all their capital savings. Those who have money just above the cut-off point might reasonably decide that they would like to replace their television set with a new or better one. It could happen that the car someone has had for many years has become worn out and irreparable. It would be acceptable to use one's funds to change that car for something in better condition, but not to buy something extravagant merely to use up the savings and qualify for supporting income.

Common-sense dictates what can and cannot be done but the general idea is that it cannot be permitted for anyone to use up money unreasonably, merely to qualify for benefits. Such an action might well disqualify an applicant. The local Citizen's Advice Bureau can offer advice about this sort of problem.

Appealing against Decisions

Anyone who feels aggrieved that they have not received a fair decision is entitled to appeal. Tribunals are set up to hear such cases and it is always recommended that appellants go along to the hearing, personally. If people feel intimidated by such procedures they can request someone to represent them. Some law centres or the CAB can provide personnel to do this 'handholding exercise'.

Additional Payments

Extra weekly payments can be made in addition to basic income support for special reasons. If it is shown that there is a medical reason for a special diet, laundry costs, or for heating or necessary travel, then modest extra amounts may be added. A doctor's letter is useful to support such applications, but remember that whether or not the doctor thinks the request is reasonable, he or she may be entitled to charge for writing such a letter.

Any person who believes that they may be entitled to weekly additions to their incomes can ask for details at advisory centres. Those who are successful are likely to belong to one of a number of special categories: aged eighty or over; registered as blind or with poor sight; needing frequent bathing for medical reasons such as incontinence; requiring special heating either because of their own physical conditions or because their homes are especially draughty; needing more than the usual laundry facilities for special causes such as incontinence.

The Social Fund

Payments from this fund for special items are no longer made outright. If agreed, they are now made as loans and only in cases where the local DSS office has used its discretion and has agreed that the loan should be made. The Social Fund is cash limited which means it is not a bottomless pocket. It could well be more difficult to get loans, even for essential items, as the year goes on and the money is used up.

Advice given in these pages can only be of a general nature and correct at the time of writing. With so many recent changes in legislation it is worth taking your queries to an advisory centre to establish whether the correct income is being obtained and, if it is not, the machinery can then be set in motion to put things right. Most of these offices do work under great pressure, but persistence pays off. It may all take time but people get their dues in the end.

Housing Benefit

This benefit was designed to help people on low pensions or incomes, whether working or retired, to enable them to pay their rent or rates. We can get housing benefit whether we live in privately rented or council owned accommodation.

Getting Help

There are times in our lives when we may need financial help to get us over a crisis. We offer a helping hand to those in need when we are in a position to do so and no one loses dignity by admitting they are themselves in difficulty. There is considerable funding available to those in genuine need and a browse through the pages of the *Charity Digest* in the library may prove to be a source of help.

Husbands, Wives and Tax

There have been recent important changes which mean that wives are now taxed independently, becoming taxpayers in their own right. This is a sweeping change and means that both wife and husband are each separately taxed on their own income. They will each be eligible for a non-transferable personal allowance and those who are older than sixty-five will have a higher allowance level. This new arrangement should be of benefit, certainly to the wife and almost certainly to the husband and wife jointly. One further aspect of these changes is that where there was a joint annual exemption from Capital Gains tax this will now be allowed to each partner, independently.

Luxuries or Necessities

The probability that prices will continue to rise makes it sensible to buy high priced items while earnings are at an optimum level. Once the retirement years are reached, income very rarely goes up and it may feel needlessly extravagant to spend large sums of money merely to improve comfort. But is it for an item which is going to help you in the care of your home or your garden or is it something you have long wanted and can afford? If it is then go out, get it and enjoy it.

The whole matter of finance is very much a question of individual situations. You must obtain specialist advice so that you get the maximum benefit from your capital and income and so derive the utmost enjoyment during the new and exciting time ahead of you.

30 You and the Law

There are individuals who reach retirement having had little need of the law and scant knowledge of it, unaware of their responsibilities or liabilities. They may be alone for the first time through divorce, separation or bereavement, having always had someone else to deal with the numerous legal documents or forms which are a part of the lives of all citizens.

Working in a Citizens Advice Bureau I have seen men and women arrive in a state of panic because an officious letter has arrived which they, understandably, have misunderstood. Using plain English would help all of us and thankfully there is less 'gobbledegook' than there used to be.

People may live out their entire lives without needing a solicitor, other than when they buy or rent a property to live in or to work from. Comparatively few will have experienced the ordeal of appearing before a magistrate, registrar or judge. But many situations could result in a need for expert opinion from either an advice centre or solicitor and possibly a barrister too.

Read the Small Print

Letters from the gas and electricity boards, from landlords or builders, contracts for the hire-purchase of a television set, or a car, a holiday booking form, these are all documents which need to be clearly understood. Where appropriate, we should always respond in writing, keeping copies, confirming verbal discussions and instructions so that we have proof of what has been agreed.

Liabilities

We have responsibilities as we go about our daily lives and if our actions cause hurt or harm to anyone, we may be liable for any damage or part of it. If we habitually give noisy parties, keeping our neighbours awake or make slanderous statements about an individual or pluck flowers from a front garden, we may be found to be in breach of the law.

Criminal Injuries Compensation

If you should be so unfortunate as to become the victim of a crime of violence, you may be compensated for your injury and any expenses incurred. Apply as soon as possible, the amount may be modest but you lose nothing by trying for it.

Grandparents' Rights

The relatives of a child, including the grandparents, are not without rights. If there is some dispute over a child, either following divorce, separation or the death of a parent, grandparents may have rights of access. Visit the CAB or consult a solicitor and determine what your legal position is.

The Law Protects Us

To a degree, we are protected by the law, for instance a door-to-door salesman must allow us a specified period of some days after a purchase so that we have the opportunity to change our minds. If we fall from a bus or taxi through the carelessness of the driver or if we are ill after eating a meal in a restaurant, we might sue for damages.

Buyer Beware

Most sales contracts are made on a reasonable and fair basis but many salesmen earn their living by the commission on the sales they make. This system means that to ensure a good income they often have to adopt persuasive techniques which may put unfair pressure on potential purchasers. Many vulnerable pensioners, perhaps housebound, lonely or busy with home duties, have fallen for a glib sales patter and an item they cannot afford. They later find they cannot justify the purchase and go through worried days and nights, anxious about finding the money to pay for the new commitment. But, in fact, they could have changed their minds and cancelled the order.

Where hire-purchase agreements are made they must offer a certain protection. They are revokable within a short period of time, allowing the purchaser the opportunity to think things over and back off if they later decide that they were too hasty. If this happens to you, always revoke in writing and send the letter by registered post. And always keep a copy.

Medical Complaints

Medical personnel must carry comprehensive insurance so that if they are accused of negligence they would have some protection should the patient sue. The care shown to a patient must be that of a reasonable and competent medical professional person. Negligence is difficult to prove but there are cases where litigation is justified and which results in compensation. Comparatively few patients want to go to court, usually only needing explanations for what has happened and having been irritated by the guarded responses which members of the medical and allied professions may have given. Informal complaint proceedings against general practitioners through Family Health Service Authorities, when time is given for detailed explanations on both sides, usually result in everyone going away satisfied without recourse to expensive formal hearings or court procedures.

Visit the Courts

Once retired and with time to spare you might pay a visit to the law courts to hear some of the cases. It can be both informative and entertaining, provided you are not personally involved. If it is your own case, whether you are defendant or appellant, it is stressful and the best advice I could offer anyone is to steer clear of taking legal action wherever possible. It can be costly in money and health and litigation can go on for years. In some areas, law centres or the CAB can provide personnel who will do a 'hand-holding' exercise, going to court with a nervous or inexperienced client.

A Friendly Tip

A solicitor visited our house, informing us as he left that we were risking the need for his professional services. We had a loose paving stone on the front steps; if someone were to trip on that step and suffer injury, we could be sued for damages. Our laxity in getting the paving stone repaired might even invalidate our personal liability insurance policy. In that event, if the damages and costs of the case were heavy, we risked having to sell valuables and possibly our home in order to be able to pay. The next day we had the step cemented back into position and enjoyed peace of mind.

If you like visiting auction sales be careful not to make any of the movements which could be interpreted as a bid for an article. My father found himself the buyer of a grand piano after he rubbed his ear at a sale.

Inadvertent Damage to Property

If the roots of a tree reach out and damage the drains of the next door property, who is responsible? The damage and repair could be extensive and expensive. If branches from a neighbour's tree overhang your garden can they be cut down and to whom do they belong? If water seeps out of a swimming pool and damages the home next door, who is liable for the resulting damage?

These are all examples of cases which have been before the courts; they may differ only slightly in detail but they could produce very different judgements.

Local Bye-Laws

Legislation can vary in different parts of the country. For example, if there is a shortage of water then some local authorities might forbid the use of water hoses. There might be restrictions regarding the fouling of public parks and gardens by dogs or about the area where bicycles may be ridden.

Your local town hall will have a legal department which can be very helpful to enquirers. The legally trained staff can provide the answers relative to particular properties and local bye-laws. CABs are to be found in most areas and can give advice on law as well as on a comprehensive range of subjects of a general nature. Where recourse to the law has to be made they may also recommend local solicitors in whose abilities they have confidence.

The Law a Safeguard

Above all else, the law is meant to be reasonable. Parliament operates to change, update and modify legislation for the whole country. For example, the Occupier's Act, 1984, places the onus on the occupier to be responsible for any injuries caused by the state of the premises if they are aware of any danger and have reason to believe it exists, have reasonable grounds to believe that a trespasser may come into the vicinity of the danger or if the risk is one against which it is reasonable to take precautions and offer protection.

We may not take the law into our own hands and use unreasonable force, even with a burglar. Spike Milligan found this out the hard way, ending up in court and being sued by an intruder who had been injured.

Signing Contracts

If we have contracts to sign, we should understand the meaning clearly, taking nothing for granted. Nor should we allow anyone to tell us that we 'need not read on'. We must feel assured that a contract says precisely what we intend it to mean. If some of the conditions are unacceptable it is quite legal to alter printed contracts and sign where altered, provided this is correctly done and witnessed.

A marriage contract, whatever the age of the partners, can settle the rights to a property. But there are certain commitments within a marriage which cannot be altered. There are recognized obligations which make a marriage real and more than a partnership agreement. For example, any attempt to eliminate sexual relations would invalidate a marriage.

Attempts are often made to simplify the language used in drafting contracts and similar official documents. Legal jargon is a special kind of parlance, however, and it is not comprehensible to everyone.

Needing the Law

When a husband handles all the paperwork his wife is doubly disadvantaged if he deserts her. This happened to Ellen who at the age of fifty had never even had to sign a cheque. She had to learn to be resourceful and turned her talent for making sweets and chocolates to good use after her marriage broke up. She made up her mind to go into the business of selling her produce to restaurants and hotels as well as the public and rented a small shop, converting the back into a kitchen. What she did not realise was that she entered a special legal category once she sold her goods for profit. Soon she found herself deep in correspondence with various town hall officials and was almost overwhelmed by the paperwork and the bewildering official language. Inspectors arrived to look at her kitchen and she had to observe every last regulation, spending a good deal of money in so doing. Her kitchen had to be 'legally' hygienic and her transport had to be both safe and hygienic.

As a manufacturer, tenant and employer she found herself in need of financial and legal advice. Ellen had for a customer a young woman who was a solicitor and she also had an accommodating bank manager. Between them they put Ellen on the right track and she now has a thriving business.

Offers to Sell

Going into a shop to buy something may seem simple but both buyer and seller incur contractual obligations. The seller must sell goods which are suitable for the purpose for which they are sold; the buyer contracts to pay the price asked. Sale goods must be sold under special conditions. Generally the law operates to help the buyer but when sellers are unscrupulous they may get around the law, leaving the hapless buyer in a vulnerable position and with no legal redress.

The Biggest Deal of your Life

You may want to move when you retire and will need the services of a solicitor for contracts when you sell and when you buy. If you purchase an apartment, there will be a contract of maintenance and you must be sure that you understand exactly what the terms are, what you will be paying and what you expect to get.

Buying or selling a property is one of the most important transactions anyone ever makes. Everyone concerned is therefore expected to take special precautions and the law offers little protection to buyers or sellers who do not exercise care.

A woman, almost blind, was duped into signing a document giving her nephew the right to sell her house. He was an unscrupulous fellow and she simply did not realize that she was signing something of such great importance. When her house was sold over her head she took the case to court but it was held that every property owner must exercise the greatest caution when signing a document and it was the owner's responsibility to know what she was signing. Unfortunately, she lost the case and tragically, her home.

Estate Agents' Commission

Consider with care a decision to contract with someone to sell a house. Sales commissions on houses are high and it is not commonly realized that if agents are granted sole selling rights they are legally justified in demanding their commission even if the owner has found and negotiated directly with a purchaser.

Legal Costs

It is both reasonable and practical to ask a solicitor for an estimate of the likely cost of any work to be done since it is better to know, even approximately, what amount one is committed to pay. Conveyancing charges for the transfer or purchase of property are likely to be calculated to a fixed scale. Vetting a contract could be a simple matter with moderate charges, but it may be difficult to estimate the cost for more complex legal issues, particularly if the opinion of a barrister is to be sought. Get an estimate in writing if you can, so that there is no room for argument later. A solicitor will need to know what is involved and this may mean half an hour or so of preliminary discussion, giving both solicitor and client the opportunity to assess each other. Many firms provide a fixed fee interview for a few pounds. Be sure to take with you all relevant papers and write down in advance, as clearly and as briefly as you can, the details you think the solicitor will need to know.

It is not uncommon for people to be dissatisfied with the work of their legal advisers or their charges. Costs must be justified and applications for reviews of complaints should be made through the Law Society. (See Useful Addresses.)

Those on supplementary pension or with low income and savings will be able to get legal aid, either free or at a reduced charge. The CAB can advise which local solicitors offer this service.

Your Rights

Stores have the right to protect their goods and stealing is a crime for which most managements will prosecute but innocent people are sometimes accused of shoplifting. If a store detective or assistant asks someone if they have paid for the goods in their possession and does not receive a satisfactory reply, they are entitled to prevent the shopper from leaving the store. But they do not have the right to search bags without consent.

The apprehended shopper will usually be requested to go to the manager's office and will be asked if bags may be inspected. Where customers have been followed out of the store and then asked to open bags, they may refuse and ask to go somewhere private. A customer who declines to open bags or to go to the manager's office may be detained until the arrival of the police. It is illegal to use force to detain someone and if humiliation or embarrassment has been caused to an innocent customer, then compensation could be claimed. Once the police appear on the scene, they may search a person who has been accused of theft. Anybody facing prosecution should seek professional legal advice without delay.

Guardianship

We who are retired often still have one or both parents to think about. A proportion of such elderly people may no longer be fully responsible and for their own sakes may need to be 'received into guardianship' if they are deemed to be suffering from a mental disorder. Two doctors must agree on the condition and the application may be made by the nearest relative or by a social worker who is qualified in mental health work. Advice about what this entails can be given by the social services department, a law office or the CAB.

Driving Offences

If you are stopped and questioned regarding a motoring offence you may volunteer a statement but ask for that statement to be written down and say that you intend to check, date and sign it as being correct.

People who receive convictions for driving offences need to

know what the restrictions will be for them in the future. They should consult the Clerk of the Court if they are uncertain about the strict meaning of the terms of their conviction.

The Law and Euthanasia

The question of euthanasia becomes a public issue from time to time, the dilemma being whether or not it should be legalized. Some people will argue that each of us has the right to determine when we wish to die. Others say that voluntary euthanasia is not suicide and no one can elect to be killed by another person under any circumstances whatsoever. They will say that to lay such a task upon doctors is unreasonable because neither they, nor anyone else, is likely to be qualified to reach independent judgements about the state of mind of individuals at a given time. And, the treatment of patients is aimed at the continuation of life.

Requests for euthanasia might, for instance, be made at a time of transient depression. The patient may be mistakenly convinced that they have some sinister condition which in fact, they do not have. Alternatively, if life cannot be sustained with dignity and there is no possibility that it will improve in the future then perhaps there is reason to opt for euthanasia. But there is a strong argument that this view undermines the very fabric of our society.

Meanwhile, the realities are that where life has become too painful to endure and where there is no hope of recovery, euthanasia may well, on occasion, be carried out and be regarded as providing a blessed relief.

Ombudsman

The Parliamentary, Health and Local Ombudsman services have been set up to deal with complaints from individuals who believe that they have suffered an injustice from the action, or failure to act, of councils or authorities. Complaints in writing should be made through a Member of Parliament or local councillor who will refer them to the relevant ombudsman.

The grievance may be remedied although councils cannot be forced to act if they decide that they do not wish to do so.

Justice of the Peace and Councillors

Anyone who aspires to be a justice of the peace (JP) or a councillor should write to the relevant authorities and make known their backgrounds. Preferably, you should do this at the latest by your mid-fifties. JPs generally retire at seventy although a proportion may go on for a further two years. One who is serving this final term is Harry, who in his seventies still maintains a full-time interest in business activities. He, with his energetic wife Renee, leads a busy social life, continuing to raise funds for charities as they have done for thirty years and more.

Being a councillor means that evenings are often busy and one example is John who, in his sixties is also a JP, Commissioner of Taxes and holds other honorary posts. He became Lord Mayor of Westminster and he and his delightful wife, Helene, had the Queen Mother to lunch. The couple are also actively engaged in their successful family business.

Both of these men readily concede that they owe much of their success to the support they have been given by their wives.

More women are taking the leading role today, becoming JPs, councillors and Members of Parliament. There are more women in the legal profession with increasing numbers becoming judges. This more even sharing out of responsibilities can only be good news.

When seeking advice, your local law offices or CABs are the sources of much useful assistance and information. Otherwise, one of the following bodies may be of value: the Consumers' Association provides useful information on everyday issues; the British Standards Institution can test products to ensure that they meet with accepted standards; the Office of Fair Trading holds information on matters relating to consumer problems.

If you have concerns about any matter with legal

implications, do seek advice. Feeling disgruntled or stewing over wrongs can do no one any good and we want these retirement years to be not only free of care but carefree.

31 Making a Will

Who should make a will

It is simplicity itself to make a will and much aggravation and injustice can be caused by a failure to make one. None of us has a freehold on life, just a leasehold of an indeterminate term, hopefully a nice, long and healthy one. So why should people feel a reluctance to make decisions about how and where their possessions should go? Some avoid the thought of anything to do with the end of life. Writing a will, however, signals nothing of the sort. It is a sensible step to take, yet a surprising number fail to get around to it in time.

In the UK, last year, over half a million people died and of these, more than 400,000 left no will, that is, died intestate. Many had wives, husbands or others to whom they would have wished to leave their possessions. Those who are left behind in such circumstances may not only face lengthy legal disputes and wrangles, but with sinking hearts could see their estates dwindle in value as legal fees eat into them. The only way to ensure peace of mind for the future and a trouble-free time for inheritors, is to make decisions about disposals and put them down on paper, legally.

There are endless misconceptions about what happens to property when it is passed on to another person and inheritance law is quite complex. Advice is needed in order to be sure that wishes are stated according to the law. But once it is decided how and to whom one's estate should go, those wishes can be transferred to paper and will be carried out in due course. Be sure that you have correct names and titles and state the relationship of beneficiaries. If there are changes in circumstances there is no problem for a testator to alter a completed will by adding new instructions, known as a codicil to the will. Any additions or alterations must be signed and legally witnessed.

Intestacy

The difficulties which arise when a person dies without leaving a will can cause problems which were most likely unforeseen. Consider the wife whose husband had always put off the business of writing a will and who dies suddenly. She will face a disturbing time just when she can least cope with it and will have to prove that she is entitled to inherit. It may have been assumed that all the husband owned would automatically go to the wife, but this is not necessarily so. Other members of the family, not only close relatives but distant ones, could come forward to lay claim to a portion of his estate and there could be delay and embarrassment. It is always a shock when this happens. Even if in the end the wife inherits her husband's property, there may have been a lapse of time during which all of the assets, bank accounts and so on are frozen, often leaving the wife in financial difficulty. If other claims do succeed, then the wife may be in the position of having to sell the family home in order to pay off the claimant.

The legal rules of intestacy declare precisely how estates may be divided up, the surviving widow or widower, with or without children getting a predetermined amount, before the balance is distributed. This may be just what was wanted by the testator, but on the other hand, intestacy could cut out any bequests that a person might have wished to make, perhaps to a dear friend, a relative or to a favourite charity. A properly drawn-up will should clearly express all the bequests a person wanted to grant.

Remember, unless the will is properly drawn and witnessed according to legal requirements, none of the owner's wishes need be regarded at all. There are exceptions to this, not relevant to my readers, pertaining to the armed forces in times of war, for example.

Inheritance Tax and Capital Gains Tax

Considering the frequent changes and complexity of inheritance laws, it is not surprising that few members of the public fully understand them. It is a pity that not everyone realizes how much their estates can be diminished for their heirs, how much the tax man can siphon off and how much could be preserved by careful and early planning.

Since the matter of inheritance arises only on death, it is really a tax on the beneficiaries who have to find the tax once they become owners of the estate. Substantial proportions of inheritances may be payable in tax, depending upon the total value. There is a zero rate band and below this there is no tax liability. Above this threshold, inheritance tax is payable at increasing rates according to the residual value of the property and it is usual to find a charge of more than a third of the value of the estate. The free-of-tax, zero rate goes up annually and is generally in line with the rate of inflation. In the case of large estates, it might amount to some 80 per cent of the residual value.

Regardless of the value, there is no inheritance tax payable between husband and wife, but after the death of the surviving spouse, the tax comes into effect. Inheritance tax rates depend upon the lapse of years since the date of any gift and death of the donor. For example, any property given away would attract no inheritance tax at all, provided that the donor lived on for seven years after the date of the gift. The inheritance tax liability reduces by percentages until after the seventh year, when it is nil.

It is commonly supposed that anything given away before death is tax free. Apart from some tax free concessions, any assets of substantial value are subject to tax. Present legislation means that capital gains tax is due on the increase in value of a gift since it was acquired. For instance, if parents wished to give a valuable antique, jewellery or a house to their children, there would be capital gains tax payable by the donor, dependent on the increased value since the parent acquired it. This amount could be reduced by way of index linking and rebating.

Rise in Property Values

The escalation in the value of property in recent years has made a lot of difference to the amount of inheritance tax to be paid. People who never imagined that their estates would be of sufficient value for their heirs to have to pay any tax, now realize that not only will tax be due, but that the amount could be quite considerable.

Mitigating Tax

One way to mitigate inheritance tax and death duty is to take out an insurance policy to cover part or whole of the anticipated bill. This may be an efficient tax saver but it will certainly need the expert advice of an accountant or insurance broker. People should only consider this type of insurance if it can be comfortably afforded and does not cause them any hardship.

Wills can be Complex

Go to a solicitor to have the intricacies of law regarding wills explained, especially if there is a sizeable estate. If the estate is of modest value and there are no difficult decisions to make and all is simple and straightforward, you could get one of the prepared will forms which may be bought from stationers. However, please exercise caution, the wording which you think is so direct and clear may not have the legal meaning which you intend or it may be ambiguous. Once completed, a will has to be signed by the testator and countersigned by two independent witnesses who are not beneficiaries. Books can be found in the library which provide step-by-step guides on do-it-yourself wills; read one if you want to know more about the subject.

Legal Advice and Charges

Citizen's Advice Bureaux can offer general advice about wills but for specific details it is essential to go to a solicitor. Their charges vary between £50 and £200 pounds for drawing up a will but could be considerably more where complex estates are involved. It all depends upon the amount of time that has been taken during the interview and how much work there is involved in writing the will itself. Think carefully beforehand and write down all that you wish your will to contain, because less time is then taken up during the consultation.

Banks, apart from offering advice about wills and estates can also act as executors. They have fixed scales of fees, usually according to the value of the estate to be distributed.

32 Accentuate the Positive

We do not have Freehold

None of us has more than a leasehold on life and even that is of an unspecified duration. According to scientists our lives are limited genetically and we run out of time at around 100 or 110 years. Even if all the causes of death were eliminated we could not, they say, continue much beyond 110. Our cells, other than nerve cells, may replace themselves for many years but not forever, nor do the replacements make us any younger.

Eventually the genetic clock winds down within the time limit of the survival of the cell. That is inevitable and a rather comforting thought. Immortality is not for us and life is renewed in our descendants who, in the natural course of events, we leave behind.

We can control to a degree how we live but there is one option that we are denied. That is the manner and time of the end of life. Unless we deliberately choose when this will be, the final stage, although we may know that we are approaching it, remains unpredictable and will come in its own time. If we think of it at all, we hope that we will slip away quietly and with dignity, surrounded by a warm and caring family and friends. We also hope that we may bear bereavement bravely and find reason to go on living, once close and loved people have gone.

We all like to think that we will face the news that we are nearing the end of the road with courage and a cheerful demeanour, making things easier for those we will leave behind. Families and friends want to know how long there is left for someone dear to them. They need time in which to prepare for a final parting, to say what must be said.

Part of the training of medical staff is learning to convey news to patients and their families that may be hard to bear. Such duties can impose a great strain despite the training. Some of the staff are naturally warm and sympathetic people who are able to comfort those to whom they have to impart distressing news. Whatever that news may be, it is hard to foretell how it will be received.

When no further communication seems possible it is still worth holding the hand of a dying person and speaking softly to them. Many people return hand-pressure long after it is thought that all consciousness has gone. Hospice nurses encourage this kind of contact, believing that it is an experience that brings comfort to those who have little time as well as to those who are closest to them.

Hospices

In hospices, patients are mostly fully aware that their futures are likely to be brief and face the world with calm acceptance. Patients so often cheer those who visit them with smiles and assurances that there is 'no need to worry, everything is alright'. They comfort their visitors, asking them not to be sad, put their affairs in order as though they were going on a trip and often slip away in peace. Death is not seen as a frightening occurrence to those who are at peace with themselves and are prepared for it.

Some have friends or relatives they have no intention of making peace with, in this world or the next. Shortly before she died, I visited a relative in her late-eighties who being very ill knew that she did not have long to live. She was busy compiling a list and when I asked what it was for she told me, 'This is going to be my funeral and these are the people I don't want there'.

An acquaintance of ours had been ill for many years with leukaemia, despite which he had lived normally and held down a job he enjoyed. He was never apparently despondent and spoke of the bonus time he had been given, during which his son had graduated from university, married and had children. 'With luck, I may even get to retire,' he had said.

And retire he did at sixty to enjoy some leisure years. In the final months he knew just what was ahead and asked for all the family photos to be brought into the hospice so that he could organize and mark them with dates and names. He said it was an ideal task to be undertaking, one that he had never found the time for. Memories flooded back as he went through the snapshots and the more formal photos. They gave him so much pleasure, allowing him to reminisce about the years gone by. 'Darling,' he said affectionately to his wife, 'You would never get around to it.'

Faith in Religion

Religion plays a big part in comforting some patients. Because of their faith many find it easier to accept whatever may come. No matter which religious order one may belong to, there is the sense that there is far more to this world than ever we dream of and that we are all part of a great purpose and order in the universe.

Suzanne was a happy women in her mid-fifties with keen anticipation of her approaching retirement when she received the news that she had terminal cancer. She reacted with bitterness to this shocking news at first but then prayer calmed her and she and her husband made carefully considered plans for the estimated six months of life ahead. She continued at her secretarial job and the couple enjoyed a family Christmas with their twin daughters of twenty-four and their twenty-two year old son. In the spring, Suzanne, helped by a friend, planted bulbs in the garden and when they had finished, opened a bottle of champagne to celebrate. A practical woman, she told her husband that he should re-marry, even nominating a close friend, a widow as a prospective wife. She was courageous to the end, sustained by her faith and her loving family.

Giving the Facts

Patients under anaesthetic are often aware of much that is going on around them. Albert thought he was in for a simple operation but in the theatre his surgeon soon recognized that his condition was serious and discussed this with his team. Back on the ward, Albert awoke to full realization that he was desperately ill, telling his daughter that he knew all about it. Care should be taken that knowledge does not reach sick people in this way.

Whispers and discussions near the bedside but just out of earshot of patients who are supposedly asleep or under sedation can be unbearable to them. Doctors will always allow time away from the bedside for questions but relatives are often diffident about bothering busy professionals. One doctor spoke of his surprise when he learned from a widower that he did not know what his wife had suffered from. He had wished to know but had never liked to trouble medical staff. It is such a comfort to families when GPs can give time and also visit following bereavement and answer any questions which relatives may have.

Living Alone

When a close relationship ends with the death of a person, the remaining partner has to get used to living alone, keeping house, cooking and shopping for one. The big differences are often easier to accept than the small everyday things and customs of many years have to change. Feelings may be mixed and if, for example one partner has had to devote years of nursing and caring for another, there can be a sense of relief mixed with guilt.

It can take some time to get used to being alone at home, eating, washing up, all without an accustomed presence and the sound of a familiar voice. One man described how he missed the homely untidiness of the kitchen as his wife prepared a meal or being scolded for leaving the cap off the tube of toothpaste. Another spoke of the gap he felt, missing, for instance, having someone to argue with about which TV programme to watch.

We may never stop missing people we have loved, but we have a positive duty to get on with life and to take an interest in the world around.

The time of bereavement is often one when people seek

comfort in religion, returning again to church, mosque or synagogue, even when they have not attended for years. Religious views are positive about grieving, setting up an approved structure and lending a dignity to the deceased and to the living. Visitors to a house of mourning can give comfort but mourners need time for private grieving and the chance to be quiet and to recover from the shock of loss.

When visiting the bereaved most of us feel at a loss for something to say. But if people feel genuine concern they rarely go wrong and gentle enquiries will not be rebuffed. In the case of the loss of an elderly person, it can be comforting to reminisce about pleasant memories and speak of the qualities which made the mourned person so valued. Bereavement brings families and friends closer and the joint shedding of tears can overcome old quarrels, reminding us all that life is of comparatively brief duration, too short for discord.

It is hard to accept that someone has died and that one will not see or hear them again. But death is an integral part of life and the intangible inheritance bequeathed, love, friendship, a sense of values, these do not die. They may be cherished, used and handed on to more people.

A Time Limit and Euthanasia

When there is painful illness and death is certain, questions arise in the minds of medical advisers as well as families, as to whether there should be a release from this pain. To avoid being a burden we ourselves might try to authorize those in charge that there should be some assistance to end life.

It is no longer an illegal act to attempt suicide. But it is strictly against the law to assist someone to make such an attempt and this might result in a charge of murder. The British Medical Association has said that in their view this law should remain unchanged. Doctors remain bound by the present legislation and subject to all the restrictions imposed in this respect. They cannot agree to increase a drug dose which might endanger life or in any way hasten a death. If they disobey these strict injunctions they violate medical ethics and lay themselves open to prosecution.

A British Medical Report relevant to these matters was published in 1988. The working party responsible for it included eminent consultants among whom were a geriatrician and a paediatrician, as well as the medical director of a hospice. The Report specifically states: 'Patients cannot and should not be able to require their doctors to collaborate in their death. If a patient makes such a request then there should be a presumption that the doctor will not agree.'

Withdrawing Treatment

There was, however, agreement within the medical profession that doctors could withdraw treatment once this has become a burden and is no longer of any benefit to the patient.

This leaves doctors with considerable leeway. Faced with a terminally-ill patient suffering great pain from which there is little relief, the doctor might order that there be no further life-prolonging help. This opinion could be taken in a case where the quality of life had deteriorated to the extent that it was of no value and the British Medical Association supports such views.

Upholding the Law

Many people would hold that the law can be illogical. A life can be deliberately abbreviated by withholding medicine or treatment and yet permission to administer a drug to end a suffering existence must be withheld. The difference may be subtle but it is quite definite.

The British Medical Report goes on to say that it is within the law for medical personnel to give terminally-ill patients painkilling drugs with the primary intent of relieving pain, even if it is known that the effect of such medication might be fatal. The Report continues with a recommendation that when a patient is defined as being in a 'persistent vegetative state' and considered by relatives as being beyond understanding, the artificial means of keeping them alive should cease. Even so, no patient or relative can ask a doctor for drugs which may have the effect of hastening death. That must be a doctor's decision alone and based on clinical judgement.

The Old Man's Friend

When a man aged ninety-four was admitted to hospital in a frail and weakened state, suffering from advanced pneumonia, the ward sister found two young doctors fighting for his life. She remonstrated with them for not allowing the exhausted old man, who had failing health and functions, to slip gently away to a quiet and peaceful end.

Tender Loving Care Only

In some hospitals, the staff do hold the view that there are times when the end should be allowed to come for those patients with absolutely no hope of either a cure or a return to normal life. These patients might be suffering with extreme dementia, from more advanced forms of cancers or some other terminal condition. They may have their records specifically marked as not to be resuscitated or with the initials well known in hospitals or hospice wards . . . 'for TLC only'. For tender, loving care only.

The Voluntary Euthanasia Society commissioned a survey which found that more than 70 per cent of people who were questioned believe that the law should permit adults to be helped to die if they were suffering intolerably from incurable disease. The Society proposes that a person's wish about living should be expressed as a special 'will'. This statement of intent should be signed in the presence of witnesses and the sanity of the person should be confirmed in the presence of independent doctors who will also vouch that there has been no pressure to make this life and death decision.

The argument for voluntary euthanasia is that the dying person's own beliefs and needs should have priority and be regarded as having serious intent. Should there be rights for people who would infinitely prefer to die under certain circumstances? Should the option be denied to them out of deference for the sanctity of life itself? Some terminally-ill people cling to life at all costs. But others say that they believe it would be more compassionate to respect an independent decision of this nature and grant their wishes to end life.

There are arguments both for and against. Certainly, there are many good and sound reasons why we should not legalize euthanasia. If this procedure was to be made legal, then the door could be open to all sorts of malpractices. The greatest care must be exercised so that there is no encouragement to commit crimes. But when one has seen a beloved relative suffering intolerably during the weeks preceding certain death, it seems inhuman that such suffering should be permitted to continue.

Case Precedence

There are numbers of cases on record where compassionate and deeply-caring relatives and friends have put an end to the suffering of their loved ones. They have risked prosecution and faced punishment. It is a painful experience to watch a dear person suffering greatly and the temptation to provide release must often become overpoweringly strong. But it is not a pleasant thing to contemplate the legal consequences of a compassionate, albeit a criminal, act. That would produce suffering of another kind. Those who consider such action must be very sure in their minds that they are doing the right thing. It is not an act which can be readily condoned.

Upholding the Law

Many judges take a positive view and may determine to make exceptional, lenient rulings in certain cases, but they must always uphold the law. There is considerable support from members of the public who have personally experienced the slow and painful end of loved ones and would wish for a legally permitted, assisted end to life under certain circumstances.

Should the Law be Changed

Notwithstanding all that is said and written on the subject it is reckoned that a very considerable number of deaths are attributable to euthanasia. Where doctors and families respond to genuine pleas for help and relief from doomed and suffering patients by breaking the law in order to spare them more pain, then perhaps the law should be changed. Other countries have bowed to public views in this regard.

It is a most solemn thing to take life. Perhaps it is even more solemn to give up life. But if circumstances combine against us, should we not all be permitted to take the responsibility for our own manner of dying, provided that we decide this at a time when we are in our right minds?

A Civilized Society

It is the mark of a civilized society that it takes care of the weak, the old and the sick, regardless of the cost. Will future societies afford the time and the money necessary to maintain these highest of ethical standards? Do we want resources to be devoted to prolonging life at any cost, possibly at the expense of health services for the younger members of our society? That will be a matter of debate for future generations.

Life is a marvellous gift and by the time we qualify for retirement we will have seen plenty of ups and downs and if we did not experience sorrow we might never fully appreciate how sweet the good times can be.

There is a song that tells us to 'accentuate the positive, eliminate the negative'. For sure, that is what we should all do.

Useful Addresses

Abbeyfield Society
186 Darkes Lane,
Potters Bar,
Hertfordshire EN6 1AB

Accommodation

ABC of Shipping
Charing Cross Shopping
Concourse, The Strand,
London WC2N 4HZ

Sea travel

Actors' Charitable Trust
19-20 Euston Centre,
London NW1

Grants
Accommodation

Age Concern
Bernard Sunley House,
Pitcairn Road,
Mitcham,
Surrey CR4 3LL

Advice
Publications
Promotes issues

Aged Pilgrims Friend Society
175 Tower Bridge Road,
London SE1 2AL

Care
Accommodation

Age Research
49 Queen Victoria Street,
London EC4N 4SA

Advice
Publications
Grants

Alexander Society of Teachers
10 London House,
266 Fulham Road,
London SW10 9EL

Teaches Health Promotion

Alzheimer's Disease Society
Bank Buildings,
Fulham Broadway,
London SW6 1EP

Advice
Grants
Welfare information

Useful Addresses

AMI Healthcare Group Plc   Private health care
4 Cornwall Terrace,
Regents Park,
London NW1 4QP

Anchor Housing Association   Equipment
Oxenforth House,   Care
13–15 Magdalen Street,   Homes and hostels
Oxford OX1 3BP

Animal Welfare Trust   Homes for pets
Tylers Way,   Grants
Watford By-Pass,
Watford, Hertfordshire

Army Benevolent Fund   Grants
41 Queens Gate,
London SW7 5HR

Arthritis and Rheumatism   Advice
Council for Research   Information
41 Eagle Street,
London WC1R 4AR

Arthritis Care   Adapted accommodation
6 Grosvenor Crescent,   Visiting service
London SW1X 7ER   Grants

Association of British Travel   Advice
Agents   Information
55 Newman Street,
London W1

Association of Carers   Advice
112 The Broadway   Information
London SW19

Association of Crossroads   Advice
Care   Help
10 Regents Place,
Rugby,
Warwickshire CV21 2PN

Useful Addresses

Association of Professional　　Advice
Music Therapists　　Information
The Meadow
68 Pierce Lane
Fulbourne
Cambridge

Asthma Allergy Treatment　　Advice
Centre　　Treatment
12 Vernon Street,
Derby DE1 1FT

Back Pain Association　　Advice
31–33 Park Road,　　Training
Teddington,　　Publications
Middlesex TW11 0AB

Back Store　　Equipment
324A King Street,　　Relief of back pain
Hammersmith,
London W6 0RF

British Association for Hard　　Advice
of Hearing　　Information
7–11 Armstrong Road,
Acton,
London W3 7JL

British Balloon and Airship　　Leisure activity
Club
c/o Travel Gas
122 Fazeley Road,
Birmingham B5 RS

British Canoeing Union　　Leisure activity
Mapperley Hall,
Lucknow Avenue,
Nottingham NG5 FA

Useful Addresses

British Deaf Association
311 Grays Inn Road,
London EC1X 8PX

Advice
Information

British Diabetic Association
10 Queen Anne Street,
London W1M 0BD

Advice
Grants
Holidays and Welfare

British Federation of Land
and Sand Yacht Clubs
23 Piper Drive,
Long Whatton,
Loughborough,
Leicestershire

Leisure activity

British Gas
Dept MB
Rivermill House,
152 Grosvenor Road,
London SW1V 3JL

Free gas checks for elderly
who live alone

British Geriatric Society
1 St Andrews Place,
London NW1 4LB

Advice
Research

British Gliding Association
Kimberley House,
47 Vaughan Way,
Leicester LE1 4SG

Leisure activity

British Heart Foundation
102 Gloucester Place,
London W1H 4DH

Advice
Research

British Holistic Medical
Association
179 Gloucester Place,
London NW1

Advice
Information

British Red Cross Society
9 Grosvenor Crescent,
London SW1X 7EJ

Casework
Care
Training

Useful Addresses

British Standards Institution Advice
2 Park Street,
London W1

British Surfing Association Leisure activity
Room G5,
Burrows Chambers,
East Burrows Road,
Swansea SA1 1RF

British Tinnitus Association Advice
105 Gower Street, Information
London WC1E 6AH

BUPA Private health insurance
Provident House,
Essex Street,
London WC2

Cancer Prevention Research Help
Trust Research
36 Roehampton Vale,
London SW15 3SF

Cancer Relief National Advice
Society Care homes
Anchor House, Macmillan nurses
15–19 Britten Street,
London SW3 3TY

Chartered Society of Advice
Physiotherapists Addresses
14 Bedford Road,
London WC1

Chest Heart and Stroke Advice
Association Information
Tavistock House North,
Tavistock Square,
London WC1H 9JE

Useful Addresses

Church of England Pensions Board 53 Tufton Street, London SW1P 3QP	Advice Grants
Citizens Advice Bureaux National Association 115 Pentonville Road, London N1	Advice Information
Constant Management Services Ltd Roman House, Newport Road, Albrighton, Woverhampton WV7 3HG	Careline Emergency link
Consumers Association 2 Marylebone Road London NW1	Information
'Contact' 15 Henrietta Street, London WC2E 8QH	Information Visits for elderly
Counsel and Care for Elderly 131 Middlesex Street, London E1 7JF	Advice Information
Court of Protection 25 Store Street, London WC1E 7BP	Legal protection in case of mental breakdown
Cruse Clubs 126 Sheen Road, Richmond, Surrey.	Help for bereaved
Disabled Living Foundation 380–384 Harrow Road, London W9 2HU	Advice Equipment

Useful Addresses

Distressed Gentlefolks Aid Association Vicarage Gate House, Vicarage Gate, London W8 4AQ	Advice Grants
Education Broadcasting BBC, London, W1A 1AA	Advice Publications Training
Elderhostal Okanagan College, 583 Hastings Avenue, Pendicton, British Columbia, Canada.	Holidays Education
Elderly Accommodation Counsel 1 Durward house, 31 Kensington Court, London W8 5BH	Advice Accommodation
Family Welfare Association 501 Kingsland Road London E8	Advice
Freighter World Cruises Inc Suite 335, 180 South Lake Avenue, Pasadena, California 91101, USA	Sea travel
General Council of Osteopaths 4 Suffolk Street London WC1	Advice Addresses

Useful Addresses

Grace and Compassion Benedictines Holy Cross Priory, Cross-in-Hand, Heathfield, Sussex TN21 0TS	Advice Grants
Grandparents Federation 78 Cook's Spinney, Harlow, Essex CN20 3BL	Advice Information
Greenpeace Freepost 30–31 Islington Green, London N1 8BR	Advice Environment information
Guild of Aid for Gentlepeople 10 St Christopher's Place, London W1M 6HY	Advice Grants
Harrison Homes 46 St James Gardens, London W11 4RQ	Accommodation
Help the Aged 32 Dover Street, London W1A 2AP	Advice Information Grants to projects
Holland, Mrs P. 15 Andrew's House, Barbican, London EC2Y 8AX	Advice Music therapy
Hospital Saving Association Hambledon House, Andover, Hampshire SP10 1LQ	Non-profit insurance scheme

Useful Addresses

Institute of Complementary　　Advice
Medicine　　　　　　　　　　　Information
21 Portland Place,
London W1 3AS

Jewish Blind Society　　　　　Advice
221 Golders Green Road,　　　Help
London NW11 9DN

Jewish Welfare Board　　　　　Advice
221 Golders Green Road,　　　Accommodation
London NW11 9DW　　　　　　Grants

Law Association　　　　　　　Information
113 Chancery Lane　　　　　　Advice
London WC2

London Association for the　　Advice
Blind　　　　　　　　　　　　Help
14 Verney Road,
London SE16 3DZ

Medway Homes　　　　　　　　Counselling for carers
Balfour Road,
Rochester, Kent.

Methodist Homes for the　　　Advice
Aged　　　　　　　　　　　　Housing
Epworth House,
25 City Road,
London EC1Y 1DR

Mind – National Association　 Advice
for Mental Health　　　　　　Information
22 Harley Street,
London W1N 2ED

Useful Addresses

Mutual Households Association Cornhill House, 41 Kingsway, London WC2BE 6UB	Advice Housing
National Benevolent Fund for the Aged 65 London Wall, London EC2M 5TU	Advice Grants
National Caving Association c/o 3 Valletort Road, Stoke Plymouth, Devon PL1 5PH	Leisure activity
National Council for the Conservation of Plants The General Secretary, The Pines, RHS Garden, Wisley, Woking, Surrey.	Conservation Flowers
National Federation of Housing Associations 30–32 Southampton Street, London WC2	Advice Housing
National Federation of Pensioners' Associations 91 Preston New Road, Blackburn, Lancashire BB2 6BD	Advice Publications
Office of Fair Trading Field House Breams Buildings London EC4	Advice Information

Useful Addresses

Open UniversityEducation
Walton Hall,
Milton Keynes,
MK7 6AA

Parascending ClubsLeisure activity
18 Talbot Lane,
Leicester LE1 4ER

Patients AssociationAdvice
11 Dartmouth Street,Publications
London W1

Pre-Retirement AssociationAdvice
19 Undine Street,Publications
London SW17

Private Patients PlanHealth insurance
PPP House, Upperton Road,
Eastbourne,
East Sussex BN21 1LH

Radar – Royal AssociationAdvice
DisabilityHelp
25 Mortimer Street,
London W1

ReachRetired executive
89 Southwark Street,employment
London SE1 0HD

Royal Air Force AssociationAdvice
Portland Road,Grants
Malvern,
Worcestershire WR14 2TA

Royal National Institute forAdvice
the BlindPublications
224 Great Portland Street,
London W1

Useful Addresses

Royal National Institute for the Deaf 105 Gower Street, London WC1E 6AH	Advice Publications
Royal Yachting Association RYA House, Romsay Road, Eastleigh, Hampshire SOS 4YA	Leisure activity
Saga Publishing Limited The Saga Building, Middleburgh Square, Folkestone, Kent CT20 1AZ	Advice Travel Publications
Sports Council 16 Upper Woburn Place London WC1H 0QP	Advice Training
Travel Companions 89 Hillfield Court, Belsize Avenue, London NW3 4BE	Advice Information Shared holidays
University of the Third Age Parkside Gardens, London SW19	Education
Voluntary Society of Euthanasia 13 Prince of Wales Terrace, London W8	Advice Information
Will To Charity 84 Claverton Street, London SW1V 3AX	Publications Lists of charities

Index

Doctors are not indexed because they are mentioned with such regularity throughout the text.

Abbeyfield   293
abortion   126
accident-prone   140
accidents   297
activity, social   21, 34
acupuncture   273
additives   68
Age Concern   101, 114
age no bar   27
   and genetic inheritance   131
   not a problem   137
alcohol   152, 213
Alexander method   39
   principles   272
allergies   272–3
aluminium   152
Alzheimer's   132, 142
ambitions   27
analgesics   165–6
angina   212
angioplasty   217
annuities   302
anorexia   197
antibiotics   163–4
apnoea   249
aromatherapy   273–4
arteries   131, 212
aspirin   159, 165
Association British Travel Agents   87
Automobile Association   95

bankers, advice on finance   303–4
Barnard, Dr Christiaan   200
bereavement   327, 330
Beveridge Report   257
bi-focals   311
blood pressure, high   51, 127, 138
bowling   50
breathlessness   175

British Medical Association   270, 331–2
building societies   304
bunions   231

caffeine   187, 215, 216
cancer   134
   of lung   145
   reducing risk   145
caravanning   78
carers   279, 312
cataract   219
charity commission   94–5
   digest   94
   holiday camp   98
chiropractic   274
cholesterol   212
collecting   53
constipation   138, 181
contact lenses   222–3
   dangers of   223–4
   tinted   224
convalescing   177
Coppard, Vera   85
corns   230
correspondence courses   45–6
cosmetic surgery   207
cycling, and TV   178

dancing   175
day-centres   286
dentists   226, 259
dental care   260
depression   148, 151, 166, 250
   clinical   148
diabetes   143
   impotence   127
   in family   133, 134, 143, 230
diets   185, 191–2

Index

doctor/patient relationship 255
dozing 252
dreams 252
drinking 187
drivers 95
drugs 140, 146, 215
  combination 161
  instructions 159
  over-the-counter 159
  reaction 160

eating, healthy 180
education 36
Elderhostal 41
electrolysis 209
emergency cash abroad 85–6
emergency phone-link 299
energy 32
erection, during sleep 252
euthanasia 319, 331
  Voluntary Society for 333, 334
exercise 33, 171, 175
exfoliants 201
exploitation at work 22
eye-tests 219

faith healing 274–5
family 12
  case-history 111, 112
  Family Health Service
    Authority 222, 226, 259
  links 111
  longevity 133
  privacy 295
  problems 114
  units 295
feet, painful 228–9
fish-pond 70
fitness 168
Fleming, Sir Alexander 163
flying, tips on travel 87–8
food 180
  to avoid 185
  variety 181
foot-care assistants 233
fractures 141

gardening 57
  clubs 65
  courses 63

gadgets 60
  tips 63–4
  watering 62
genes 133–4
gerontophobia 154
glaucoma 220
gliding 73
gout 229
grandchildren 111
  their health 134
grandparents 311
  rights 113–14
  to adopt 109
graphology 275
greenhouse 68
Greenpeace 66
guardianship, of elderly 318

haemorrhoids 165, 244
Hagerman, Fritz 170
hair 208–9
hang-gliding 73
Harrison, Lisa 65
Hartmann, Dr 249
health care 72, 255
  costs 256
  private care 264
  promotion 144
  service 10
hearing 224
heart attack 144
  bypass 216
  exercise for 171
  problems 211
  transplant 216
herbs 69, 216, 275
hire-purchase 312
hobbies 48
holidays 72, 75
  abroad 76
home, abroad 290
  care and safety 286, 297
  case histories 289, 291
  one's own 289
  returning to retire 290–1
Homestart 99
homeopathy 276
homosexual 125
  marriage 125–6
hormone replacement therapy 162, 240

349

Index

hospice 328
hospital 260
  in-patient 268
  Hospital Saving Association 265
  private 267-8
hotel residents 295-6
housing 294
  associations 292
  benefit 308
  sheltered 296
hygiene 186
hygienist 226, 260
hypnotism 276
hypothyroidism 257-8

illness, inherited 132
impotence 127-8
income support 306
incontinence 235
  case history 237
  corrective exercise 240-1
  laundry service 284
  preventive measures 240
  sexual relationship 238
independence, encourage 141
inflation, effects of 91
inheritance tax 323-4
insecticides 68
insurance 82
  health 132, 265
  medical 83
  tax relief 269
intestacy 323
investment, bank 303-4
  building society 304
  stock-market 304
  unit trusts 305
ionisers 276
iridology 276

job, part-time 89
  satisfaction 21-2

karate 39-40
keep-fit classes 176
ketama 40
Kirlian photography 275

land-yachting 73
laughter 166

law 310
  courts 312
  local 313-14
  society 317
legal aid 317, 325
  costs 317
  liability 311, 313
  responsibility 66
leisure 72
lesbian 125-6
life expectancy 5
  styles 11
living alone 330
Livingstone, Ken 161
longevity 135, 137, 212
luggage 83

Mackarness, Dr Richard 273
make-up 210
marriage break up 110
  case-history 110-11
masturbation 251
medical conditions, predisposed 132
medicine 158
memories unreliable 154
memory recall 139
mental illness 147
micro-wave ovens 183
milk 251
minerals 187-8, 204
mobile, keeping 141
mobility 287
moisturisers 199-200
monogamy 121
Monro, Dr Jean 273
moped 73-4
music therapist 52

narcolepsy 249
naturopathy 277
Neighbourhood Watch Scheme 299
Newman, Paul 98
nocturnal myoclonus 249
noises, preventing sleep 253
nursing home 297

obesity 194
occupation, changing 89
occupational therapists 170, 283
ombudsman 319

Index

open university 46
opium 165
opticians 219
osteoarthritis 229
osteopathy 277
osteoporrosis 141, 162, 262
overweight 189
oxygen 138

pacemaker 216
pain 156, 165
paracetamol 166
parascending 74
Parkinson's disease 151
patients, and doctors 255
   in hospital 261
penicillin 163
pensions, state retirement 303
   transfer abroad 87, 302
pets 48, 54
pharmacist 205, 260
photography 39, 52
physiotherapists 170, 283
piles 244
plants, conservation 67
pneumonia 139
polysomnogram 249
pools, fibre glass 69
   garden 69–70
posture 138
pot-hole 74
privacy, intrusion of 17, 112
problems, marital 122–3
   psychological 120–1
property 301
prostate gland 238–9
psychic healing 274

quarrels, patching up 106

Reach 101–2
recreation 72
rehabilitation 141
rejuvenating 200
relationships 105
   need attention 111
   with children 107–8
relaxation 245–6
religion 329, 331
respite, for carers 282, 286

retirement, early 2, 23
   sex in 129–30
role-playing 28
rowing 74

sailing 74
Samaritans 151
saunas 51
savings, national certificates 305
Scrabble 55
scuba-diving 75
sedatives 250
serotonin 251
sex, abuse 117–18
   counsellor 123–4
   differing taste 124
   hasty performance 123
   importance of 116
   no age bar 126, 214
   problems 116–17
sexual barrier 118
   case history 118–19
   conflicts 122
   happiness 118
   inadequacy 119–20
   infections 128–9
   intercourse 251
   relations 315
   resentment 126
   security conscious 298
shock shingles 258
shoes 230–1
shop-lifting 317
sight 219
skiing 75
skin, composition of 198
   conditions 202
sleep 246–7
   patterns 247
sleepiness 248
sleeping pills 151
slimming pills 162–3
smoking 145, 176, 213
snoring 255
social fund 308
social workers 114
speech therapists 225
spiritual healing 274
St. Johns Ambulance Service 96–7
stair-lift 291–2

Index

steroids 161
stockmarkets 304
stress 148, 214
stroke 144
students, mature 29–30, 43
sunflower seed oil 186
sunshine, effects of 201
support services 282
surgeries 257
swimming 177

taxi-card scheme 287
teaching handicrafts 100–1
tinnitus 225
tranquillisers 162
transcendental meditation 278
transvestite 124–5
travel alone 84
travel companions 85
travellers cheques 86
trees, loss of 63–4
   miniature 65
   planting 66
tryptophan 251
turkish bath 51–2

unit trusts 305
University of the Third Age 44–5, 81

vacation with study 40–1
vitality depressed 172
vitamins 188, 203–4
voluntary bureau 99
   drivers 95
   work in hospital 97
volunteers 103

Walton, Dr Anne 22
water skiing 75
wigs 209
Williams, Dr Roger 164
wills 322
work, case history 92–3
   hospital 97
   importance of 89–90
   incentive to 16
   part-time 89–90, 92
   satisfaction 17
   voluntary 93

yoga 39, 278
yoghourt 164